Essentials in Christian Faith

Essentials in
Christian Faith

by John B. Harrington

PROFESSOR OF PHILOSOPHY
LEWIS AND CLARK COLLEGE

Harper & Brothers • *Publishers* New York

ESSENTIALS IN CHRISTIAN FAITH

Copyright © 1958 by John B. Harrington

Printed in the United States of America

Library of Congress catalog card number: 58-6128

1. Christianity - Philosophy
2 Theology, Doctrinal

To MY FATHER AND MOTHER, MY
WIFE, CAROLYN, AND OUR
DAUGHTER, ALICE CATHERN

*One generation shall praise thy works to
another, and shall declare thy mighty acts.*

Psalm 145:4

Contents

Contents

Contents

Contents

Preface

This book is not written for professional theologians or philosophers. It is intended rather for serious seekers from many different backgrounds who wish to think through the basic tenets of Christian faith. Reading these pages can never be a substitute for further study of available first-hand materials, and to this end a list of suggested reading will be found in the Appendix. But the student in college or university or the concerned layman sometimes finds the reading of original scholarly documents a difficult task. Therefore it is the purpose of this book to introduce the general reader to some of the main currents and trends in theology and the philosophy of religion in our day. A glance at the Table of Contents will indicate to the reader what I consider some of these main currents and themes to be.

It has been impossible in a volume of this scope to include discussion of all of the topics which properly belong here. Obvious omissions are treatment of prayer and worship, Christian ethics in any detailed way, and the intricate relation between Christianity and political and economic affairs. I believe, however, that general principles will be found for application to these concerns. The reader is encouraged to follow his own interests by reference to literature which is readily available in these fields. Adequate coverage of these subjects would require the writing of many volumes. Thus, even in my discussion of those topics included here, I attempt to be *suggestive* rather than exhaustive.

More than a decade ago I began teaching a course at Lewis and Clark College entitled Basic Christian Beliefs. Before that, as an adviser to church youth groups and as a pastor, I had been attempting to help young people and adults achieve a firmer grasp on and a clearer expression of their faith. Out of give-and-take discussion, my own materials in mimeographed form began to take shape. These I placed in the hands of students to supplement their reading in order that we might be free to carry on a continuing informal conversation in class. Encouraged by students and various friends and colleagues, I was led to draw

Preface

these materials together into this volume. It is my sincere hope that students enrolling in college and university courses will find it helpful, as well as thoughtful young people and men and women generally.

One central difficulty delayed the actual writing in the early stages: making up my own mind as to exactly what kind of book I wished to write. Gradually it dawned on me that I could not succeed in writing in cool, dispassionate, and objective fashion from "outside" the Christian faith. I am a Christian brought up in the Reformed tradition. One cannot escape the background that has nurtured him, nor would he wish to. I frankly and gratefully acknowledge the focus of interpretation and faith which I have known in some degree since boyhood.

But I am also trained in and engaged in teaching in the field of philosophy. Can a man or woman be *both* Christian and philosopher? It is my conviction that this is possible for reasons that unfold throughout the course of this volume.

This does not mean that those who read this book need be professional philosophers. Every person is a philosopher insofar as he holds certain beliefs about the world, God, and man. But he needs to submit his beliefs to the light of critical scrutiny and communicate his faith clearly to his own generation.

The Christian, who is also philosopher in this broad sense, takes his stand "inside" the community of faith. He issues an invitation for other folk to come over and "see life steadily and see it whole" from this vantage point. Taking persons and history as the most significant clues to the nature of reality, he then seeks to discover how these may illuminate *all* of existence. Running throughout this book will be found expression of the enduring theme of biblical Christianity: God active in human history, especially through the person of Jesus Christ, to bring about reconciliation between man and Himself. Our attitude would be not dogmatic but "confessional." This is the kind of invitation we would issue to all who read this book and honestly seek to come to grips with the esential problem of human existence. For we begin with man as he *is* and his human predicament, and then attempt to discover what answers the Christian faith offers to concerned men and women in ours or any age.

I have tried conscientiously to acknowledge indebtedness to various authors and books, as will be evident throughout the text. There is, however, that climate of thought and life within which we live that unconsciously influences what we think and what we are. These past two or three decades have wrought a veritable revolution in religious and philosophical thought. The effect of these dynamic changes will be evident to the reader of these pages. It is my hope that he too will catch some "feel" of what is in the air these days.

Preface

Specifically, I would express my gratitude to thoughtful students who have honored me with their friendship and stimulated my thought through their searching questions and critical observations. Also I wish to thank President Morgan S. Odell and Dean Charles W. Howard of Lewis and Clark College for their cordial encouragement of this project. To colleagues as well, in many different departments of the college, I owe my thanks especially for assuming larger shares of committee responsibility and the like so that I could be freer for writing. For this writing has been done early and late in odd hours wrested out of a full teaching schedule. I appreciate the help of Professors John L. Anderson, Hideo Hashimoto, and Christine Pattison of the Department of Religion and Dr. Philip S. Bashor, my immediate associate in the Philosophy Department. My former student, Frithjof Bergmann, Instructor in Philosophy at Princeton University, read parts of earlier versions and offered invaluable criticisms. Invaluable assistance has been extended by the Lewis and Clark Library staff, especially Mr. Lloyd C. Dry, who tracked down many an elusive reference. I wish also to thank Mrs. Hazel Torgerson for her tireless and thoughtful work in preparing the manuscript for publication and my secretary, Miss Dorothy Baxter, for help in correspondence.

Above all, as is the case with all my life and work, there would have been no book if it were not for my wife, Carolyn, who read every word and encouraged me through every chapter along the way. And my appreciation also is expressed to our daughter, Alice Cathern, who had to put up with what she chose to call "Daddy's book mood." It goes without saying that none of these persons is responsible for what I write here or for the way in which it is expressed. I assume full responsibility for lapses and errors in what I hope may prove to be helpful suggestions to members of this generation.

JOHN B. HARRINGTON

Lewis and Clark College
Portland, Oregon
December, 1957

xiii

Essentials in Christian Faith

Chapter I

Man and His Moral Dilemma

A writer in a popular magazine has written the following words: "We are all, if you will pardon the expression, headed for Hell in a handbarrow. If ever the people of the world stood in need of spiritual revival, it is now. We are beginning to poison the face of the earth with our miserable presence. The brakes are off. The cart of the world slides down the way greased with greed, hatred, ambition, lies, self-seeking and avarice toward the pit." [1]

The author of these words makes no pretense of being "a religious man." In fact, for him it is precisely religion in its organized forms which has in part caused the situation he deplores. He is careful to state that it is not "religion" for which he is looking. For, in his opinion, religion throughout the history of our culture has advanced its control over human beings by the instruments of bigotry and persecution. Yet, out of despair over the current human situation, he says: "The voice for which my heavy spirit is yearning must reach us all. . . . For if it is not heard, we are lost. Something there must be that we love other than ourselves. Some goal . . . beyond our material enrichment and the lust for power and position, some rewards founded upon goodwill, selflessness, and the innate

[1] Paul Gallico, "This Man's World: When Will the Spirit Revive?" *Esquire* Magazine, May, 1948, pp. 35, 114, 116-118.

dignity of the human spirit . . . honor . . . humility, decency, courage." [2]

It is significant that a thoroughly sophisticated modern like Paul Gallico, writing in the pages of a periodical not usually devoted to such subjects, should disclaim all religious pretensions and yet in the same breath use the language of religion. He reaches out for a frame of reference around which to organize human striving toward realization of goals and values. But even more profoundly than this, he states, "something there must be that we love other than ourselves." This is deep-rooted desire for total commitment to an object of devotion. His very questions are those of personal and ultimate concern in which there is probing beneath the surface of superficial human existence to some solid core of being. Here expressed is the kind of tension which men and women feel when they sense the wide gulf between their lives as they *are* and their lives as they *wish* they were. Their basic yearnings are religious in nature. Yet they are somehow afraid to call them religious. For apparently we have a predicament on our hands—with "the cart of the world [sliding] . . . toward the pit." If we are involved in a predicament, do we understand what it is? Can we find a way out? Are there religious answers? Or is religion itself only part of the disease instead of a cure?

Clearly, the only kind of religion which can challenge and attract thoughtful men today will come to grips realistically with the actual situations in which men live as individuals and groups. Religion worth its name claims to bring some constructive answers to the deepest and most pressing problems of human existence. Of course, some religions seem incapable of facing man's situation as it is. These kinds of religions offer false answers to false problems since they embrace neither what man is nor what he may legitimately hope to be. But the search on which we are embarked here is for authentic religion which brings genuine answers to real problems.

[2] *Ibid.*

Man and His Moral Dilemma

As the main themes of the first five chapters develop, three phases of the predicament of modern man will be discussed: his moral, his philosophical, and his personal dilemmas. The purpose of this first chapter is to examine the dilemmas which demand moral decisions of pressing urgency. The second chapter, which continues concern about man's moral problems into considerations of bases for solution, is entitled Living Creatively with Uncertainty. Chapter III will pose man's predicament as involving philosophical decisions about the nature of man himself in relation to the wider universe, under the title Man Faces His World. Chapter IV will offer some positive suggestions about this philosophical problem and is called The Search for a World View. Chapter V will be concerned with Man and His Self. Here man's personal predicament of tension and anxiety, in view of the specifically Christian interpretation of his nature, will be considered.

There keeps pressing in on thoughtful persons a question that is essential to the entire study of basic christian beliefs. It has to do with the Christian understanding of man and his human predicament as moral, philosophical, and personal. Is this interpretation valid in its fundamental insights and of value in coping honestly and effectively with our individual and social situation where we actually live day by day? If Christianity's way of posing the central questions of human existence is false and irrelevant, then the claims of its answers, which comprise the structure of Christian belief, become meaningless and irrelevant. Thus this baffling but important task of probing into our individual and social life in these times confronts every serious participant in the events of today's world. What is wrong with men and societies? How can we begin to grasp solutions to our dilemmas?

MAN'S MORAL PREDICAMENT

But how shall contemporary man's most pressing problems be characterized in more detail? First, *the predicament of modern man is moral.*

3

The American thinker, Thoreau, about a century ago, watched some workmen erect telegraph poles for the building of lines of communication across the continent. He wondered whether, with this new instrument, Maine would have anything important to say to Texas, or Texas to Maine. Man had perhaps only developed, he said, "improved means to unimproved ends."

The more intricate instruments of our own century and the human ingenuity which has contrived them pose an even more pressing question: Shall our wisdom about ends keep pace with our skill about means? The very energy heart of the physical universe has been cracked wide open. Meanwhile man stands in the midst of a civilization he has won at such cost, with all the powers of suns and planets held as means in his two hands. In his mind he is framing a moral decision about ends, in fact, a decision that has to do with sheer survival. The symbols of today are the atomic bomb and the hydrogen bomb. We have not yet discovered the symbols of the future.

Once Albert Einstein sent an urgent telegram to his fellow scientists: "The unleashed power of the atom has changed everything save our mode of thinking and we thus drift toward unparalleled catastrophe. We scientists who released this power have overwhelming responsibility in this world life and death struggle to harness the atom for benefit and not for humanity's destruction."

Everything has changed save our mode of thinking. This is startling expression of the perennial moral predicament of man in every age: serious thinking about ends and means. In that thinking we are realizing more pointedly than ever before that life itself is more than thought. Human personalities are wholes. Thought always leads to conduct. What men think is always spilling over into what they do. Educated men and women have been telling themselves that knowledge is more important than conduct and that technical skills possessed by clever people render them superior to moral obligations or social responsibility. Elton Trueblood has expressed the problem in this way: "Our predicament is but a com-

4

mentary not on instruments and instrument makers, but on human inability to employ both scientific knowledge and technical skill with moral and spiritual discipline that products of our human genius shall be used for the welfare of the human race rather than their harm and destruction."

Thus events of these past few years seem to have brought man to the very edge of an abyss. Beyond him beckon the possibilities both of life and death. But, for many a keen observer of today's human scene, the deepest abyss is *inside* man's own being: the threat of meaninglessness for human existence here and now and tragic hopelessness and despair which haunt the human mind.

The fact is, however, that many do not know or care that modern man has a moral dilemma on his hands. The most serious predicament would therefore appear to be that men do not realize they are involved in a predicament. For behind all the practical and immediate decisions of our personal, social, business, and political life, there moves the dynamic power of a different and more basic order of decision.

This is not to imply that busy people, engaged in meeting the many pressing demands of earning a livelihood and fulfilling their social obligations, are always aware of having made decisions of a different and more fundamental sort. Yet, however vague and unconscious these may be, principles, purposes, goals, and values of one sort or another do have important bearing on practical, day-to-day decisions and conduct. Living itself forces us to make choices, to take one course of action as contrasted with another, to give reasons for the direction in which we have decided to move rather than another.

But in order to decide such matters, we must form some scale of values or standards against which to measure our motives and actions. We praise with such statements as "He is a good man," and we blame by saying, "That's not fair," or "What you propose is unjust." But what are we expressing when we make such utterances? Are they the result of conscious deliberation in which universally valid principles are applied to concrete practical situations? Or are they simply the expressions of inner feelings, wishes, or desires? In the one case, values are said to be objective. In the other, they are said to be subjective. Values are objective if they do not depend on the inner feelings, wishes, or desires of individual persons. Values are subjective if they do depend, either entirely or in part, on the inner feelings, wishes, or desires of individual persons.

These contrasted views are integral parts of the moral dilemma of modern man. The difficulty is not simply that men have found no goals or standards by which to come to some agreements on patterns of personal and social conduct. Rather, it is the fact that men do not believe there *are* such goals or standards to be discovered. This is to say, many men do not now hold to the belief that the world is a moral order. For as W. T. Stace has expressed it:

> . . . the belief that the world is not a moral order is the same as the conception that moral values are subjective. For a value is subjective if it depends on human desires, feelings, or opinions. It is objective if it does not depend on any such human mental states. And if moral values depend on human psychology, then they do not exist in the universe apart from the existence and the thoughts of human beings. There was no good or evil in the world before there were any men, and there will be none after men cease to exist. The non-human universe which is our dwelling place has in itself nothing either moral or immoral. It is indifferent to our human values. It is a non-moral world.[3]

Somehow the view has come to pervade the minds of many modern men and women that the universe is basically neutral or indifferent to human aspiration and striving. Despite the fact that it is an illogical conclusion, countless men believe today that the physical sciences especially indicate that the world is a huge machine governed by physical forces within which man and his values are simply products. More will be said in Chapter II about the far-reaching practical effect of conclusions such as these. For

[3] W. T. Stace, *Religion and the Modern Mind,* Philadelphia, J. B. Lippincott Company, 1952, p. 104. I am indebted to Stace for the basic analysis of relativism presented throughout these pages.

now, we may note similar illogical conclusions which many today draw from the social sciences of psychology and sociology.

Most students in today's colleges and universities catch some glimpse at least of current developments in these fields; in fact, influences from these disciplines pervade every phase of contemporary culture. The first-hand impressions which students gather from these studies do not always agree with the views of competent social scientists. For the latter, as scientists, claim to do no more than describe the conditions under which individuals and groups behave in certain describable ways. Even the environmental factors which occasion men's *beliefs* and *values* are the legitimate objects of scientific investigation—providing this also purports only to describe, under assignable conditions, what effects result if given influences are present.

The social scientists do not, as scientists, claim to evaluate the resulting behavior or to state the validity of men's beliefs or standards, once they have occurred. Yet many a beginning student in these fields misunderstands the function of the social scientists at this point. Unfortunately, this misunderstanding is aided and abetted by some social scientists themselves. According to some psychologists, for example, what we think or value is merely the rationalization of our impulsive drives. A belief in God is only the infantile cry of the child for the protective love of a father, say the Freudians. And it has become commonplace to claim that the brooding pessimism of a Schopenhauer or the driving surge of a Nietzsche against dull conventionality can be explained by reactions against unfortunate relations with the opposite sex or rejection of small-town pietistic morality. All persons, it is believed, seek to sublimate the drives that are within them. Some compose symphonies; some build industrial empires; some espouse the cause of Christian love; some embrace metaphysical doctrines; some write poetry. None of these is any truer or even more valuable than any of the others, is the conclusion; for all are simply caused by one set of conditions or another and it is enough to describe what these are.

7

Essentials in Christian Faith

SUBJECTIVISM AND RELATIVISM OF VALUES

This point of view, converted into a systematized generalization beyond the limits of scientific investigation itself, becomes the articulate position called *subjectivism*. Questions of values illustrate the issues at stake here. What is value? Are there any absolute values? Do values have an objective status in the universe? For these are not themselves psychological questions which the social scientist might put to individual after individual in the attempt to discover what conditions usually produce certain attitudes or emotional tendencies. They are questions which reach beyond scientific description into interpretation of the world and the life of man within it: his goals and standards.

Subjectivism is the convenient name given to the considered view that values are not properties of objects outside us. Values here have no objective status in the universe; for we do not live in a world that is a moral order. They are rather just words used to describe certain experiences inside people. These experiences differ widely among persons of varied background and training. There are no universal values on which men can agree as binding on all. No ways can be discovered, therefore, according to subjectivism, by which the value judgments of various persons may be compared—let alone validated—by reference to any agreed-upon standards.

More pointed still is the view that subjectivism inevitably leads to *relativism,* adopted by many sociologists and anthropologists. It states that man's views of the nature of reality are simply the product of many complex social and cultural conditions. These are said to determine the specific values, ideas, and concepts which characterize men's world outlook. The result is that men and women are not merely confined within the limits of individual experience, as with subjectivism; they cannot step outside the orbit of the particular given culture within which they have received the conditioning influences which comprise their training. For among the factors determinative of men's world views and religious convictions and

8

accepted goals are group pressures, established mores, political processes, economic needs, technological developments, and the like. Men's moral ideals are thus the projections, upon the screen of the wider world of human relations, of the miniature pictures of the legal, political, economic, and cultural structures and patterns of the particular society within which they happen to live. Any attempt to discover universal standards binding on all men is thus a futile enterprise, according to this point of view, and ought to be given up.

Whenever man's moral predicament is discussed among students or other groups, invariably these issues of subjectivism and relativism are raised. The conversation may begin with the question whether or not we do in fact have a moral dilemma on our hands concerning the goals toward which our instruments are to be directed. All will appear to assent that we are faced with such a dilemma. "Must men, women, and young people direct their conduct toward good ends?" Yes! But then the inevitable question emerges sooner or later when someone remarks: "But by what standards can we make our judgments of good? For, of course, these always vary from individual to individual, from circumstance to circumstance, from age to age, from culture to culture."

It is the "of course" which is the significant refrain, echoed and reëchoed without question or challenge throughout the group engaged in discussion. Christian and non-Christian, religious and irreligious, alike seem to agree that "of course" morals are relative without realizing the deeper implications of what they are saying. For they detect no inconsistencies between their view that morals are relative and their religious faith, which affirms that this world is in some sense a moral order. Moreover, does theory in this instance agree with practice? Do decent folk of our acquaintance act as if there were discoverable standards of value and at the same time deny that in theory there really are any such standards? Thus our moral dilemma discloses itself in two interrelated phases: first, to be discussed in this chapter, the theoretical concern about the meaning of this doctrine of ethical relativity which is held and proclaimed so confidently; and second, consequences which this theoretical issue has for the practical conduct of affairs among men and nations, especially for those of Christian conviction. For taken together these two phases comprise the moral predicament of man in this or any age. We shall discuss the latter issue in Chapter II and also make some constructive suggestions concerning the direction in which the solution lies.

First, as to the meaning of moral relativity, W. T. Stace points out that the sentence so often uttered, "Morals are relative," may be understood in two entirely different ways. It is essential to keep these two meanings separate, for the failure to do so "is the root cause of much muddled thinking on the subject."

The first meaning of the sentence, "Morals are relative," states a fact that can hardly be denied: namely, that moral beliefs and standards do actually vary from age to age and from culture to culture, and are thus relative to the particular cultures within which they emerge. But its second meaning states much more than this. For those who utter it intend to say that the moral values of a particular society are *right* for that society. The confusion arises because, having accepted the first meaning as true (that standards do vary), many people suppose that the second meaning is also true (that the moral values of a particular society are right for that society but perhaps not right for another society). Bent on "proving" moral relativity in the second sense, many then go on to cite "evidence" which actually supports only the first meaning. They list case after case of discoveries made by anthropologists. But all such data as this show is that established mores or customs do in fact vary from society to society.

But then they move on from this first factual assertion to draw a conclusion which properly belongs to the second meaning of the sentence "Morals are relative." In John Graham Sumner's phrase, "The mores can make everything right." This would mean that what suits one group is right. Entirely the opposite modes of behavior may suit another group and these, also, are right. None are right, really, because all perspective for self-criticism has been lost and no meaningful statement can be made about what men ought to do. Self-criticism and dynamic correction of existing evils in a given society depend upon recognition and commitment to standards which transcend current practices. Otherwise the injustices, inequities, sicknesses, and degradation which infect a given society continue to fester as incurable sores. For to keep saying, as so many do in our day, that the moral values and practices of a society are right is to hold that there are no bases at all upon which morality may be established or moral affirmations make any claim to truth.

This situation is logically parallel to reasoning about the development of scientific knowledge of the physical universe out of primitive and (as now realized) false beliefs. For example, we now hold that the sun is the center of our universe, but there was a time in which men believed that the earth was the center of the universe. Do we then conclude that the sun at one time is the center of our universe and that at another time it is not? Yet the logic of this argument is exactly the same as the popularly accepted argument for moral relativism. Such an argument might proceed this way: In our culture we hold that private vengeance in retaliation for wrong done to us is immoral. But in other cultures and times private retaliatory vengeance is moral. The conclusion seems to be that private vengeance is bad in our culture and good in another. The logic of the argument about the sun is the same as that about private revenge. Most of us simply *see* the fallacy involved in the argument about the sun; for we acknowledge a distinction between our beliefs about the events and order of nature and the way these actually are. Yet in this argument and in the one about morals, as widely accepted among students and others, the conclusion is drawn that any and every belief is true in and for the society which holds it.

Conceivably, moral relativism might be true on quite other grounds, but its conclusive truth does not follow from the fact of wide variety between the standards and practices of different cultures. These other grounds, on which relativism could be logically established, involve basic decisions as to the very nature of the universe itself and of the nature of man, his beliefs, his values, within that universe. For the fundamental questions are these: Do we live in a universe that is a moral order? Are such universal and intrinsic values of justice and love grounded in the nature of things? Do men as persons find reality and power beyond their own striving to give direction, support, and significance to the human enterprise? How may these be found? What are the consequences for day-to-day living? These are not simply moral questions. They are also philosophical and religious questions, toward which we must press for meaningful answers.

Chapter II

Living Creatively with Uncertainty

"If it could be shown that we do *not* live in a moral order, that is, that subjectivism is true, and that relativism follows as a consequence of subjectivism, this would be a convincing argument for relativism." [1] But most of those who believe in relativism ground their conclusions on the first meaning of the sentence "Morals are relative" on the fact that beliefs and standards do vary from society to society. And lined up against the relativists of this sort are the *absolutists,* who claim that values do not vary as accidents of taste or circumstance but rather comprise fixed standards and principles which they believe to be true. These are assumed to be universal and objective truths about values. Obviously, the danger here is the opposite of that tentative skepticism which so often affects the relativist. For the absolutist easily becomes the authoritarian dogmatist who claims irrefutable finality for given systems of value.

The bewildered student of human affairs thus finds himself caught in the middle between extremes. He takes "All or nothing at all" as his theme song. He is convinced that he must subscribe to systems of value which, under the sanction of religion especially,

[1] W. T. Stace, *Religion and the Modern Mind,* Philadelphia, J. B. Lippincott Company, 1952, p. 119.

13

make claims of utter, unquestioning obedience upon him. But if not this, many students conclude, then the only other alternative is a skepticism in which all the rules are off and there is no certainty to be found in any case. Thus it is either dogmatism or skepticism, apparently, with no possible middle ground between.

CONSEQUENCES OF RELATIVISM FOR PRACTICAL AFFAIRS

It is at this strategic point that the second phase of the moral dilemma emerges: the consequences which the theoretical issue of the meaning of relativism have for the conduct of affairs among men and nations. The immediate effect for many who find themselves caught between extremes is paralysis or the complete indifference of ethical neutrality.

One day an eight-year-old blurted out a phrase at the lunch table she had heard somewhere: "Oh, it's one of the ten-shuns of the inter-um!" "One of the tensions of the interim," the sentence finally emerged. Are we living in an interim, a time between, and in a state of mind of suspended animation between certainty and skepticism? Elton Trueblood writes in his book, *Foundations for Reconstruction*, "The most common and the most damaging reaction to the shattering events of our time has been the emergence of an *interim mentality*. Emotionally we are a people waiting for a catastrophe."

Students sit down to talk about goals, values, and ambitions only to ask with indifference, "What's the use of a job, or preparation or education, or planning?" To use C. S. Lewis's phrase, we are a people "hag-ridden by the future." If only events out in the world would show promise of reaching a happy solution, and we could see where we are going, or could be certain about what values to hold and what goals to seek, *then* we could get on with our work day by day, we say. But in the meantime . . . and our voices trail off into vagueness.

The crucial practical moral dilemma confronting thoughtful persons, who are caught thus in our day between skepticism and dogmatism, is that of learning to live creatively with uncertainty. Can men and women learn to live with it, accepting it, coming to grips with it as a brute fact in the world all around us? Can they do this with our despair or disillusionment or shrug of the shoulder that says: What's the use? Can such realism that faces the facts of an uncertain, bewildering world be dynamically related to an ultimate hopefulness in certain principles regarded as absolute and unchanging?

In answer to the strange moods of the interim mentality, Elton Trueblood suggests a positive step. "We can make the decision to organize our lives as though they are to go on, and thus make the fundamental wager. We shall build best if, while we are fully aware of the danger which surrounds us, we proceed on the hypothesis that organized life will continue and that we are building for the generations."

Or to put it in the language of a feature article on landscape gardening: "Accept the immutable. Have fun with the variables." For there are certain factors about the plot of ground purchased for a home which are beyond immediate human control. Wishful thinking cannot change the unalterable contour of the land, or the soil, or the amount of sunlight, or neighbors' meddlesome children or pet dogs. But facing these peculiarities, in full realization that it is useless to struggle with wasted energies on unalterables, then the prospective homeowner can "have fun with the variables." Following the shape of the ground, he may set out his rock gardens, plant his flowers, shrubs, and trees.

In planning the shape of individual and social life also, we run head-on into certain set limits and conditions within which we must work for constructive change. Ideal goals seem unattainable and principles to which we are committed unrealizable. Meanwhile, in the face of baffling decisions which confront us, we fret out our days because often we have not learned to live with limitation, relativities, and uncertainties—always *this* side of these goals. This, on the practical side, is the crux of the moral dilemma which confronts us all in this or any age.

Jan Struther cites and comments on a couplet which expresses the same perspective:

> When you are an anvil, hold you still.
> When you are a hammer, strike your fill.

There are, she suggests, two balanced but related qualities of mind needed to meet man's moral predicament. One is patience. The other is courageous action. The problem is how to distinguish, in day-by-day experience, those moments which require patience from those which require action. Forces beyond conscious human control may strike at any hour. These demand our *anvil* moments, when all we can do is brace ourselves against the shock. But there are other situations in which clearly we have the power to act. Then we need all the firmness, energy, and singleness of purpose we can muster. We must strike quickly, strike hard, and, above all, strike in the right place. "With these two qualities," suggests Jan Struther, "*patience* and *strength*—we can endure all things and achieve many."

But countless men and women find it an intolerable task to live thus creatively with uncertainty, which involves critical and discerning judgment in knowing when to stand and when to act. Some find themselves, as we have suggested, suspended in the middle between extremes in either paralysis or indifference. Others, having taken seriously the fact of cultural relativity, sometimes turn to skepticism, in which they believe there are no final or absolute values to which human beings may commit their lives and destinies. Still others express a deep-rooted need for certainty in their commitment to values to such extent that they call upon the power of established authority and tradition to guarantee the rightness of their own beliefs. Thus peace of mind, a feeling of security, faith in detailed codes and institutions, are often purchased at the price of the sacrifice of critical judgment or mutual understanding.

16

Living Creatively with Uncertainty

Strangely enough the contemporary relativist, as we have characterized him, adopts his relativism because he thinks he stands thereby for freedom against the sterile conventionality of existing ways of believing and behaving. But as a matter of fact, if he were consistent, he would readily admit that he possesses no dynamic for constructive change because what actually is the custom within a given culture is right. For the insistent pressures of current moral and social conventions, exercised through groups, institutions, and patterns of mores, determine what is right. In effect, these "relativities" have become "absolutes" over which he can exert no control. Thus the extreme relativist and the absolutist find themselves in exactly the same position of uncritical acceptance of the *status quo* which paralyzes appropriate action based on sound judgment. For both the extreme relativist and the extreme absolutist, these consequences emerge: (1) Questions of value cannot even be discussed because the answers are fixed—in the one case by pressures of convention and in the other by externally imposed authority. (2) In the long run, questions of value are meaningless because, for both extreme views, questions of value reduce to questions of fact as to what is or is not "the thing to do." Hence for both views, the questions "What is really most valuable? What ought men to do?" simply disappear.[2]

OBJECTIVE RELATIVISM

But in response to the issues we have raised, there is another alternative, which in theory overcomes these difficulties and asserts (1) that values can be discussed and (2) that value statements about what men ought to do are meaningful. Furthermore, in practical application this point of view makes it possible to live creatively with uncertainty and to work constructively, within given limitations and relativities, toward the realization of values and principles held as objective. This position is called by various

[2] Philip Wheelwright, *The Way of Philosophy*, New York, The Odyssey Press, 1954, pp. 420 ff.

names, but the light it throws on man's moral dilemma is more significant than labels. The term *objective relativism* indicates its intended meaning more accurately than any of the others used among writers in the philosophy of value.[3] For the objective relativist attempts to synthesize the insights of both objectivism and relativism. Yet he would assert that his is no mechanical compromise theory which takes objectivism from one philosopher and relativism from another. He believes rather that both objectivism and relativism are extreme exaggerations that stress certain phases of value experiences to the neglect of others.

According to Beck the objective relativist holds that he has found a single answer to two different questions that bother the objectivist and the relativist in turn. The objectivist asks: If value judgments are just the expressions of likes or dislikes of many different individuals, how can we account for agreement about values shared by many diverse groups and cultures? The relativist asks: If values are objective qualities which men can discover and know, how can we account for the wide diversity of judgment about values as between groups and cultures? Each of these has a grasp on an essential aspect of the human value situation. The objectivist is concerned about agreement, but at the cost of overlooking the diversity that obviously exists. The relativist is concerned about diversity, but at the cost of overlooking agreement or near agreement, which also obviously exists among many groups.

But the objective relativist would insist against the extreme relativist that the fact of agreement, among some groups at least, is important. In short, as Wheelwright [4] puts the case, questions of value can be discussed; for (1) values are real and objective, and furthermore, (2) questions of value are meaningful. But on the other hand, against the extreme objectivist, the objective relativist

---

[3] For definition and discussion of this point of view, see *ibid.*, and also Lewis White Beck, *Philosophic Inquiry*, New York, Prentice-Hall, Inc., 1952, pp. 212 ff.

[4] *Op. cit.*, p. 423.

holds that the other phase of the value situation must not be over-looked, namely, the fact that (3) values are relational or contextual since they always do have their origin within the living and limiting conditions within which men make their moral decisions. Even though values are thus relational or contextual, they are nonethe-less real and hence open for meaningful discussion. We would sum-marize briefly the case for objective relativism or contextual objec-tivism as presented by Wheelwright in his clear and concise fashion.

1. *Values are real and objective.* The argument which supports this assertion consists, according to Wheelwright,[5] in showing "that diversity and fluctuation of value-judgments is no logical disproof that values may objectively exist." Two analogous cases are then cited. First, size. Two different individuals may see a given object and come to diverse conclusions about its size. Yet, sensibly, these two persons do not claim that the object has no size at all. Rather they proceed to measure so that each can check his impression with the object itself. Or, second, diverse experiences of color or tempera-ture may occasion real dispute about exact shades of blue or the exact degree of warmth in a room. Here also measurement is resorted to, although, in the case of color or temperature, it is less direct than measurement of size. These measurable qualities are, of course, matters of relationship and always occur within contexts which include the persons who experience them. Yet these primary and secondary qualities, as they are called, are real and agreement can be reached concerning them.

May the same be said of "tertiary qualities" of objects of expe-rience: beautiful, ugly, good, bad, noble, revolting?[6] Can these values be referred to any objective standard in the same way or at least in any analogous way? The objective relativist insists that they can. Values may be in part dependent on the interests of the person who holds them and within the context of environing con-ditions within which they occur. Yet the holder of this view insists

[5] *Ibid.*, p. 421.
[6] *Ibid.*

that values are not exclusively private or personal. They are known in a way just as valid and basic and objective as the objects of facts about the world of nature. At the very least, they can be discussed.

2. *Value statements are meaningful.* Wheelwright develops an imaginatively suggestive point of view concerning the meaningfulness of value statements.[7] Some contemporary writers insist that value statements contain two elements: one, *declarative,* stating that the speaker either likes or dislikes a certain object in a certain way; and, second, a *nondeclarative* element in the form of a command which enjoins another person to share the approval or disapproval. Wheelwright's point is that in all genuine value judgments, this latter nondeclarative element is not basically a command to somebody else. Rather it is a self-command. He writes:

> Let each reader test this for himself by introspective reflection. Think of some *discovery* of value and consequent obligation—e.g., when one recognizes what one owes to a friend in need and accepts the obligation to help him. In a practical situation like this the value at issue is perhaps never formulated in words. Whether it is or not, it involves more than factual discovery. "I *want* to help my friend." Of course there is this too. But there may be an even stronger contrary pull—"It is so inconvenient to give him the help he needs!" The question is not the factual one of which motive is, at the moment of considering them, stronger. The reasoner does not reduce the question to the simple factual form. "Which do I actually want to do more?" Even if he uses that form of words, there is surplus of meaning which they do not express. That additional element of meaning comes not as a discovery of fact, but as a discovery of command; and not a command issued by one individual to another, but a command issuing somehow out of the situation, or it may be from beyond the situation, and which the reasoner beholds as an obligation to be fulfilled—or better, as a vocation, *a being called.* A real value judgment is always in part an answer to the command, a "So be it!"[8]

[7] *Ibid.,* pp. 423-425, for discussion of the views of Charles L. Stevenson. See his *Ethics and Language,* New Haven, Yale University Press, 1944, Chap. II.

[8] Wheelwright, *op. cit.,* pp. 425-426.

Living Creatively with Uncertainty

What is the source of command in which concerned persons may reach decision and constructive action? Here I move beyond Wheelwright's explicit statements into the context of basic Christian belief. From the perspective of the committed Christian, this source of moral imperative is the God of Justice and Love as disclosed in Jesus Christ. The fuller implications of God's relation to the moral life and the role of Jesus Christ, in his person and in his teaching, must be reserved for discussion in later chapters. For now it is sufficient to say, as we have suggested above, that man's moral questions at their deepest levels of concern keep pointing toward questions which are philosophical and religious. The most fundamental of these is: Do we live in a universe that is a moral order? Are values such as justice and love grounded in the nature of things? Do men find reality and power beyond their own striving to give direction, support, and significance to the human enterprise?

Men and women of Christian commitment stake their faith on an affirmative answer to these questions. For it is the Christian conviction that we *do* live in a morally ordered world and that human beings find fulfillment in response to the demand from beyond themselves to realize more fully justice and love in every phase of human relationship.

But this is not to claim that men and groups of men, in their limitations and self-seeking, ever completely succeed in meeting the demand for justice and love, nor, within the pressure of many conflicting needs and loyalties, that what men believe in specific terms to be good always is good. Nor does this view deny the fact of wide variety among the detailed standards and practices of different ages and cultures. For Christianity is not an abstract system of detailed codes for conduct, prescribing in exact terms what men and women must or must not do under any and every circumstance. If this were the case, it would be a kind of legalism in which one moral rule could be applied automatically to each kind of moral situation. But obviously your neighbor, and you yourself, have many different needs of varying degrees under changing times and con-

21

ditions. If you respond dynamically to the command from beyond yourself to embody in your everyday living the principles of justice and love, you will not be told thereby exactly how to meet your neighbor's needs. For no matter how devoted you may be in your *whole* person, exactly what to do in detail to actualize these principles will depend upon the circumstances and the times and the strength and sensitivity of your own commitment of intelligent judgment.

It has been stated that objective relativists hold that values are real and objective, and that value statements are meaningful. These two claims are made against extreme relativists in the conviction that value judgments can be discussed and the search for fuller realization of values demands the complete commitment of concerned men and women. The Christian perspective moves beyond these considerations to state that the source of moral imperative is the God of Justice and Love as disclosed in Jesus Christ. But a third statement is implied in what we have been saying. This assertion is made against the claims of the extreme absolutist.

3. *Values are relational or contextual.*[9] Here also the Christian perspective, as already indicated, is consistent with objective relativism. How can the values of justice and love be declared to be meaningful, real, objective, and yet conditioned within the contexts of changing times, shifting circumstances, and varying cultures?

THE SOURCE OF MORAL OBLIGATION FOR CHRISTIANS

Christianity is a movement let loose in human history that expresses itself according to the needs of the successive social and cultural environments within which it comes to live. To follow the Christian way of life involves far more profound commitment and insight than simply "following the teachings of Jesus," as many in our day insist. For an exact pattern of goodness, developed for the first century, cannot be reproduced in the twentieth. Ours is a different world. Jesus cannot therefore be copied slavishly by all

[9] *Ibid.*, p. 426.

people, in all places, in all times—as if religion, or morality either, were lived mechanically by rote or dull imitation. For, as will be discussed in later chapters, "to be like Christ" and to enter into relationship of creative good will with God and man, within the moral order of the universe, strikes much deeper than that. Although Jesus' specific moral precepts do not tell us precisely what to do in our personal and social relationships, it is the Christian conviction that the Spirit which is released through Him into human history is the dynamic source of power and insight for all effective moral criticism and reform.

George Bernard Shaw once said: "The only man who behaves sensibly is my tailor; he takes my measure anew everytime he sees me, whilst all the rest go on with their old measurements, and expect them to fit me."

Each succeeding generation therefore must discover the significance of that Spirit anew and apply the insights gained therefrom to new situations in freshly creative ways. As to how this shall take place, once commitment has been made to the principles of love and justice, only intelligent judgment within the context of urgent and practical need will determine.

This is the story of the dynamic relation between the Christian movement and the Western world. For example, Paul, and many another like him, brought Christianity into the Greco-Roman world without any explicit intention of directly changing established social patterns. Yet he helped release into the world forces powerful enough to aid in altering the basic structure of Western civilization. For example, Paul was not interested in education, as such, but yet Christianity became the sponsor and custodian of education throughout the so-called Dark Ages. Paul built no hospitals, yet the motivating spirit of Christian love was to keep open houses of mercy through hard and cruel times. Paul overthrew no totalitarian governments, but the creative power of Christian justice stood opposed to despotism everywhere. This is not to suggest that Christians completely measured up to their ideal standards, or even

23

do today; for on many occasions it is used as sanction for cruelty and injustice. The demands for fuller insight, love, mercy, and justice than man has yet known always outreach the measures of his achievements and stand in constant criticism of cultural patterns and modes of conduct among individuals and groups.

What we are suggesting here is that, for the Christian, the theoretical problems about values and practical commitment become one deep-rooted concern. In terms of conviction, there is no basic contradiction between this kind of commitment to certain moral principles regarded as universal, objective, and absolute and the relativity of detailed application to varying needs and conditions of everyday living. For even men's value insights themselves become sharper, clearer, more compelling, in the midst of the context of day-to-day living. Thus the search for values and men's continuing conversation about the meaning of values is never closed but always imaginatively open. If we claim, with the extreme relativist, that there are no objective values, then there is nothing to discuss. And if, with the extreme absolutist, we say that one code or pattern of value is to be regarded as literally absolute, then in this case also we cannot talk about it. In neither instance is there fundamental dynamic for social change because what *is* is right.

Yet whether we wish it or not, new physical forces and their possibilities for mankind's benefit or destruction have changed everything "save our mode of thinking," as Einstein stated in the telegram quoted earlier, "and we thus drift toward unparalleled catastrophe." It cannot be doubted that there is close connection between the prevalent moral relativism of our age and the current moral chaos among men and nations. According to relativism, standards of one society are final within that society. But as between cultures or even nations, no moral values are binding on all. In practical terms, therefore, the result is international chaos and constant threat of conflict. Neither, on their terms, is there any possibility of solution; relativism means at its roots that *we do not live in a moral universe.*

24

Living Creatively with Uncertainty

The pressing demand upon men of moral concern today is the discovery of moral principles to pull the scattered fragments of human life into a unity. Failing to find such principles, as Gerald Heard suggests, even technical science itself is doomed and all our culture will fall. We shall be defeated, he says, "where defeat is final—in our minds. Our power to think constructively, to make sense of experience will fail. The human intellect will be bankrupt."

But in the meantime? Shall men give way to the tentative skepticism of "the interim mentality"? Or embrace a dogmatic authoritarianism? Can we live hopefully, meanwhile, in the midst of uncertainty, committed to ultimate principles, without despair or disillusionment? What shall we think? What shall we believe? On what view of the nature of things can we act? For our thinking about man's moral predicament, in both its theoretical phases and practical applications, involves the question: Do we or do we not live in a moral universe? What sort of world is it in which we live? Can man's life matter in so vast and mysterious a universe? Is it friendly or indifferent to man, his aspirations, his values, his achievements? These are questions which comprise man's philosophical predicament. To this we turn in the next chapter.

Chapter III

Man Faces His World

The German pessimist, Arthur Schopenhauer, is said to have gone out for a stroll one evening through the streets of Berlin. Fatigued from his walk and weighed down with thoughts of the unintelligibility of the universe and the dark mystery of man, he sat down on a bench to rest. A policeman, seeing this shabbily dressed figure, mistook the great philosopher for a beggar or tramp and demanded, "Who are you? What are you doing here?" Schopenhauer, still concentrating on his problems, answered in desperate tones, "I wish to God I knew!" [1]

There is a profound difference between the policeman's matter-of-fact questions and the way in which Schopenhauer, in his philosophical and personal preoccupation, understood them. The officer of the law wanted a catalogue of data so as properly to classify an unidentified human figure on a bench; name, address, occupation, proof of social respectability. But Schopenhauer was asking himself questions about his own ultimate destiny in the midst of a vast and mysterious universe. He symbolizes the quest of man in every age for significant answers concerning the nature of the universe and of his own status within that universe. Who are you? What are you doing here? Does your life matter in such a universe? Is it

[1] Norman Pittenger, *The Christian Way in a Modern World*, Louisville, Cloister Press, 1944, p. 1.

the kind of world that makes response to your aspirations? Or is it fundamentally indifferent to your striving? Is it a *moral universe* that supports human values and therefore renders them objective and yet dynamically related to day-by-day decisions and acts? And what of the reality of God and human awareness of His self-disclosure in nature and history? Do we live in the sort of universe in which this is possible? Or are all these questions senseless and meaningless, the cries of children in the lonely dark for comfort and security when they ought to realize that none can be found?

Some would say that the lives of individual persons do not matter. Nothing matters in any ultimate sense. For all there is, is matter. You yourself are nothing but a *thing,* such as a bit of steel or stone; or just a collocation of atoms, swirling centers of forces and energies. You are a cog in a machine. At most, you are simply one event within a mechanical universe, a process among many natural processes, such as the mathematically precise movements of a planet or the growth of a biological organism.

Others would tell you that you are nothing but a bundle of reflexes—a knee jerk. You are a puppet on a string. Or cynically, some would offer you these estimates of yourself: You are an insignificant insect on a pigmy planet blindly whirling through space. You are a "ridiculous parasite on a dying speck of matter in infinite space and infinite cold!" You, as a man, are a high form of cosmic accident. You are simply

> An infant crying in the night;
> An infant crying for the light,
> And with no language but a cry.[2]

Do you like this picture of yourself and of the universe in which you live? Is it true or is it false? Whether men and women consciously admit it or not, this is the philosophy by which countless thousands actually live in our day. There is a child's song:

[2] Tennyson, *In Memoriam,* Section 54, stanza 5.

Oh, a-hunting we will go,
A-hunting we will go!
We'll catch a little fox,
And put him in a box—
And then we'll let him go.

What has happened to values? According to subjectivism and relativism, these are shut up within the "box" of men's own inner feelings and desires. As for ideas, these also are simply ideologies expressive of the narrow interests of men and groups of men. And as to the being of God, many in our day have "put Him in a box." For God is all shut up inside our minds somewhere. God is simply a man's own inner thoughts—a voice from within. But what of the on-moving processes of the universe outside us, the realms of nature and history? According to some current philosophers, they grind on their way determined by the laws of their own necessity. Values have no objective status; for this is not a moral universe in which we strive and make our decisions. Ideas do not refer to anything "real" behind this façade of things and events we experience with our senses. The natural universe knows nothing of any God. For outside this little circle of light, with its human aspiration and striving, lies that vast and dark area of impersonal forces and energies within which event moves relentlessly into succeeding event. And what of human history beneath the blank heavens? As someone puts it, the complex life of men and societies looks like "the swarming of ants in the gleam of a million million suns." Values, ideas, God? Put them in a box, safely tucked away within the inner minds of men. But, it is said, they have nothing to do with the world of nature as it actually is. The universe is so overwhelmingly large; the minds of men—their values, their ideas, their God— so ineffectually small.

THE PHILOSOPHICAL DILEMMA OF MODERN MAN

Archibald MacLeish has written a poem about a circus tent. The armless man was lighting a match between his great and second toe, and Madame Sossman was just ready to place her head in the lion's mouth, when, all unannounced, the big top was blown away by a sudden squall. "And there," says the poet,

> . . . There overhead, there, there hung over
> Those thousands of white faces, those dazed eyes,
> There in the starless dark, the poise, the hover,
> There with vast wings across the cancelled skies.
> There in the sudden blackness, the black pall of
> nothing, nothing, nothing,—nothing at all.[3]

This is the philosophical dilemma of modern man as he faces his world: the human race, staring into the starless dark—into nothing at all. As was said earlier, scientists have opened the heart of the universe. And men somehow have concluded that within that searing heat and blinding light the real nature of things is disclosed. It seems to be the sort of impersonal universe they were afraid it was all along. And unfortunately some, in their bewilderment and overwhelming fear, have simply given up trying to discover what the universe is, essentially and really.

But the philosophical dilemmas of modern man are not easily solved. They involve patient and persistent search on the part of men and women who are convinced that there *are* answers to be found and who are willing to undertake critical and imaginative examination of prevalent ideas about the nature of the world. In this chapter we shall therefore present a brief account of the nature of the philosophical enterprise in which all of us share. In Chapter IV, we shall discuss the search for a world view. There the question will confront us: Is that philosophical enterprise a meaningful and fruitful one? For some in our day would define its function in a certain highly specialized way. But in Chapter IV, positive suggestions will be made as to how, in pursuit of the philosophical quest for some answers as to the nature of the universe, we may avoid tentative skepticism and agnosticism on the one hand and

[3] Archibald MacLeish, "The End of the World," *Poems 1924–1933,* Boston, Houghton Mifflin Company, 1933.

closed dogmatism on the other. Also, we shall explore the significance of what it means to be a Christian who yet, in the light of his faith, seeks to carry on the persistent search for answers concerning the reality of the wider world in which we live.

THE NATURE OF PHILOSOPHY

As to the nature of philosophy, it is easier to show what philosophy does than to construct a pat definition of what it is. This is so in part because philosophers themselves do not agree as to how to define the term. For one school of thought may omit what other schools would regard as essential to an adequate definition. But the main reason why it is easier to show what philosophy does than to define it is this: philosophy is not a thing or an entity. "Philosophy" is nothing in itself. It is a word used to describe what happens when people undertake a specific conscious activity. It is the intellectual enterprise called philosophizing.

Philosophy lives in men's minds. It becomes articulate in their words and embodied in their actions. In this broad sense, every man is a philosopher; for each one of us is constantly engaged in the process of developing and expressing in one way or another what he believes. The following characteristic functions of philosophy begin then to emerge.

1. *Philosophy is the sum of beliefs.* William Ernest Hocking writes: "We mean by a man's beliefs all those judgments, from certainties or convictions at one extreme to mere impressions at the other, upon which he customarily acts. Beliefs are the opinions a man lives by, as distinct from those he merely entertains: in this sense they constitute his philosophy." [4]

Beliefs do make a difference. There has developed among us of late a strange and potentially dangerous attitude toward beliefs. Some say it does not matter what a person believes because actions are more important than opinions. But actions are a direct result

[4] William Ernest Hocking, *Types of Philosophy,* New York, Charles Scribner's Sons, 1939, pp. 1-2.

of ideas. Ideas, held strongly and passionately by consolidated groups of determined people, may occasion catastrophic changes in the social order. Every person, for better or worse, does possess a body of ideas or principles around which his life is organized. The sum of these beliefs comprises his philosophy.

Someone asked Daniel Boone, the intrepid explorer, if he had ever been lost. After a moment's silence, he replied, "No, I have never been lost. But I was bewildered once for three days." Caught in the midst of confusing and conflicting pressures, men and women today are bewildered. Minds have become numbed. "What do I believe?" some ask themselves. Or more profoundly still, "Am I capable of believing anything?" And then, "Why is it so important?"

In answer to such questions as these, there are words of G. K. Chesterton which are quoted in many introductory textbooks in philosophy. But they are still apt. "There are some people—and I am one of them—who think that the most practical and important thing about a man is still his view of the universe. We think that for a landlady considering a lodger it is important to know his income, but still more important to know his philosophy. We think that for a general about to fight an enemy it is important to know the enemy's numbers, but still more important to know the enemy's philosophy. We think that the question is not whether the theory of the cosmos affects matters, but whether in the long run anything else affects them." [5]

In his *Pragmatism,* William James states that he agrees with Mr. Chesterton in this matter and adds that ". . . the most interesting and important thing about you is the way in which it [your philosophy] determines the perspective in your several worlds . . . the philosophy which is so important in each of us is not a technical matter; it is our more or less dumb sense of what life honestly and deeply means. It is only partly got from books; it is our individual

[5] G. K. Chesterton, *Heretics,* New York, Dodd, Mead & Company, 1923, pp. 15-16.

way of just seeing and feeling the total push and pressure of the cosmos." [6]

Everybody possesses beliefs whether he is willing to acknowledge it or not: all those opinions he lives by and on which he customarily acts. These constitute his philosophy.

2. *Philosophy is the special science of examining beliefs.* Philosophy, in this more precise sense, consists in the critical and systematic attempt to think one's way through to a wellgrounded set of beliefs. For the philosophical frame of mind, no ideas are exempt from the clear white light of critical scrutiny. This is the case even with those religious beliefs which we hold sacred. Each of us needs to keep asking and reasking, "Where did I get that belief? From a teacher, a friend, parents, some authority? From my own personal experience? Do I hold it simply because someone else has commended it to me?"

George Macdonald has said: "Each generation must do its own seeking and finding. The father's having found is only warrant for the children's search." This is not to discredit authority of various sorts as the source of our beliefs. For most of our ideas come by way of authority or suggestion in the midst of our everyday contacts. Philosophy as abstract reasoning cannot itself furnish us with the materials of conclusive belief about ourselves or our world. Walk through the backyard in the dark and step on a rake carelessly left on the ground. Just so, beliefs "hit" us in the midst of day-by-day experience. What, then, does philosophy do in relation to everyday living?

"Now a faith, all ready-made, is something philosophy cannot provide men with. Only experience can do that, and it is a slow and painful process. But philosophy can help our inquirer in that hardest of human tasks, learning from experience. And it can clarify the faith that is already in him, and help him enlarge that

[6] William James, *Pragmatism*, New York, Longmans, Green, and Co., 1907, pp. 3-4.

faith by experience: and it can make him more humane and less fanatical and dogmatic. . . ." [7]

Granted that our beliefs come to us from all sorts of sources, including those of authority or suggestion, philosophy can aid us in discovering what the actual grounds are upon which human beliefs are based, and then what grounds are good grounds. In this way we engage in a coöperative effort to understand our convictions, render our thoughts explicit and systematic, and imaginatively project into this wider world the consequences which follow from the ideas we hold.

3. *Philosophy is the fine art of asking relevant questions.* Philosophy thus is a process of critical search for a pattern or unity below the flux of experience—distinguishing the true from the false, fact from fiction, reality from illusion. Men of philosophical mind are never content with partial, fragmentary answers, although they may have to put up with such answers so long as they are finite human beings. But the search is the thing. To be philosophical means to be possessed of an attitude, a frame of mind: curious, free, open, steady, imaginative. In the midst of the search, certitudes may begin to emerge.

Like Socrates, the "gadfly" harassing respectable and comfortable folk with endless questions, the philosophically minded person today probes beneath everything which everybody else takes for granted. People say concerning questions of fact: "That is true." The philosopher asks: "What *is* truth?" Your friends say to you about matters under investigation: "I am not guessing here; I know." The philosopher wants to know about all such claims: "By what criteria may anyone legitimately claim to know? What is knowledge?" These are questions generally included under that formal field of philosophy called *epistemology,* or *theory of knowledge.*

Then there are questions of axiology or value, which we dis-

[7] John Herman Randall, Jr., and Justus Buchler, *Philosophy, An Introduction,* New York, Barnes & Noble, Inc., 1952, p. 12.

cussed in Chapters I and II. Your neighbor points to a mutual acquaintance and says: "He is a good man." You may not wish to dispute your neighbor's judgment. But, as a philosopher, you are moved to ask certain prior questions about the bases of all such judgments. When is a man good—any man? By what standards may you judge a person good? What is goodness? These are the questions of the branch of philosophy known as *ethics*. The problems of *aesthetics* are raised every time anyone exclaims: That is beautiful! For again the philosopher asks the searching question: "By what standards may you make judgments of value in the field of the arts? What is beauty?"

A comment frequently on our lips is: "That is real." That is a real friend. He is a real man. This may be a legitimate claim in many instances. But often it is spurious. We keep blurring the distinctions between the real and the illusory. Beneath all men's day-by-day confusions lie the deeper questions in which the philosopher is interested. These are the philosophical questions *par excellence*, the problems of *metaphysics:* What is reality anyway? What is the real in itself in relation to which everything else receives its significance? The specific questions of *ontology* are here involved: What does it mean to *be*—not to exist as this or that, but to be at all? What is being, as such? Is there some ultimate reality— the very stuff of the cosmos which is the source and ground of all existence? What is the nature of the universe? And what is man in the midst of it all? What is the essential being of man?

Finally, in a moment of worship a man says: "I have found God. Now I know where my destiny lies and my salvation." The philosopher, as a man, may also claim that he too has undergone such immediate experiences and is convinced of their authenticity. But, if he is interested in the philosophy of religion, he presses on to ask the constructively critical questions: Is there an ultimate being we call God? Does the evident need of man for a final source and ground of his destiny find cosmic response? Are the asserted convictions of religion genuine or illusory? Is this a moral universe?

Man Faces His World

Are the highest values we know rooted at the heart of the universe or are they doomed to eventual extinction? And is death the end or is there more for which we may hope?

Through the centuries this process of persistent questioning has been formalized into the several fields of philosophical investigation such as those we have just mentioned. But their pursuit has often been technical and sometimes a confusion of terms and subtle distinctions. This is the point where "personal" philosophy becomes the kind of enterprise which professional philosophers engage in. But in the long run the professional philosopher is attempting to utilize the tools of a technical discipline to deal with the very same questions which are the concerns of personal philosophy.

The difference between the two is one of precision and thoroughness of investigation. The value of the technical variety is purely instrumental. That is, it is a means to the end of more adequate understanding of the world. Sometimes this perspective of technical philosophy is lost. Then philosophy becomes highly abstract logical and semantic analysis written primarily for the edification of other professional philosophers. But where this perspective is preserved, technical philosophy is helpful for every serious student in his effort to understand the significance of human existence within the larger world which is his home.

Chapter IV

The Search for a World View

Thoughtful men and women keep putting persistent questions to the world in which they find themselves. It is not necessary to be a professional philosopher or even a professional in religion to be curious about such matters. Every one of us may attain those moments of deepest reflection when we ask: What is truth? What is goodness? What is beauty? What is reality? What of the Being of God? What does it mean to be a man? But may we legitimately expect to find definite answers?

This is the center of the philosophical predicament of man. What kind of world do we have on our hands? Is man forever destined to look into the blank heavens and "the starless dark," into a mechanical world that makes no response to his hopes and dreams? Are his ideas, his values, and his God just subjective notions, "shut up in a box?" Is the world any different for the Christian in contrast to the secularist? In any case, are there any answers?

Is the objective nature of things as they actually are knowable? Is there an answer which is the truth about the universe and the significance of the things, events, and persons within it? Is there likewise a distinctive key or clue corresponding to each of our questions, so that we may know of a certainty what things are good, beautiful, real, or divine? These are all-important phases of the metaphysical quest through which men hope to discover the general nature of reality and the significance of man, his knowledge, and his values within the totality of everything we call reality.

Three matters of serious concern will be discussed in this chapter: (1) Is this philosophical enterprise in its quest for answers a fruitful and meaningful one? (2) How, positively, may we pursue the metaphysical quest for some answers as to the nature of the universe? (3) How may a person of Christian conviction view the wider world in which he lives?

THE PURPOSE OF PHILOSOPHY

Is this philosophical enterprise a fruitful and meaningful one? Many a person gives up the metaphysical quest at this crucial stage, for he had hoped perhaps to find *one truth* clearly labeled. Now, to his bewilderment, he discovers down through the ages a veritable procession of varied answers. Each carries its own banners stating its claims. Each demands to be heard. The total effect is confusion and contradiction. Instead of providing answers to doubts and settling perplexities, these clamoring voices only succeed in raising more doubts and driving perplexity toward skepticism, disillusionment, and cynicism. Are there no answers? There are too many answers. And this is just as bad as no answers, says our seeker. For it must be either all or nothing at all! Philosophies and theologies cannot prove anything because they try to prove too many different and conflicting things. The final step for such a person is then to give up once and for all any attempt "to see life steadily and see it whole." One is thus a prey either to continuing skepticism, which holds that no knowledge at all is possible, or agnosticism, which claims that knowledge of metaphysical reality is impossible even though we may know many immediate objects of scientific investigation and practical pursuit. And for some the quest ends in blind grasp of some insistently dogmatic and authoritative faith preached with fervor and emotional appeal.

But, most likely, such a person as this continues to carry around with him the inherently metaphysical assumptions of his own uncritical beliefs. He does, whether he explicitly admits it or not, tacitly acknowledge and use one view or another about the world and his place within it. Yet he protests that technical metaphysics or even any personally undertaken attempt to find a world view is a foolish waste of time. For it is an impractical enterprise that bakes no bread, builds no houses, cures no diseases, fights no wars. Let us get on with the world's practical business, then, concludes our man of common sense.

An influential group among current philosophical movements develops into precise, articulate expression these common-sense protests against all metaphysical speculation. These philosophers do not so much comprise a school of thought in the usual sense as a trend or movement which since the 1920's and 30's has had more widespread and profound effect than we can yet measure. *Logical positivism,* or *logical empiricism,*[1] is the most intellectually aggressive movement yet to arise within technical philosophy, and yet its implications have cut a wide swath in practically every field of interest: scientific, ethical, cultural, and theological. Its advocates have occasioned searching criticism especially of traditional and commonly accepted notions of moralists, theologians, and metaphysicians. More specifically, logical empiricists attempt to revise the function of philosophy itself in such a way as to render any attempt to discover the ultimate nature of the universe as a whole a senseless undertaking.

The legitimate task of philosophy, according to this view, is analysis of the logical relations, the language forms, and the methods of the experimental sciences. Philosophy is not concerned with producing the factual materials of knowledge, for that is the

[1] Brief discussion of this movement will be found in the Appendix to this chapter, pp. 49-55. Those readers who are concerned about this problem of the status and value of the metaphysical enterprise would do well to examine the claims of *logical empiricism.*

task of the sciences themselves. Rather, philosophy has as its main purpose, as Ludwig Wittgenstein states it, "the logical clarification of thoughts." It should give up, once and for all, the unfruitful metaphysical speculations in which traditional philosophers and theologians have been engaged for some 2500 years. For these dealers in fancies and dreams have fondly imagined that they could know and state in understandable language the actual nature of things as a whole. But once philosophers realize that these attempts at speculative metaphysical knowledge are to no avail, then they will get on with the important work of critical analysis. So with all of us, whether we express our philosophical ideas as professionals or amateurs, we ought to exercise extreme care as to precision of meaning. What do you mean, what can you possibly mean, when you utter words such as spirit, soul, good, being, freedom, immortality, faith, God? Do these terms make sense, or are they literally nonsense?

THE METAPHYSICAL QUEST

Can we pursue the quest for some of the answers as to the nature of the universe? Is there a fruitful method of procedure? The critical philosophy of the logical empiricists does not render the metaphysical quest impossible or worthless. But their radical rejection of metaphysics puts us on guard against any presumptuous claims to absolute and finally demonstrable truth. For the method used in the search for a world view is different from that employed in the sciences. The way in which a metaphysical system is developed lies closer to the imaginative creativity of the poet, novelist, or artist than to the precise experimentation of the chemist or physicist.

Of course, such a theory of the nature of things is not merely imaginative. It must somehow explain, gather into itself, render intelligible, whole masses of material which comprise these human experiences of ours. In this sense, a metaphysical view becomes a *hypothesis,* not a completely verified truth, but the most fruitful suggestion yet envisioned, on the way to confirmation. The alert and sensitive interpreter of the world will become aware of the widest possible range of facts and results of investigation in every conceivable field of knowledge. But, as has been pointed out, this does not mean ". . . that the philosopher first gathers all facts and all knowledge together, and then proceeds to interpret them by picking out what is important and significant. . . . For human thought never operates by first assembling all the facts or data, and then asking them to deliver their meaning. Philosophic inquiry resembles all other human inquiry in seizing upon some organizing hypothesis as the tool with which to search for further data; the interpretation goes on with the discovery of fresh facts which are relevant to it." [2]

In everyday practical affairs, as well as in the sciences, unsolved problems continually confront us. As we develop ability to solve problems, our guesses concerning possible solutions become more and more precise. These guesses are hypotheses which are projected beyond the given facts in acts of creative but disciplined imagination. This is a crucial stage in scientific investigation. Here there are no set rules of procedure, for here the scientist is more like the artist than the technician. Of course, mere imaginative illumination is no guarantee of truth; for there lies ahead, for the investigator, precise deduction of the consequences which would follow if his hypothesis were true, as well as actual verification by experimental procedure.

But now we combine these concerns and methods which the scientist exhibits in the creative projection of possible solutions to his problem with those of the philosopher and artist, as described throughout these paragraphs. There emerges the approach of the metaphysician who would deal in what Stephen C. Pepper has called "world hypotheses." "The peculiarity of world hypotheses

---

[2] John Herman Randall, Jr., and Justus Buchler, *Philosophy, An Introduction,* New York, Barnes and Noble, Inc., 1942, p. 13.

is that they cannot reject anything as irrelevant. When certain inconvenient matters are brought to a mathematician, he can always say, 'These are psychological (or physical, or historical) matters. I do not have to deal with them.' Similarly with other students of restricted fields. But students of world hypotheses can never have that way out. Every consideration is relevant to a world hypothesis and no facts lie outside it." [3]

While a world hypothesis becomes a point of view from which it is possible to grasp with the mind's eye the broad reaches of life and experience, still it begins from observation of a small segment of that experience. The man in search of a world view becomes sensitively aware of certain kinds of objects in his world and of his responses to them. These are uniquely his own and in a sense set limits to his perspective. But he is a man and not a god. If he is going to discover any truth at all, he can do so only by being himself and developing to the uttermost the possibilities of his own unique point of view.

But this beginning with his own experiences does not condemn him to perpetual subjectivity. He is on the way to objectivity— seeing the world as it is. Since he cannot know everything, he must select from those things he does know certain significant keys or clues which suggest to him the nature of reality. To illustrate with a figure of speech, it is like projecting a miniature color slide onto a huge screen. For in the metaphysical enterprise, that selected segment of experience with its distinctive key or clue is thus frankly projected onto the "screen" of the universe and becomes an *analogy* suggestive of the nature of the whole of reality. Metaphysics in this sense is then not a demonstrative science but an analogical art.

Again Pepper, by means of what he calls the "root-metaphor method," describes the way in which metaphysics works:

The method in principle seems to be this: a man desiring to understand the world looks about for a clue to its comprehension. He pitches

[3] Stephen C. Pepper, *World Hypotheses*, Berkeley, University of California Press, 1948, p. 1.

41

upon some area of common-sense fact and tries if he cannot understand other areas in terms of this one. This original area becomes then his basic analogy or root metaphor. He describes as best he can the characteristics of this area, or, if you will, discriminates its structure. A list of its structural characteristics becomes his basic concepts of explanation and description. We call them a set of categories. . . . Since the basic analogy or root metaphor normally (and probably at least in part necessarily) arises out of common sense, a great deal of development and refinement of a set of categories is required if they are to prove adequate for a hypothesis of unlimited scope. Some root metaphors prove more fertile than others, have greater powers of expansion and adjustment. These survive in comparison with the others and generate the relatively adequate world theories.[4]

Let the reader ask himself: "What do I really take in my experience as the most significant clue to the nature of things?" This stage of reflective awareness is crucial for anyone who is curious and deeply concerned about the sort of universe in which he is living. Is dirt or personality the clue to the nature of reality? Is the world like a machine contrived to operate by laws of strictly determined precision? Is it like an organism, growing, responding to an environment, whose every part is intimately related to every other part? Or is mind, conscious, intelligent, purposing, as we find it in ourselves, an analogy of a central reality called mind or self or will at the heart of things? Or is personality, in all the richness and fullness of individual existence and of social life which comprises human history, suggestive of the most fruitful root metaphors? Whatever key or clue you choose, you are following the same basic method: imaginative insight that begins from human experience but does not end there; for in this fashion some apprehension of the being of the universe comes within man's grasp.

In the sciences a fruitful hypothesis is not simply richly and imaginatively suggestive. It must be testable by available procedures of experimentation before it can be regarded as the most probable explanation of the facts under investigation. In metaphysics, as

[4] *Ibid.*, pp. 91-92.

has been indicated, a world hypothesis is closer to the creative expression of the artist than the experimental work of the scientist. Yet in the words of Lewis White Beck: "Unlike a work of art, however, a metaphysical hypothesis is supposed to be factually true. It must justify itself not by its beauty or style, but more in the way in which a scientific theory is justified: by comprehending, explaining, and rendering integral and intelligible a mass of otherwise chaotic experiences." [5]

But, paradoxically, a world hypothesis cannot be verified by the precise methods employed in the experimental sciences, that is, predicting what consequences would follow if the hypothesis were true and then proceeding to test these in the laboratory. If we are to avoid the conclusions of the logical empiricists that the general hypotheses of metaphysics have no cognitive meaning at all, then we must find another way of testing them.

This other test is usually called the method of *dialectic*, or dialectical experiment. It says to you: Ride your hypothesis until any mistakes show up; if they do, then correct it. It may be that you will not be obliged to abandon your hypothesis altogether, but only to modify it. For each fruitful root metaphor or analogy in which the hypothesis is expressed may contain some valuable insights. You will not wish to turn your back on these but rather to use them in the continually creative process of further search. No one hypothesis devised by the human mind can grasp the whole of reality in a single piece. Your obligation then is to find that world hypothesis which is as adequate as possible. But you cannot be satisfied if you have deliberately excluded any phase of experience from your purview.

Our metaphysics thus needs to be one which will enable us to make sense of the whole range of human experience—religion, art, political and economic activity, the life of the spirit and the life of the body,

[5] Lewis White Beck, *Philosophic Inquiry*, New York, Prentice-Hall, Inc., 1952, p. 250.

metaphysics itself and the physical and historical sciences, the life of the town and the life of the country, sport and manual skill, contemplation and action. All these and more may indeed be arranged in a scale of ascending values but the goodness and worthwhileness of none of them may be denied. Any metaphysics which takes the easier course of explaining one or more of them away, always and fundamentally for the sake of easing its problems and concealing its failure, stands by that condemned as one which disintegrates life with an unsteady vision.[6]

THE CHRISTIAN'S WORLD VIEW

How may a person of Christian conviction look at the wider world in which he lives? Is it possible to be both a Christian and a philosopher? What is a "Christian philosophy?" Does such a view of the universe, man, and his values move us any closer to solution of man's philosophical predicament? Does a Christian in his basic perspective differ at all from the secularist as he asks the selfsame questions: "What are you? What kind of world is it in which we live?" Can the Christian discover within human experience fruitful root metaphors, clues, analogies by which we may catch some glimpse of the nature of reality?

Unfortunately, even many folk who espouse the Christian faith have surrendered, if they ever seriously undertook, the philosophical task of seeking to find the nature of reality. They believe in God and avow allegiance to certain doctrinal ideas, moral teachings, values which they hold to be central to the Christian life. But their God, their ideas, and their values are also cozily shut up within the "box" of their human minds, ways of living, and, often, of a certain theological tradition. For they do not ask in all seriousness what wider consequences their accepted beliefs, ideas, and values have for the whole range of human experience. What possible light do these tenets throw on the nature of the world of forces and energies which comprise the physical universe? Does it make

[6] J. V. Langmead Casserley, *The Christian in Philosophy*, New York, Charles Scribner's Sons, 1951, p. 198.

a genuine difference whether or not God, who is the Creator and Sustainer of all things, exists? And what of man, his mind, his ideas, his values, and human history? Are these conceivably different in their basic make-up for persons of Christian conviction? Or do the secularist, who lives on the supposition God does not exist, and the Christian who believes that God does exist, hold the same views of the larger world, man, and his values?

Karl Heim expresses concern about this situation in which modern men's Christian affirmations seem to have little bearing on their philosophical interpretation of the world. This is especially the case within the developing tradition of Protestantism. For, says Heim, the history of Protestantism took "an unhappy turn" when, during the nineteenth century, Protestant theology severed its connections with philosophy so that it might become an independent field of study.[7] Since that time, it has become more and more reluctant to face the problem of the nature of the wider universe. Rather, Protestant theology has been content to abstract from the overall picture of reality that one segment which concerns the history of man's salvation.

This account depicts how man, created by God, falls, and then is redeemed. Concentrating on this, theologians believed they could safely leave the rest to the secular sciences. Here involved are, of course, the central themes of theology as distinguished from philosophy.

The reader is advised to consult various dictionaries and glossaries and other sources suggested in the general bibliography for definitions of such terms as theology, philosophy, science, art, and religion. For now, we may define theology as *the reasoned attempt, on the part of men already committed to a given religious faith, to say again what that faith means in the light of the needs and problems of each succeeding generation.* For a long time, Protestant

---

[7] Karl Heim, *Christian Faith and Natural Science,* New York, Harper & Brothers, 1953, pp. 26-27.

theology could safely concentrate on the central theme of man's salvation, says Heim, and leave the remaining parts of the world picture to secular sciences without conflict; for all the rest, philosophy and natural science, was just "the handmaiden of theology."

Today, Heim suggests, the situation is completely changed. The confession of faith of the Reformers, if stated at all nowadays in academic halls, makes a peculiar and grotesque impression. It is, says Heim, much like "a last remaining fragment of wall, all that is left standing of a medieval cathedral in a half-destroyed town, appearing as a foreign body amidst the newly erected blocks of offices and flats of a modern city." [8]

Again Heim paints this graphic picture in illustration of the isolated status of theology: "During the last war a deep impression was made when, after an air raid on Mayence, all that remained standing of a church dedicated to St. John the Baptist was a fragment of a doorway on which were inscribed the words: 'Repent ye: for the kingdom of heaven is at hand!' But this ruin from the past could not be left standing like that permanently. Either it could be built up again into a complete church of a design which fitted in with it, or it would have to be pulled down and cleared away." [9]

Then Heim makes practical application to our current educational and cultural situation:

In a present-day university, with its research institutes and clinics, the theology of the Reformation makes a similar impression. Either this ruin from the past must be cleared away—that is to say there is no room left for theology in a present-day university—or else this fragment left over from another conception of reality must be built up again and completed so that it forms a comprehensive world picture. Unless this is done, it has become meaningless. Only when the whole is again visible, of which this fragment forms a part, will it be possible to discuss it seriously. But the question here is not the relatively unimportant one

[8] *Ibid.*, p. 27.
[9] *Ibid.*

of the position of theology in the structure of the present-day universities. Something far more important is at stake, namely the credibility of the Christian message in the world today.[10]

Beyond the theological task, therefore, essential as that is, lies a further concern of thoughtful men and women in our day. What light do the central affirmations of Christian faith throw on the wider universe, nature, history, man, his values? This is the concern of philosophy.

Professor W. P. Montague has written: "If God is not, then the existence of all that is beautiful and in any sense good, is but the accidental and ineffectual by-product of blindly swirling atoms. . . . A man may believe this dreadful thing to be true, but only the fool will say in his heart that he is glad it is true. For to wish that the things which we love and strive to realize and make permanent should be only temporary and doomed to frustration and destruction, is to wish there should be no God."[11] And what of yourself within this larger universe? This is the issue reduced to its simplest terms. You have your basic choice. Either you are a physical thing like stone or steel or atoms produced by nature's mechanical processes or you are something much more: a living personality who can think, feel, and aspire. "Man is but a reed," wrote Pascal, "but he is a reed that thinks." Start with yourself, then, and what you think you are. Do not seek abstract arguments to prove to yourself what you are. Be pragmatic, if you like. If you believe you are just a thing, then act like one. A thing can't ask questions? A thing can't think? The very fact that you ask what you are presupposes that you are the kind of reality that can ask questions. You can think; you do not simply react as physical forces react; you respond.

Men of Christian conviction continue to develop a philosophical view of the universe and men. They say to you: "If you exist as

[10] *Ibid.*
[11] W. P. Montague, *Belief Unbound*, New Haven, Yale University Press, 1930, Chap. III.

a person, then our universe must be the kind of universe that can produce persons." It is a person-producing universe, not only a thing-producing universe. Man is at home in that universe. Man is not "a lost cause," as the pessimistic Joseph Wood Krutch says, with no place in the natural universe. Man belongs. There must, therefore, be some power at the heart of things that is capable of producing and sustaining persons. That power must be equal to the task. Certainly that reality is not less than personal and must be much more than personal. That power, that meaning, at the very center of everything, we call God. Do you believe this? Or do you believe that the universe is a huge machine and you simply another physical force? Whichever is your belief, act on it and discover which way life makes sense.

Christian philosophy thus takes analogies drawn from the life of individual persons and the broad sphere of human history as the most significant clues to the nature of reality. The whole of things is interpreted from this perspective. The one who takes this view in effect says to the rest of us: "If you want to see life steadily and see it whole, come and look at it from this vantage point." This is not to claim absolutely conclusive "proof." Rather the question is: How well does the evidence converge around this hypothesis, as compared with other alternative world views?

How effectively does the Christian world view enable us to understand the nature of the universe, to solve and handle our problems, to thrust forward dynamically into new areas of concern? As Casserley puts it, the process of verification in metaphysics consists in asking two questions: "Has our doctrine breadth, inclusiveness? Has it momentum?"

What light is thrown on the nature of man, his ideas, his values, his beliefs, his aspirations, his tensions, his anxieties, his attempts at self-justification, his pride, his sin, his rightful place in the scheme of things? To these concerns about man and his self we now turn.

APPENDIX TO CHAPTER IV

THE LOGICAL EMPIRICISTS

The logical empiricists base their views upon a specific theory of meaning or meaningfulness, called the "verifiability theory.of meaning." Putting this theory to work, a representative of the movement would say to you: "Consider the statements you make. Do they purport to convey information? Are they declarative sentences that communicate knowledge?" If they do, then they are *cognitive* sentences, and they may be said to be either true or false. Before you can consider whether any of your statements are true or false, you must ask: "What does it mean?" To answer this question, you must be able to show how the truth or falsity of such a statement can be determined. If you can show the specific conditions under which it would be shown to be true or false, then that statement has meaning or makes sense. If you cannot show the conditions under which it would be true or false, then the statement is meaningless or nonsense.

Cognitively meaningful statements, for logical empiricism, are of two basic kinds: those which have *formal* meaning, and those which have *factual* meaning. (1) The truth or falsity of formal statements may be determined by examination of the logical structure of the statements themselves. Such a statement may be a *tautology* in which the predicate merely restates the subject. Examples are: "All bachelors are unmarried." "Two plus two equals four." Statements of this sort are used in logic or in mathematics and do not depend on any matter of fact. (2) On the other hand, factual statements are verifiable by reference to what is observable by the senses. For example: "That book is red." "That cat is black." Interpreted most broadly, factual meaning may be said to be exhibited if we know what would constitute verification no matter whether there are obstacles of a practical sort or not. However, if there is no possible way of discovering the truth or falsity of a statement, then it is nonsense or meaningless no matter how persuasive we may be in expounding plausible and attractive theories in metaphysics or theology.

In the view of logical empiricism, when the verification principle of meaning is seriously and rigorously applied, the only claims to knowledge which stand up are those of the experimental sciences. No matter what theoretical methods may be involved, these always come back to the starting point of observation by the senses. This is not the case with the statements of metaphysics and theology. These may begin with observation and develop hypotheses purporting to explain the world's nature or God's, but such hypotheses cannot be verified. The difficulty is not simply that these speculative theories may be false. Actually, according to this view, they are neither true nor false, and, in any case, none of them makes any real difference in practical human experience. The questions to which these theories are presumed to be answers ought not to have been asked in the first place.

The reason is that, for logical empiricists, the very concepts employed in fields such as metaphysics, theology, or ethics are pseudo-concepts. A genuine concept, by contrast, is a predicate used in a statement that conveys information and is therefore cognitive, such as "red," "square," "heavier than ten pounds" in the sentences, "That necktie is red," "That figure is a square," "That sack of potatoes is heavier than ten pounds." In each of these cases, the predicate applied to the subject is appropriate; for even if the statements were false, the concepts employed are still genuine. But if I should say, for instance, "The sum of the angles of a triangle is red," the predicate "red" would be a pseudo-concept employed in a pseudo-judgment. Just so, the concepts of ethics as well as those of metaphysics and theology cannot be the assignable properties of anything. They are not completely useless, however, for they are tools which enable us to express our feelings or to affect attitudes in other people. Thus while these concepts do not possess cognitive meaning, they do have *emotive* meaning. As noncognitive, they are neither true nor false in any universal sense, but they may provide those who use them with emotional satisfaction, peace of mind, or a sense of security.

The logical empiricists would thus warn those who indulge in metaphysical or theological statements not to claim truth or falsity for them or to try to give logically compelling reasons for holding them. For those who try to do so are only self-deceived. They believe they are stating genuine propositions about the nature of reality or the self or God. What they are actually doing is to express their own feeling-states, desires, hopes, visions. Therefore, let such visionaries honestly admit they are dealing in "such stuff as dreams are made of" and not pretend that they are philosophizing. If they enjoy this sort of fairy-tale-spinning, that is their privilege. But all genuine problems of human concern would be better handed over to the scientists for solution. In the words of Moritz Schlick: "Thus the fate of all philosophical problems is this: Some of them will disappear by being shown to be mistakes and misunderstandings about our language, and others will be found to be ordinary scientific questions in disguise. These remarks, I think, determine the whole future of philosophy." [12]

What answers can we make to these ground-shaking criticisms? Are the rather technical and detailed arguments of the logical empiricists simply the conclusions, in complicated form, of the skeptics and agnostics? Surely, to say that metaphysical and theological speculations ought to be retained simply because they are traditional is not a convincing answer to practical-minded Americans. We would agree, perhaps, that much complicated doctrine ought to be scrutinized carefully and some of it eliminated or revised. But are we prepared to go the whole way with David Hume? For that critic of the eighteenth century wrote: "When we run over libraries, persuaded of these principles, what havoc must

[12] Moritz Schlick, "The Future of Philosophy," *The College of the Pacific Publications,* 1932, p. 60.

we make? If we take in our hand any volume; of divinity or school metaphysics, for instance; let us ask, *Does it contain any abstract reasoning concerning quantity or number?* No. *Does it contain any experimental reasoning concerning matter of fact and existence?* No. Commit it then to the flames; for it can contain nothing but sophistry and illusion." [13]

Is this the choice that confronts us? Either we reject the logical empiricists' insistence on the primacy of scientific methods or we agree with them in rejecting altogether any attempt to discover what kind of world we are living in. Some thoughtful folk today claim that, stated in this bald and extreme form, these are the alternatives and no compromise is possible. Others say that the alternatives are not so sharp and mutually exclusive as has been pictured and that it is not necessary to make a choice between them of all or nothing at all.[14] Certainly logical empiricism is an influential factor in the current climate of thought. Everyone who claims to know what is going on in today's world must in all seriousness take account of the whole trend it represents. This is particularly the case with those possessed of deep religious as well as philosophical concern. But we would be on guard against uncritical acceptance of the logical empiricists' total rejection of the metaphysical and theological enterprises. In order to attain a balanced view, it is essential for us to keep in mind certain criticisms, both positive and negative.

1. Besides their work in technical fields of logic, semantics, and philosophy of science, the logical empiricists have made worthwhile contributions of wider application. This is particularly the case in their stress on the need to clarify the meanings of terms and definitions which we use every day. Analysis of language is a basic task in our attempts to examine all phases of human

---

[13] David Hume, *An Enquiry Concerning Human Understanding*, in *Hume Selections*, Charles W. Hendel, Jr. (ed.), New York, Charles Scribner's Sons, 1927, pp. 192-193.

[14] See Hunter Mead, *Types and Problems of Philosophy*, New York, Henry Holt and Company, 1953, p. 267.

experience and to convey to other people what we have found. So it is with concepts which we employ whenever we try to state the significance of our moral relationships or religious beliefs, or views concerning the nature of the universe. What do we mean when we utter such terms as good, duty, freedom, mind, spirit, being, truth, divine, God? How may we avoid the extreme pretensions of those who claim for their own opinions final and absolutely authoritative truth? The empiricists wisely would warn us not to mistake our particular formulations of opinion for what is actually the case in the world of events in which we live.

The logical empiricists have also correctly stressed the fact that many of our statements of moral judgment or philosophical or religious belief *are* emotional. We do express our likes and dislikes, our attitudes, our hopes and dreams. Or we frequently try to persuade others that they also would find emotional satisfaction in judging as we judge or believing as we believe. But often our most serious offense is that we pretend to ourselves and others that our judgments are completely free of emotional bias or personal prejudice and that we are stating objective truth about things as they actually are.

2. There are some difficulties involved in the views of logical empiricism. For its advocates themselves make claims to finality when they hold that any statements not confirmed by sense data are purely emotive; are senseless, meaningless, and have no rational significance whatsoever. The following negative criticisms begin then to emerge:

Despite the fact that the logical empiricists wisely caution us always to clarify the meaning of terms and statements we ask in turn some searching questions about the verification theory of meaning itself. What does it *mean?* The logical empiricist says that the meaning of a sentence is exhibited by showing the specific conditions under which it would be verified as true or false. But surely this is an arbitrary limitation to claim that every kind of statement must measure up to this criterion. A sentence, whether in everyday discourse, or in the language of the metaphysician, need not be meaningless simply because it cannot be verified by the same methods as employed in the experimental sciences. To state of a given sentence that it can be verified as true or false is not to say whether or not it is meaningful.[15]

All you are doing in such a case is to characterize that sentence as a certain type, i.e., as an empirical sentence, one that can be verified as true or false by reference to sense experiences. Its meaningfulness is quite another matter. For every kind of statement need not be of the same sort as used in the sciences. At least for a long time now, the utterances of metaphysicians, as well as those of literary artists and thinkers, have been regarded as meaningful. It may be, as we shall attempt to show, that the "truth" of such utterances is of a different order, just as the methods employed are different from those of the sciences. But this does not relegate these utterances to the realm of the unintelligible or the irrational.

Moreover, far from demonstrating that metaphysics is impossible, the logical empiricists actually are involved in the metaphysical enterprise themselves. They attempt to rule out all metaphysical theories as senseless. But what in fact they are doing is to argue against certain specific metaphysical theories. Even if they would eliminate some of the theories which have come down to us through long centuries of tradition, still they cannot avoid having some view or other as to the nature of the world in which we all live. They, as do all of us, make some basic judgments about the character of man, his values of good and beauty, knowledge and the claims of truth, the universe and what things are real within it. Indeed, no man can escape acting as though certain things are more real, more significant, and more meaningful than others. To act like this is to presuppose, whether we wish to or not, a metaphysical point of view. It is the obligation of an honest man, especially one who in his empiricism expresses reverence for

15 See J. L. Evans, "On Meaning and Verification," *Mind*, January, 1953.

the facts, to acknowledge in all honesty the facts about his own implicit assumptions.

Logical empiricists reply to this criticism that the empirical method does not involve making metaphysical claims, even tacitly. But careful reading of the literature in this field would indicate that metaphysics is involved if metaphysics means the examination of the presuppositions which these philosophers in all seriousness take as the ultimate.

Chapter V

Man and His Self

Paul Scherer tells about a young man, steadily and interestingly employed on the editorial staff of a weekly business publication. One day he is sitting comfortably in his home at his own desk, with the radio turned off and all the conditions of peaceful and secure existence well established. Yet out of these pleasant surroundings issue these words: "I suspect there are a good many persons who are irritated more than soothed by the flow of life around them. I am up against a blank wall in a sense far more real than I care to admit. Evenings I get drunk, or rub the snout of my gregariousness against the fur of other animals about me, in an almost frantic effort to get relief from myself. Something has been taken out of me. The great majority of days are so filled with banality that all talk of purpose, meaning, and high morality seems a strange sort of cant."[1]

Here is a contemporary, a dweller in cities, modern, educated, sophisticated, altogether adjusted and secure, if outward appearances are any guide. He has, of course, thrown religion overboard because he has decided it is too drab a business for his tastes. Now, as Scherer reminds us, he sits there biting his pencil and dully

[1] Paul Scherer, *For We Have This Treasure*, New York, Harper & Brothers, 1944, p. 129.

wondering what it is that has been taken out of him. Yet, strangely enough, toward the end of his article, in a kind of diagnosis of his own trouble, this young editor writes something of the things for which he dreams and hopes: "It seems to me the essential source of my trouble is a need for some unshakeable conviction of the importance of living, and of the way a man should live. In strong measure I am fascinated by the incalculable. There should be some adventure and uncertainty in life. I prefer to pit myself against hazardous moments, to try myself to the utmost, to have the greatest possible variety out of my journey from the hamlet of birth to the City of Death." [2]

MAN'S PREDICAMENT: PERSONAL AND RELIGIOUS

Contrast "Something has been taken out of me" with "the source of my trouble is a need for some unshakeable conviction of the importance of living." This young man has come close, whether he would acknowledge it or not, to grasping the nature of man's personal predicament. He is also within reach of the essential genius of creative religion, even though he may be unconscious of it. Moreover, this is the temper and core of Christianity: that within the depths of man's own self, out of profound and intimately personal need, emerge the possibilities of his being taken hold of by a Power and Being from beyond himself. Out of lostness and estrangement issue reconciliation and renewal of a man's very self, of perspective and resource for the demands of everyday living.

Man faces thus a dilemma which is not only moral and philosophical but also one that is profoundly personal. In terms of the first, we have stated that in all genuine judgments of moral value there is involved a *command*. This is not basically a command to somebody else. It is a self-command that emerges somehow out of the actual situation within which the individual man lives and makes his decisions. Or perhaps it issues from beyond the situation.

[2] *Ibid.*, p. 132.

It may be a command "which the reasoner beholds as an obligation to be fulfilled—or better, as a vocation, a *being called.* A real value-judgment is always in part an answer to command, a 'So be it!' " [3] At the roots, therefore, of his very being, lives a man's self, making response to other selves and, according to religious conviction, to a wider Self. This is a relationship between man and God: Man and his self in vital community with a divine Self, an I with a Thou.

As for the second form of predicament, man in his philosophical quest for a world view also comes to that profound moment when his very self is involved. The questions "Who are you? What are you doing here?" demand an answer which reaches below the level of the abstract and theoretical or even the practical and expedient on which a man earns his living and deals with the meaning of existence. Not just any man is concerned but every man—you and I. This is to move on an intimately personal dimension which, implicitly at least, is religious. Man faces, therefore, a dilemma about his self. It is at its roots a religious predicament. He must find solution to this also and relate what he discovers to his concerns for values and for a philosophical world view. It may be that the very source of insight for all the rest wells up out of the depths of his own life as a personal self.

For it becomes clear that philosophical concerns, and even those about values, are of two closely related but distinct kinds: the technical or formal, and the personal or *existential.* It is with the latter type, the existential, that religious concern begins to distinguish itself from the moral or philosophical. The word *begins* is important at this point. For clearly men asking personal questions may still move within the field of philosophy as such without distinctively religious involvement. But what we are saying is that as soon as any person, whether he is consciously philosophical or not, asks questions about his own deeply intimate relationship with

[3] Philip Wheelwright, *The Way of Philosophy*, New York, The Odyssey Press, 1953, p. 426.

reality and with the sources of value judgments, then he is at least on the verge of religion.

Beneath even the formal problems of philosophy surge those questions which are intimate and thus existential. These are the questions which each individual asks about himself and his own relations to the world. Here his central problem has to do with his full human existence. To each searching general question of ultimate significance he adds: "Does it concern *me*, deeply and intimately?"

The epistemological query is: What is truth? This may become the existential question: How may *I* live in the light of truth? The problem of what knowledge is contains within it the self-searching question: What decisive obligations do the search for and the possession of knowledge place upon me? Inescapably personal questions are also involved in the formal problems of *axiology*, or value. The ethical inquiry: What is goodness? penetrates into the conditions of a man's own moral existence. What does it mean for me to be good? Why do I choose this way rather than that other? What are the enduring bases of my own decisions? The aesthetic question is: What is beauty? This leads to the personal question: How may I help create the conditions of sensitive response to beautiful things?

So it is also with the problems of metaphysics and the philosophy of religion. Here also the abstract may become intimate. The questions of *ontology* are: What is reality as a whole? What is the structure of being as such? But men may also ask the existential question: What is the meaning of being for me? In what sort of universe do I actually believe I am living? Does it actually make a difference that it is of one sort rather than another? And what am I as a man?

Three closely related phases of man's personal predicament will be discussed in this chapter. First, we shall undertake a discussion of the persistent question, "What is man?" Second, we shall review some live options among perspectives on man's nature which move through our western culture. Third, we will make brief statement of the distinctive view of Christianity concerning man's being as a self, including what it conceives to be the core of man's personal dilemma as centered in anxiety and sin.

THE NATURE OF MAN

What is man? A demented, lost man, suffering from shock and amnesia, wandered onto the platform during a lull in the proceedings of a huge national veterans' convention, held out his arms beseechingly to the crowd, and asked, "Please, please, can anybody here tell me who I am?"

You say he had lost his identity. There was no persistent unity of experience into which everything else could be tied together. He had lost his *self*. Perhaps this is what a self is: the way in which an individual personality functions all together as a single unity or identity, a wholeness persisting throughout all the various moments which comprise his human span of life. But is there any such core of identity? Do I share, in common with all other creatures of like kind, certain qualities or essential characteristics? Can anybody tell me who I am?

We look out across the world and see in imagination all sorts of men, women, young people, and children: about two and one-half billion of them. There are people in every succeeding moment doing the things or undergoing the experiences which, in all their complexity and variety, belong to this human lot in which we all share. There are folk being born, starting life, breathing, eating, crying, growing, walking, talking, desiring, feeling, living, hating, fighting, working, appreciating, thinking, worshiping, marrying, begetting, conceiving, and giving birth to children. Some live in homes; some are homeless. Some have plenty to eat; some have little. Some have found comparative comfort and security; some are suffering, bleeding, dying in hunger, want, and despair. Some are living in indifference to the needs of others. Some agonize in deep concern and constructive action for the welfare of their fellow men.

60

Man and His Self

Who are all of these? They are different from their fellows and yet sufficiently alike to be classified as a single species: Homo sapiens. Present-day peoples are divided into five racial groups: white, or Caucasian; yellow, or Mongolian; black, or Negroid; brown, or Malaysian; red, or Amerind. They are further divided into nations and blocs of nations; and yet they are organized into all sorts of groups: families, communities, political parties, economic and professional societies, unions and trade associations, churches, clubs, and lodges. Each man, woman, or child is distinctively different from all the others. Yet all have a common biological origin and constitution; live in constant interrelation with a physical and cultural environment; make response with common urges and needs; move toward similar goals and hold comparable concepts, ideals, and values.

Man studies himself by means of the several sciences and thus sees his existence on different levels. No one of the perspectives presents an untrue picture. Yet no one of them is completely true. But, with the help of all, a composite picture emerges.

1. As a part of the *physical* order of nature, then, a man occupies space and moves as series of events through a given span of time. He has size, shape, dimensions, weight, and color. A man, as do all organisms, absorbs from his surrounding world certain substances and transforms them into the very stuff of his own body. Chemical processes take place in the functioning of his digestive, circulatory, respiratory, and reproductive systems. The raw materials of which man is made are the same chemical elements as are found in the physical universe that surrounds him: carbon, oxygen, hydrogen, calcium, chlorine, nitrogen, sulphur, and phosphorus.

2. As a part of the *biological* order of nature, man belongs among the animals as one of nearly a million species of animals that inhabit the earth's surface. He is a thing which occupies space during a certain stretch of time. But is he more than this? Man may possess, in his skeletal structure and muscular system, essential features of a complicated machine. He may also function as a complex of several

61

chemical processes. But are these adequate explanations of man's nature?

As a matter of fact, some scientists hold to what is called *mechanism* in biological theory, according to which living organisms can be completely explained in terms of the hypotheses and laws of physics and chemistry. These theorists readily admit that at present the descriptive laws of biology cannot be derived from those of physics and chemistry, but they claim that these principles can be so derived when we possess more knowledge. Thus, according to the mechanists, a biological organism is nothing but an exceedingly complicated physical and chemical machine.

However, other interpreters believe that, at the animal level of evolutionary development, distinctive qualities of life have emerged which are new and different and thus not reducible to the mechanical or chemical.[4] An animal is, according to the latter view, more than a machine. Animals function in such ways as J. A. Thomson has summarized in these words: "A living creature differs from a machine in being self-stoking, self-regulating, self-repairing, self-increasing, self-multiplying, and eventually in being self-conscious."

3. But, as part of this *animal* order, man occupies a unique place among living beings, performs certain distinctive functions, and possesses certain physical characteristics. Man alone among the animals moves with really erect posture. This frees his arms and hands for exploration and manipulation of objects. Man's hand, with its free fingers and thumbs opposed to each other, enables him to grasp objects. And this, together with the rotation of the arm, are important conditions of man's becoming the toolmaker, the inventor of instruments of amazing intricacy. Man's brain is larger and his nervous system is more highly organized than those of any other animals.

4. In addition, there are certain *social* and *cultural* differences

[4] See Samuel Alexander, *Philosophical and Literary Pieces,* London, Macmillan and Company, Ltd., 1939, pp. 204-311; C. Lloyd Morgan, *Emergent Evolution,* New York, Henry Holt and Co., 1923, pp. 297-298.

which distinguish man as a member of the human order; for he is able to create cultures and institutions to regularize his relations with other human beings. Man contrives articulate speech, language, writing, and number systems. These extend human memory into the past, become the instruments of projection into the future, and enable man, the incurable social creature, to communicate with his fellows in words that point beyond themselves to meanings and sentences and series of sentences that express judgments and elicit responses. Man thus brings cultures into being as he formulates his communications about the world into literatures, arts, sciences, and philosophies. He is the only animal who asks questions and ventures answers in imaginative forms. Man, coöperating with his fellows in larger and larger units, alone builds social institutions in the fields of agriculture, commerce, industry, government, education, science, philanthropy, and religion. For man is distinctive in the contrivance and creative use of these social functions, of trading, governing, rearing the young, serving the needy, and worshiping what is held to be divine.

5. But man is also a *person* whose very being perhaps eludes the interpretive grasp of the various physical, biological and social sciences, valuable as these disciplines are in telling us in part who we are. We need also to turn, for education about ourselves, to the testimony of history, religion, the humanities, including the arts, literature, and philosophy. For the seriously questing student, much deepened insight may be gained simply through day-to-day relationships with other persons in their work, play, feeling, believing, hoping. What is man as a person?

Paradoxically, man is the only animal who knows he is an animal. This implies that he is capable of transcending the natural order of things and even himself and his own distinctive functions. Other animals may be conscious of the world about them. Only man is self-conscious. In this awareness of his own self, man is able to span across wide ranges of meaning and, in memory and creative imagination, speak of his own history, culture, and institutions. But he also can carry on a continuing conversation with the self who, in part at least and in company with other selves, has brought these things into existence and who therefore stands as an independent being over against the objects of his creativity. Man becomes an *I* as distinct from the kind of objects designated as *it*.

Man is capable of abstract thinking, logical reasoning, evaluation, and creative expression which come to grips with concepts and ideal values. Man is, of course, a part of the flow of events in nature. Yet he is conscious that he is involved in nature. Thus he is not totally involved but rather transcends these processes. Man can generalize. He can construct *classes* of things and events, and he can abstract common qualities from particular objects bearing similar characteristics. Man can use these abstractions, through symbolic terms, to communicate what is true or false, logical or illogical. In his discernment of objects of beauty, he can make judgments on the basis of standards or principles and give his reasons for doing so. Man can apprehend the significance of moral values and discern good from evil in human conduct. He exercises not only discernment and apprehension of values but he also is capable of creating beautiful things and making ethical decisions which bring into existence the visions entertained in imagination. Man, to construct philosophical systems, can attempt to grasp in synoptic perspective the significance of all time and existence. And he alone of all creatures finally finds objects of utter religious devotion and commits a total *self's* destiny to such an ultimate Being for all time and eternity.

In summation, we are led to say, with Edgar S. Brightman, that a self or personality is not a simple abstraction, like a number or a physical thing, that you can hold in your hand. But it is a *whole* that is complex, moving, dynamic. It is a conscious and self-conscious life in constant, sensitive interaction with its environment. A self is in vital relationship with the physical world, its geographical features of climate, land, sea, and sky. It is rooted in its own biological nature—a body with living tissue, organs, glands—in part determined by specific hereditary factors of capacity and given organic make-up. A self, a personality, lives also in sensitive response to its own psychological processes of desiring, feeling, hoping, thinking, as well as the conditioning influences of the complex social and cultural environment all around it. But it is reducible to none of these and the total significance is more than all of them acting together.

At each level, the raw materials of total responsible selfhood are provided, but they are in themselves neutral; for these factors —physical energy, hereditary factors, glandular reactions, conditioned responses, social pressures—do not of themselves determine which specific way the personality will develop. Their moral and spiritual significance depends upon what a human self does with them.

LIVE OPTIONS ON MAN'S NATURE

Before discussing the distinctively Christian view of man and the tensions of his paradoxical selfhood, we need to examine briefly two other relevant interpretations which in large measure dominate western thinking.[5] The first is the classical, rationalistic view, which is rooted in the Greek tradition and found expression in the Enlightenment of the eighteenth century and the idealism of the nineteenth. The second is the broad current movement of critical naturalism, which includes various shadings of emphasis, such as scientific humanism and religious humanism. These terms are, of course, indicative of certain trends and in a sense artificial classifications. They are not to be regarded as tight, compartmentalized categories or types; for no one interpreter or even group of interpreters is ever wholly "typical." But, understood in this sense, our discussion of these trends may help to dramatize the livest options for men and women today. It does make a difference what we

[5] See Reinhold Niebuhr, *The Nature and Destiny of Man*, New York, Charles Scribner's Sons, 1941, Vol. I, pp. 1-25, 178-203, 208-219, 228-240; and *The Self and the Dramas of History*, New York, Charles Scribner's Sons, 1955, pp. 3-61, *passim*.

believe about our own being as selves, and the test of our beliefs is that upon which we customarily act.

The classical, rationalistic view of man selects for exclusive emphasis one phase of this many-sided, paradoxical being we call human personality, that is, man's capacity to reason. By and large, this is the perspective of the Greek philosophers, Plato, Aristotle, and the Stoics. Man is thus essentially a rational being who is able to grasp general concepts and rational order, which pervades the entire cosmos. For it is not the particular objects experienced with our senses which are real, but universal and abstract forms or ideas.

The way to understand ultimate reality, then, is through the exercise of man's rational powers. This is to apprehend truth. But the true is also Good, not relative good, but absolute, unchanging Good. And to know the Good is to do the Good. Thus this kind of knowledge brings freedom to men, freedom from slavery to the limitations of space, time, the senses, emotions, impulses, appetites. To be free is to achieve harmonious balance of body, mind, and soul.

For Plato and Aristotle both, reason is the ruling part of the soul which brings this animal body of ours under control. This element of the soul is independent of the body and is immortal in its essential nature. It belongs not to the changing flux of the things of this physical world, but to the unchanging, infinite world of eternity. The basic difficulty with man is his ignorance. He is cut off from eternal reality simply because, in his finitude and limitations imposed by his senses and his passions, he does not know, rationally and intelligently, the eternal world of forms. The result of this ignorance of the essentially true and good is vice. Conversely, genuine knowledge of the eternally true and good enables men to discover and realize practical good in man's day-to-day life. For the individual, this means the achievement of *eudaemonia* or happiness.

Eudaemonia, or vital well being, is the result of that perfect balance and harmonious proportion in which a man brings all aspects of his life under the control of reason. He is functioning as a man should function, for man is the "rational animal" whose essential genius is the capacity to reason. The felt awareness of this perfect health or balance is happiness, or eudaemonia. Likewise, man can discover and bring into existence a political order for the state. For knowing perfect good or justice by his rational powers, he is capable of achieving that proportioned balance of political powers and functions which is the just social order. Here also eudaemonia, or the happiness of harmonious human existence, will be realized when each man or group of men performs his designated function for the vital well-being of the whole.

At the time of the Renaissance of the fourteenth to seventeenth centuries in Europe, there occurred a culmination of interest in the classical learning of Greece and Rome which men of the so-called Middle Ages had fostered. But now, at the very threshold of what we call the "modern" period, new ideals and attitudes emerged from this love for ancient writings. For an emphasis upon man himself became more pointed and powerful than at any other previous time in western history. These ideals and attitudes characterize Renaissance humanism: the worth and dignity of the individual man in his own right; his freedom to choose good or evil in determination of his own destiny; his confident ability to develop and use his own rational powers to deal with the pressing problems of this world; his growing capacity to create and appreciate works of art; his increasing sense of the vastness of a universe awaiting scientific discovery, and yet belief in the ability of his own intellect to grasp its structure and significance; his awareness of his own place in the scheme of things as part of the natural world, and yet "lifted above other creatures by a soul that was rational and immortal like God Himself." [6]

For in northern Europe, in contrast to the Renaissance in Italy, men such as Erasmus maintained humanism's vital connection with the Christian heritage. He was convinced of the inherent goodness

[6] George F. Thomas, *Christian Ethics and Moral Philosophy*, New York, Charles Scribner's Sons, 1955, p. 148.

of man and his ability, in reasonableness and conciliation, to establish a religion of piety based upon what he called the "philosophy of Christ." Renaissance humanism may be summarized in the words of Hamlet: "What a piece of work is man! How noble in reason! how infinite in faculty! in form, in moving, how express and admirable! in action, how like an angel! in apprehension, how like a God! the beauty of the world! the paragon of animals!"

During the beginning of the nineteenth century, this confidence in man found expression in *philosophical idealism*. Idealists discern within man himself the most significant root metaphor or analogy by which to grasp the nature of reality as a whole. For idealists hold that reality is of the nature of mind. Ultimate reality is psychical or spiritual in its basic make-up. It is rational and intelligible. It has meaning which may be grasped through the self. For there is a kind of inner harmony between reality and man whereby man does not move meaninglessly or alone in the darkness of an unfriendly universe. Rather human life "adds up," makes sense, counts in the long run. Man's existence, as is all of the natural world, is thus the expression of the universal Mind or Spirit. According to Hegel, for example, human history, at every stage of development, is the unfolding upon the plane of time and space of an eternal meaning which is the life of the absolute. For human beings, according to idealism, this has this significance: to move within this realm of absolute meaning is to leave behind us all the fragmentariness of these little, partial worlds of ours, and thus to find wholeness, completeness, and unity.

It has been said: "It is remarkable that to an enormously muddled but brilliant German professor of the nineteenth century almost every important movement of the twentieth century begins with an attack on his views. I have in mind Hegel. . . ." [7] This is the case with existentialism, pragmatism, and logical empiricism. But the movement of *naturalism* had its inception long before the start

[7] Morton White, *The Age of Analysis,* New York, New American Library, 1955 (Mentor MD 142), p. 13.

of our twentieth century. In general, naturalism is that philosophy which holds that nature is the whole of reality and that the experimental methods of the sciences give us the whole of truth. Within so broad a category as this many shades of view are included: from the kind of materialism (discussed in Chapter III) which reduces man, his ideas, his values, his God, to the functions of a machine to the broader and more accommodating views of scientific and religious humanism.

In our twentieth century, this broader view, called critical naturalism, attempts to avoid the narrow reductionism of mechanistic materialism; for matter, motion, and energy are inadequate analogies for the understanding of reality or the nature of man. Strangely enough, those who embrace this view agree with idealism in pointing to the significance of mind and the uniqueness of man, his ideas, and his values. But these are the product of nature even though emergences of new and distinctively different levels of development have taken place throughout the course of evolution. Like materialism, this perspective denies the reality of any supernatural purpose or God on whose being nature and human history are dependent for their significance. But within the sphere of nature, this space-time order, there are purposiveness and the realization of ends and goals.

Perhaps the livest option among various naturalistic views today is that of humanism. Man is the child of nature, subject to its laws and conditioned by relations to his bodily organism, his physical and social environment. Health, disease, and death are man's lot quite apart from any moral deserts. Yet man is able to deal with the obstacles with which nature confronts him. He has the capacity, in increasing measure, to control its forces and use its resources for his own benefit. To do this, man employs the tools of the sciences, both physical and social, as he becomes engineer, industrialist, educator, or physician. Especially in these days, man has come to appreciate the resources of the social sciences in the challenging task of meeting the intricate problems of human relations.

Also, in agreement with classical and Renaissance humanism, contemporary humanists hold that man is a rational being. For he is possessed of that unique ability to ask endless questions of the world of which he is a part. He can range through his memory into the rich heritage of past history and through imagination use it to interpret the future and explore the infinite reaches of the universe. Reason is an instrument to be employed functionally in devising ways of meeting human needs most effectively.

Man is a free, creative, and responsible self, according to humanism. The processes of nature may condition man's values and patterns of conduct in countless ways, but do not determine these in strictly causal fashion. For man has the capacity to control his environmental situation, to pursue growth in self-development, to guide action by consciously accepted purposes. Moreover, man is aware that he is free and responsible for his conduct and destiny.

Man is a *social* being who develops his fullest capacities of rational and responsible freedom in fellowship with other persons and groups. By his own choices, he envisions goals of justice, good will, peace, and decency and utilizes his scientific ingenuity, all the tools his inventive genius has contrived, his intelligence, his reason, his freedom and sense of responsibility, to create the good life in a well-adjusted society. For "the goal of the human enterprise is a world community of free persons voluntarily and intelligently coöperating for the common weal to the greatest extent made possible by the nature of the world of men and society." [8]

The basic difficulty with the human race would thus appear to be that we simply are not human enough. Apparently, we have not developed to fullest capacity our inherent resources needed to cope with personal and social problems. Many humanists commit themselves to the cause of human well-being in a mood of religious fervor, social passion, and confidence in the worth and dignity of man; yet nonetheless they have no use for the sanctions or con-

[8] Curtis W. Reese, *The Meaning of Humanism*, Boston, The Beacon Press, 1945, pp. 27-28.

fusions of "outmoded religion." We do not need to rely, they say, on some supernatural power to extricate us from difficulties of our own making. Rather than depending upon "indirect methods," man ought to tackle his own problems directly, linking his own individual efforts to those of other men of like mind in a social process for good. As for religion, some would claim that such imaginative projection and constructive realization of human goals and values *is* religion—all the religion needed and the only kind sufficient to bring solution to the problems which beset men and nations.

THE CHRISTIAN VIEW OF MAN

Turning to the affirmations of the Christian tradition, we are led to say that the classical, rationalist, Renaissance, idealistic, and contemporary humanistic views of man and man's predicament bear close resemblance at many crucial points to the essentially Christian views of man.

George F. Thomas, from the point of view of Christian conviction, makes comment on these perspectives:

They are not errors, they are half-truths. Man *is* a rational being, but his reason is more distorted by prejudice and more easily overcome by passion than modern men have been willing to admit. He *is* a spiritual being capable of devoting himself to the universal ends of the Divine Spirit, but he is also a selfish and sensual being. He *is* a being whose natural impulses and feelings often seem to lead him spontaneously towards goodness, but he also suffers from the most irresponsible and destructive egoism. In short, man is a complex being. The weakness of the humanistic and idealistic conceptions of him is that they have been too simple and abstract.[9]

Again with reference to the naturalistic conception of man, Thomas states: ". . . it is a simple and abstract view. It, too, has been developed by exaggerating one side and neglecting the other side. Man *is* a child of nature, an animal species subject to the laws of nature; but he is also a spiritual being who transcends

[9] Thomas, *op. cit.*, p. 150.

nature. He *is* an irrational being driven by his appetites and passions; but he is also a rational being capable of gaining a measure of control over them. He *is* a creature of time and he must die; but he is also a being who transcends time and longs for eternity." [10]

What is this man? It is the Christian affirmation that he is a creature of contrasts and contradictions, an "in-between being," who, as a child of nature, lives in continuity with the environing world. Yet he is that curious creature who transcends nature and is able in some measure to control its forces. Writers of all ages have wondered and pondered over the paradox of man's double existence. Blaise Pascal has given this answer to the riddle of human life: "What a novelty! What a monster, what a chaos, what a contradiction, what a prodigy! Judge of all things, imbecile worm of the earth; depositary of truth, a sink of uncertainty and error; the pride and refuse of the universe!"

Carlyle wrote of man's nature in striking symbols: "He is of the earth, but his thoughts are with the stars. Mean and petty his wants and desires; yet they serve a soul exalted with grand, glorious aims — with immortal longings — with thoughts which sweep the heavens, and wander through eternity. A pigmy standing on the outward crest of this small planet, his far-reaching spirit stretches outward to the infinite, and there alone finds rest."

Yet it is the Christian conviction that this paradoxical being of contrasts and contradictions is a whole self. That abstraction, man's "mind" or "rationality," stressed by the classical tradition, is not the whole of man. Nor does that other abstraction, man's body or animal organism, comprise the entirety of human personality. Neither are impulse, feeling, or even will, conceived as separate entities, sufficient characterizations of man's total selfhood. Each of these are merely focuses of the self. They are often in tension with one another, engaged in constant "dialogue," as Reinhold Niebuhr puts it. But it is the *whole* being of man who, in the

[10] *Ibid.*, p. 152.

essentially Christian perspective, belongs to the transcendent God. This is so because man is the creature of the God upon whose very Being he himself, together with all of nature and human history, is conceived as utterly dependent. Man, the creature, is made in the image of God. He is like God in his essential make-up. Yet man is a free and responsible agent who is capable, in his whole person, either of accepting or rejecting the claims of God for fuller justice and love. Thus man distorts the divine image that is within him, but he does not utterly destroy it. He does not cease to be a free and responsible person living in terms of inherent goodness. This, then, is the root of man's personal predicament. Serious as it is, his basic trouble is not one of ignorance, to be cured by sharpened intellect and the accumulation of more rational knowledge. Neither is it a matter of control of natural forces in the world at large or impulses within ourselves. Nor may we hope for cure by extricating ourselves from the everyday demands of this practical world to find refuge in some transcendent world of "spirit."

Man cannot escape his limitations of ignorance, set as he is within this world of space, time, and causal events with the obligations of day-to-day tasks upon him. But his trouble is that he thinks he can. Thus he fondly seeks to become more than man, to take control of things into his own hands, to become his own center of meaning and significance. According to Christian perspective, man forgets he is human, a creature, and tries to become "god," either in his own individual person or in the name of mankind at large. This issues in pride, arrogance, and finally in that state of rebellion called sin. It is the Christian conviction that this is the source of man's basic dilemma. It is *separation*, in his total person, from God. And the solution, so the Christian believes, lies in an ultimate reconciliation between God and man, who is created in God's own image, an image lost for awhile, and defaced, but never completely destroyed.

Christian doctrine of man, at this point, claims to be realistic about our human nature. We are enjoined simply to take a long, honest look at ourselves as we actually are. Within our selfhood there is conflict. Wherever there is conflict, there is tension. Wherever there is personal tension, there is anxiety. It is this characteristically human response to our ambivalent situation which contains possibilities for both good and evil, tragedy and triumph. Tragically, we seek all sorts of devices to find release from our restlessness and insecurity. From the Christian perspective, these attempts to find release are but measures of desperation which only serve to intensify anxiety. But we fondly believe we find solutions to the deepest dilemmas of selfhood. Men take some partial answer for the final answer; give devotion to some cause, some power or center of meaning, which is less than God. The result is delusion, despair, emptiness, meaninglessness. For it is the Christian conviction that completeness and fulfillment of total human selfhood is to be found only in the God who transcends and yet is dynamically related to all of nature, human history, and individual persons.

The spurious, self-defeating solutions we seek for our tensions and anxieties mean sin and separation. But to be found of and by the creatively loving God, as He discloses Himself supremely in Jesus Christ, who is more concerned about ourselves than we are, means genuine solution for the human predicament and ultimate reconciliation. This, at least, in briefest form is the radical claim of Christian faith to go to the very roots of men's personal dilemma to heal and restore.

More detailed discussion throughout succeeding chapters will serve to fill in further implications of these convictions. For how do we know God as distinguished from the way we know in the sciences and practical pursuits? How does He reveal Himself? What is faith and its relation to reason? What of the Being and Nature of this God of whom we speak? The significance of Jesus Christ as the way of reconciliation and atonement? What of the life eternal, the way of prayer and worship, within the Christian community, the Church, and everyday living individually and socially in the light of this reconciliation?

But for now the key to all the rest lies in this estimate which Christian faith makes of this radical separation of man from God and the necessity of reconciliation. For it is the Christian conviction that this paradoxical human being, who really seeks God above all else, cannot save himself out of his ultimate spiritual predicament. Yet he tries. He rebels. He asserts his independence. He fastens his devotion to false, partial "gods." It is thus man who, in pride and willful arrogance, separates himself from God.

If these convictions about man's religious predicament are false and misleading, what other alternatives are there for men and women today? If not the realism of biblical Christianity, then the livest alternative would seem to be some form of critical naturalism with its scientific or religious humanism. Here man's root troubles lie within himself and his own ignorance. And solutions as well are within man's own grasp. He has simply to become more rationally intelligent and more resourceful in the uses to which he puts the tools of the sciences, technology, arts, and letters toward the ends of fuller "human" existence. Which general view makes more sense? On which are you willing to act? Which gives the fuller, richer, more coherent account of man and his life within the vast reaches of an infinite universe? Is man-centered humanism the most adequate answer to man's moral, philosophic, and personal predicaments? Or is God-centered biblical Christianity? This is a decision which each must make for himself. The further discussions of succeeding chapters are attempts to assist the reader in clarifying these issues so that each may see for himself something of what the implications, the satisfactions, and the demands of Christian faith are.

Chapter VI

The Role of the Sciences

Religion does not begin with philosophy for most of us—certainly not with abstract, rational, or formal philosophy. Normally, we are not first consciously philosophical and then religious as a consequence of this; although at certain stages of our development, philosophical thinking may aid our reach toward maturer religious insights. This is true also with respect to the history of human cultures. For self-conscious, rational philosophy is a rather late arrival on the cultural scene. Rather it is more accurate to say that both philosophy and religion, together with the sciences and the arts also, spring out of men's elemental wonder and bewilderment in the face of a mysterious universe.

Each of these phases of man's attempts to relate himself to all the richness and complexity of the objective world around him fulfills its own distinctive function. Philosophy is the attempt to overcome human limitations and finitude by grasping the world with understanding as to its essential structure, its being, significance, and values. On the other hand, the sciences, evolving out of men's early groping efforts to trace out the systematic patterns of process in the physical world, now consist of certain specialized fields. Key terms in the sciences are observation, description, prediction, calculation, verification, experimentation, control. By contrast, the arts also play an integral part in man's developing culture. As he creates his music, drama, literature, sculpture, painting, and architecture, the key terms which describe his work are not understanding or description and control, but rather expression, creativity, communication, form, beauty.

But, moving beyond philosophy, the sciences, and the arts, religion is more than the intellectual assent of belief or understanding or scientific experimentation or artistic expression. It involves the response of man's whole being to that which has become his supreme object of devotion. Thus the key words which characterize religion are commitment, loyalty, worship, faith, revelation, salvation, reconciliation, God. These are matters of *personal and ultimate concern.* If you want to know what a man's religion is, then discover what it is outside himself to which, in total response of his whole self, including deep thought, feeling, and will, he has committed his entire destiny. In terms of Christian perspective, solution to man's personal predicament is found in utter devotion to the Eternal God who is source and ground of everything that is. For it is the Christian conviction that completeness and fulfillment of total human selfhood are attained through the saving power and loving concern of the God who transcends and yet is dynamically related to all of nature, human history, and individual persons. Furthermore, this solution to man's religious dilemma can be reached in nothing less than God and, at that, most pointedly and significantly as God discloses Himself in and through Jesus, the Christ. Only in God's Being can the authentic being of a man's own selfhood be restored into God's image, lost for awhile but never defaced. Out of lostness and estrangement, so the Christian believes, issue reconciliation and renewal of a man's very self, of perspective and resource for the demands of everyday living.

But naturalistic humanists, whom we have discussed, rest strong confidence in scientific methods and the capacity of intelligent men to employ the specific tools of the physical and social sciences to understand and control the forces of nature as well as those of personal and social relationships. Some even claim, as has been suggested, that if man sharpens these rational and scientific instruments to their finest precision, he can solve his human problems, including his moral and personal predicaments, without recourse to the sanctions and confusions of "outmoded religion." Naturalistic humanists tend, however, to be more moderate in their estimate of the role of the sciences than contemporary logical empiricists or the positivists and materialists of the nineteenth century. For these latter, more dogmatic, advocates of scientific method identify knowledge and science completely. Some describe this claim concerning the role of the sciences by the term *scientism*. Any experiences which are not amenable to scientific investigation, say the extreme advocates of scientism, are noncognitive and meaningless. But the trend of contemporary critical naturalism is certainly more moderate than that represented by the positivists. They place their confidence in the more generalized, more broadly interpreted "scientific spirit or attitude" of open and objective investigation of every aspect of human concern whatsoever. Nature is not reducible to matter in motion or points of energy held in tension. Rather, nature is conceived in the widest possible sense as including everything there is.

In his discussion of this view, Lewis White Beck comments:

Why, then, call "reality" by the name of "nature"? The reason for this . . . is that the naturalist asserts that the whole of reality is subject to the same kind of study that has already gone far toward mastering that part of reality which everyone agrees in calling nature. The critical naturalist says that whatever is claimed as knowledge must be justified by careful empirical enquiry, like that to which the natural sciences are devoted. Whatever any experience offers as insight into reality must be tested before it is accepted; no credence is to be given to intuitions or *a priori* insights. They are, at most, kinds of experiences that must be tested to see if what they suggest is true. As valuable kinds of experience, and as possible sources of knowledge, the naturalist is interested in cultivating, enjoying and examining them. He does not dog-matically pronounce them as absurd, as the materialists tend to do.[1]

Perhaps this is still scientism. For it is, of course, naturalism in its several varieties, which has adopted science and not science which has adopted naturalism.

In this chapter we shall discuss, first, the methods and knowl-edge claims of sciences as the outgrowth of common sense; second, classification of the various sciences; third, an example of the way in which a scientist seeks for solution to a problem; fourth, the characteristics and limitations of the sciences and ways in which the scientific contrasts with the nonscientific. Added to these ques-tions of the present chapter are those issues to be discussed in Chapter VII. There we shall think about what happens when, by contrast to the employment of scientific methods, religious (and specifically Christian) commitment and faith as ultimate concern take hold of men; the characteristic language of religious faith; and the basic harmony of faith within the Hebraic-Christian tra-dition with the functions and methods of the modern sciences. In Chapter VIII we shall consider the Bible and history and in Chapter IX, revelation and response.

These are all closely related problems for the sincere student and we dare not come to glib and superficial conclusions. For our severest temptation of presumed conflict between the sciences and religion, reason and faith, is to discount the claims of one in the name of the other, or to dismiss the entire problem as an insoluble impasse.

METHODS AND KNOWLEDGE CLAIMS OF THE SCIENCES

As to the methods and knowledge claims of the sciences, this aspect of the specialized human quest for understanding begins where all of us begin in our ordinary, everyday experiences:

[1] Lewis White Beck, *Philosophic Inquiry*, New York, Prentice-Hall, Inc., 1952, pp. 420-421.

with a world of things, events, and relationships. We all make generalizations, draw inferences, and suggest explanations in the form of hypotheses about what occurs in that world. Some of these statements represent the elemental level of common sense.

Through what we call common sense, we have built up a mass of funded knowledge, opinions, beliefs about the way things are and the ways in which members of society are expected to behave. Such common-sense knowledge rests in large measure on custom or tradition. Much of it is superficial, vague, and ambiguous intermingling of attested fact and blind prejudice. For common-sense claims to knowledge are fraught with both peril and promise. We constantly make generalizations and draw inferences from a narrow segment of observed data. Sometimes lack of access to "fair samples" leads us to make unwarranted generalizations or to draw inferences for which there is no supporting evidence. And yet it is precisely this imaginative process of thrusting out from the partially known into the unknown which makes possible the beginnings of scientific discovery through imaginative suggestions which may lead over into factually verified knowledge. This knowledge is never absolutely certain but only, at best, very highly probable. Nevertheless it is knowledge which enables us to predict and control processes in nature in terms of consciously chosen ends and goals.

Examples of the kinds of statements we utter every day may be cited. The reader will find it helpful to compare these statements with those he himself ordinarily makes in the midst of practical situations and to note how many of these are subject to exact confirmation and hence to scientific treatment. Consider the sentence "If it rains, the pavement will be slippery," and the sentence "There are 35 chairs in that room." The first is a prediction expressed in the form of a hypothesis, stating that *if* one event occurs, it probably will be accompanied by another event or state of affairs. The second statement is a complete enumeration about members of a given class of objects which is directly verifiable simply by counting. Some statements are more difficult to verify than others because the methods of confirmation are indirect and the supporting evidence less conclusive, or because they are not the kinds of statements which are subject to factual verification such as value judgments. Compare these sentences: "Light travels at 186,300 miles per second." "Sunspots are causally related to economic crises." "On July 4, 1976, the weather in Portland, Oregon, will be cloudy." "All men are created free and equal." "Beethoven's Ninth Symphony is beautiful music." "Stealing is wrong."

These truth claims and the attempt to contrast and compare them introduce us to the crucial problem of determining what kinds of statements can be verified by precise experimental methods. On the common-sense, prescientific level we act on evidence which would not be regarded as conclusive if we were engaged in a scientific enterprise. On the scientific level we must exercise more care. For there we seek exact knowledge that is formally grounded and empirically tested with such calculable precision as to enable us to predict and control, under assignable conditions, given kinds of processes in nature. That is to say, scientific knowledge is the most generalized knowledge, the most theoretically formulated. Yet it always comes back to the starting place of perceptual experience, and is thus the most carefully verified knowledge. The reason for this is that every scientific knowledge claim must be submitted to the tests of experimental confirmation and is at best only highly probable knowledge, for it is subject at any time to modification in the light of new empirical evidence.

CLASSIFICATION OF THE SCIENCES

The sort of scientific procedure we have been describing here, and with which we are chiefly concerned for purposes of our study, is *theoretical* or *pure* science as distinguished from *applied* science. The pure sciences have to do with the attainment of descriptive, objective, and mathematical knowledge of natural processes for its own sake without any immediate concern for practical application of this knowledge. The applied sciences are concerned with the practical application of this knowledge in the technological development, production, and use of instruments and machines to accomplish specific purposes in everyday affairs.

It is important to remember that there is no such single discipline as "science." There are many different sciences, each with its own precise methods and definable area of investigation. Yet these various sciences are related to each other as members of general families. Some sciences are more basic than others in the sense that the concepts and methods of one science are presupposed and employed in the work of another. For example, in the scientific study of man as a biological organism, the biologist must use some of the results of chemistry and physics, but the chemist or physicist does not need to be concerned with the work of the biologist. This is to say that physics and chemistry are more basic than biology. The more basic a science is, the simpler it is; for fewer assumptions need to be made. Also it is more general because its laws and principles apply to a wider variety of objects in nature.

Arranged in order from the more basic to the less basic, there are the formal sciences of logic and mathematics; the physical sciences of astronomy, physics, and chemistry; the organic or biological science of biology, including zoölogy and botany, with its various subdivisions; and the social sciences of psychology and sociology and, some would add, economics, political science, history, and so on. There are various other subdivisions representing detailed specialties and also some overlappings and cross-divisions, such as physical chemistry or biophysics.

We have been using the terms sciences and scientific methods in the course of our discussion. The term sciences may thus refer to the many specialized sciences; to the body of systematic knowledge, including the hypotheses, theories, concepts, and laws which have been developed through the centuries by many different scientists; or to scientific methods of obtaining the most exact, objective, verified knowledge possible under the conditions which confront the investigator.

THE WAY A SCIENTIST WORKS

An example of the way in which a scientist seeks for solution to a problem may be selected from the development of early physics: the experiments of Galileo with falling bodies. Ancient astronomy, following the lead of Aristotle, pictured the earth as at the center of the universe with the planets, contained in translucent spheres, moving around the earth. Despite the fact that fifth-century (B.C.) Pythagoreans and Hellenistic scientists such as Aristarchus (310-230 B.C.) had suggested the theory that the sun is the center of the universe, this view was regarded as far too complicated. Thus, under the leadership of men such as Ptolemy (flourished in Alexandria about A.D. 130), the movement of planets around the earth was pictured in the form of epicycles, or small circular movements made in the course of their larger circular journey.

At the beginning of our modern era, Copernicus (1473-1543) advanced the view that the sun is the center of the universe and that the earth turns on its own axis as it travels in a circular orbit, between Mars and Venus, around the sun. Kepler (1571-1630) showed that the notion of circular motion assumed by Copernicus did not fit the facts. He therefore developed the hypothesis that the orbits were not circles but ellipses and that the closer a planet is to the sun in its elliptical orbit, the faster it moves (the square of the time being proportional to the cube of the distance).

Galileo (1564-1642) was also intensely interested in the movements of the planets and, through the telescope he contrived, observed the satellites of Jupiter. But still the fixed stars seemed to be only points of light. It occurred to him that the planets must be of the same substance as the earth, masses of matter moving around the sun, and that the movements of bodies on earth could be calculated exactly. Many thinkers before Galileo had asked why bodies fall, and for many centuries it had been held that heavy bodies fall more rapidly than lighter bodies through space conceived in absolute "up and down" fashion. Galileo undertook in his science of dynamics, or "local motion," to show *how* bodies fall in precise mathematical terms; for he thought of the universe as an orderly system in which every event may be related by necessity to every other event.[2]

All scientific investigation, he believed, must include both experimental observation and theoretical reasoning. The scientist must go to nature for his data. But the data, he said, must suggest a theory called a hypothesis, or likely explanation of the problem under investigation. And out of the suggested hypothesis must be deduced possible consequences which would follow if the hypothesis were actually true. Then the hypothesis in turn must be subjected to the tests of observation and experiment. That is the way he himself worked. The empirical data suggested to him a universal theory. This he formulated in precise mathematical terms, including the possible implications which could be deduced from it. Then it was subjected to experimental test, verified, and formulated into a statement of results as a theory henceforth useful in explaining certain natural phenomena.[3] By this method, Galileo believed man could discover more and more about God's universe; for he did hold it to be God's universe. In more precise terms, the task which confronted Galileo was to develop an exact formulation of the laws of falling bodies—not why they fall but how they fall.[4]

Thus he knew that a falling body moves through space at a constantly increasing speed. His real problem was to determine the rate of increase. This is then the first step: formulation of the problem, that of determining the rate of increasing speed as bodies fall

[2] Galileo Galilei, *Dialogues and Mathematical Demonstrations Concerning Two New Sciences* (trans., Crew and De Salvio), New York, The Macmillan Company, 1914, p. 153 ff. See E. A. Burtt, *The Metaphysical Foundations of Natural Science,* New York, Doubleday Anchor Books, 1955, p. 73.

[3] Burtt, *op. cit.,* p. 81.

[4] See Sir William Cecil Dampier, *A History of Science and Its Relations with Philosophy and Religion,* London, Macmillan and Company, Ltd., 1931, p. 143.

from a height. Second, he had to suggest a hypothesis which would explain precisely how this increase of speed takes place. After a false start, he conceived the idea that the speed increases with the time of the fall rather than with the distance, as he previously had thought. His *working hypothesis,* to be verified, thus became that the speed of a falling body increases with the time of the fall. Third, was to deduce the consequences which would follow if the hypothesis were true. Fourth, he proceeded to work out methods of experimentation by which the working hypothesis could be tested. This became a practical matter of devising means of measuring speed, and this phase of the experimental process is sometimes called the *operational hypothesis.* Galileo realized that it was impractical to attempt to measure the speed of bodies falling freely through space. So he contrived an inclined plane and rolled balls down its slope. For he was convinced that balls rolling down a slope would exhibit the same velocity as balls dropped down from a height. Fifth, he deduced the implication concerning the exact mathematical relation that must hold between distance fallen and time taken for the fall; that is, the distance fallen would be proportional to the square of the time taken. Sixth, he then proceeded with his actual tests involving the rolling of balls down the inclined plane. And, finally, he formulated his results and discovered that they checked with those derived by deduction from his hypothesis that the speed of a falling body increases with the time of the fall, thus verifying, by means of his *operational hypothesis,* or experimental method, his original working hypothesis.

CHARACTERISTICS AND LIMITATIONS OF THE SCIENCES

We proceed now to discuss the characteristics and limitations of the sciences and ways in which the scientific contrasts with the nonscientific. In addition to these two types of hypotheses employed in scientific investigation, another type of hypothesis is brought into play as actually prior to the other two (prior both logically and in point of time in the process of investigation). It is called the *collateral hypothesis* and refers to the whole context of previously established knowledge which forms the background for new experimentation.[5]

It functions like a *postulate*, which is assumed to be true. Yet it is not certainly true or self-evident, but subject always to correction. For example, the scientist, Adams, worked out an explanation for observed irregularities in the motions of the planet Uranus as caused by a hitherto unobserved planet. In order to do so, he assumed the collateral hypothesis concerning Newton's law of gravitation. This collateral hypothesis, taken together with the working hypothesis (to be proved) and the operational hypothesis (defining the experimental procedure to be undertaken), forms a "family" of hypotheses. Beck summarizes the method which Adams employed by outlining the ways in which the three types of hypotheses are related to each other.[6] He does so as follows:

Major premise: Family of hypotheses	If the hypotheses about gravitation are true	Collateral hypothesis
	And if the hypothesis about the unknown planet is true	Hypothesis to be tested; "working hypothesis"
	And if a telescope is pointed at position p at time t	Antecedent of operational hypothesis
	Then a new point of light will be seen at p	Consequent
Minor premise: Experiment	The telescope is pointed at position p at time t	Affirming the antecedent of the operational hypothesis
Conclusion	The point of light is seen	Observed fact, and the consequent of the entire family of hypotheses

[5] Beck, *op. cit.*, pp. 94 ff.
[6] *Ibid.*, p. 95.

The Role of the Sciences

But behind specific collateral hypotheses, there lie certain other assumptions or postulates which form the background, so to speak, against which the scientist does his work. For the scientist seeks to discover patterns of order in nature. He believes it is a cosmos, not a chaos. His work involves search for "laws" which describe how certain kinds of events take place in case after case so that he can predict, under given conditions, new and perhaps unexpected facts. If he can do this, then he can formulate his conclusions with mathematical accuracy so as to correlate one set of measurable instances with other instances. Such laws stating these correlations are not "prescriptive" laws which would regulate in advance what must happen. Rather they are *descriptive* or *functional* laws which tell not how some event ought to happen, but what has usually been observed to happen time after time and probably will happen again.

But what of even more generalized laws, such as the principle of the uniformity of nature, which states that certain kinds of events are usually followed by certain other kinds of events? This performs, in a sense, the same function as that performed by a collateral hypothesis. It is, states Beck, a member of every family of good hypotheses. But it is unique. For it itself is not testable. "Without it, no hypothesis can be verified. With it, all good hypotheses can be tested, and if it is true, the others that are true can be distinguished from those that are false. If, on the other hand, it is false, no hypothesis can be confirmed. Without it, all hypotheses become poor." [7]

At this point, some interpreters of the relations between religion and the sciences say: "Look at the assumptions which the scientists make. After all, their work is based on faith also, just like the faith of the religionist." But this is a vast oversimplification of the issue. Scientists do have a faith in the sense of general confidence in the value of their work, just as in the case of many other specialists.

[7] *Ibid.*, p. 141.

However, religious (and specifically Christian) faith is of a different order and character, as we shall point out in more detail in subsequent chapters; for it is response of the whole person, including thought, feeling, and will, in utter commitment to the God who is the object of personal and ultimate concern. It is a matter of the motivation and purposive direction of all of our human resources, including those of the sciences themselves. As man of faith, each person is not an impersonal observer of processes and events, but a participator and experiencer.

But the purposive use of the results of scientific investigation toward ends envisaged by faith does not affect the precise findings of the sciences themselves. It is true that in the social sciences the danger of bias and the complex character of the data involved make the precise testing of hypotheses more difficult. Yet even here the basic methods of the sciences must be maintained, that of submitting hypotheses to the tests of impartial observation. In the social or in the physical sciences, the investigator *qua* scientist, even though he also be a man of faith, is an observer and must maintain the autonomy and independence of scientific method. His fundamental assumption concerning the uniformity of nature is simply one of the tools of his trade. It is a collateral hypothesis which, if assumed, makes possible the discovery of specific truths about the natural order. If it is not assumed, there is no chance of finding out what is actually the case among the mysteriously complex processes going on in this universe all around us.

What then do scientists do? In summation, what are the distinctive characteristics of the sciences, features which also indicate the limitations of the sciences? For, as scientists carry on their work, they believe the world is a cosmos and not a chaos. They proceed on the postulate that, through experimentation and observation, they can discover laws describing the ways in which certain natural phenomena behave, under controlled conditions, in case after case. Thus they formulate their conclusions with mathematical accuracy—correlating occurrences with such precision as to be able to predict what most probably will happen in the future under similar conditions.

Wheelwright cites the following six characteristics of science in summary fashion, which we paraphrase here.[8]

1. Science describes phenomena and makes no attempt, in any explicit way, to evaluate them. But, as has been indicated, the same man who is scientist is also a whole man, husband, father, citizen, moral idealist, committed man of faith. Even the cause of scientific pursuit itself may be an object of intense devotion and hence be a supreme value. But this does not affect the precise methods or results which he must develop within a given field of investigation, no matter what his wishes or feelings may be.

2. These descriptions of the sciences are selective. The objects of scientific investigation are abstractions in the sense that data with which a scientist is concerned are publicly verifiable.

Thus the somewhat private experiences of the religious mystic, the lover, and the artist are not accepted as directly evidential. In a sense they are of interest to the psychologist; but only as offering clues to the nature of the "subject"—the psychophysical organism—not as offering clues to the nature of the world with which the subject thinks himself to be in contact. Moreover, the scientific psychologist does not rest content with the subject's verbal testimony as to what he has experienced but seeks confirmatory evidence in overt behavior. Thus to the scientific psychologist the "subject" becomes an *object* of investigation. The aim in science is to eliminate as far as possible the subjective and personal element from the problem.[9]

3. Science proceeds by making as few assumptions as possible. This is the so-called principle of parsimony which found expression in "Occam's Razor," as formulated at the beginning of the fourteenth century by the English Franciscan philosopher William of Occam.

4. Science is not interested in an individual as an individual, but

[8] Philip Wheelwright, *The Way of Philosophy*, New York, The Odyssey Press, 1954, pp. 182-184.
[9] *Ibid.*, pp. 182-183.

only as he is an instance of a whole class and indicates significant knowledge about that whole class.

5. Science advances when it puts stress on the measurable. That is, the scientist must express the results of his experimentation in such exact terms that any other scientist, under the given conditions, would arrive at the same results. This generally means that scientific statements are quantitative.

6. Science assumes that every event in nature has a cause and that these causes are discoverable. This is the *postulate of determinism.*

By way of contrast, Wheelwright also cites the significant opposites of each of these six characteristics. If these belong to the scientific, then the opposite traits belong to man's nonscientific experiences. "Briefly it may be said: Experiences so far as they are (1) evaluated, (2) private, (3) full, (4) individual, (5) qualitative, (6) fortuitous, are not accepted as material for science." [10]

We have discussed the methods and knowledge claims of the sciences: first, their relation to common sense; second, the classification of the sciences; third, examples of scientific method; and, fourth, the characteristics and limitations of the sciences and hence contrasts between the scientific and the nonscientific. This leads us to face squarely further basic issues concerning the significance of the religious in contrast to the scientific impulse, to be raised more fully in the three succeeding chapters.

[10] *Ibid.,* p. 184.

Chapter VII

Commitment and the Language of Faith

The scientist is essentially the impersonal observer. But the man of faith (who may be the same individual) is distinctively the experiencer and participant. The religious response of total human selfhood characterizes the non-scientific rather than the scientific.

By contrast to scientific experiences, with their six characteristics listed at the conclusion of the previous chapter, we may describe moments of religious impulse. Here a man does evaluate, is involved in his own private states, deals not with simple abstractions but with the whole fullness of human experience, is concerned with the individual and personal, pays closest attention not to the quantitative but the qualitative, and is not bound by the determined necessities of nature but is free in some measure to make decisions and bear responsibility. It is not the special business of the sciences to offer solution to the three kinds of human predicament which we have discussed: the moral, philosophical, and personal. That is to say, the sciences, as such, may not tell us toward what goals or ends we ought to direct the products of human ingenuity, or offer us standards or principles by which human conduct ought to be judged. Nor may the sciences, as such, have concern about *reality as a whole*. Moreover, it is not the function of the sciences, as such, to solve the personal predicament of existential anxiety and the

91

estrangement of sin. For release into complete fulfillment of total human selfhood in God cannot be effected by technological manipulation, valuable as these techniques are in dealing with neurotic tensions and maladjustments. But it is precisely within the context of the religious perspective that these human deeper dilemmas become meaningful and reach hopefully toward solution. For in a genuine value judgment, as we have indicated, a *self* is called in terms of a command to answer, "So be it!" In the philosophical quest for reality, he asks, "Why? Whence? Whither?" Then a man's total self is involved as, within the depths of his own human existence, his being meets the essential Being of the universe. On the level of the personal also, this paradoxical creature called man may be led to utter commitment of the whole self to an object of ultimate concern and hence find release from disruption, anxiety, and sin. These are the sorts of concerns with which religion deals. Christian conviction claims especially to view the human situation as realistically as possible and offer reconciliation between man and himself and man and God whose image man has wilfully defaced but not quite completely lost. The sciences, *qua* sciences, cannot answer these human needs; for it is not their business to do so. But neither can committed men of faith live without the sciences to provide the tools of understanding, prediction, and control of that world of nature and of the conditions of human nature within which selfhood finds its fulfillment. In the final analysis, therefore, the inherent scientific and religious concerns do not necessarily conflict but rather comprise a working partnership essential to human well-being.

In this chapter, we shall suggest, positively, (1) characteristics and illustrations of what happens when, by contrast to the employment of scientific methods, religious (and specifically Christian) commitment and faith as ultimate concern take hold of men; (2) the characteristic language of religious faith; and (3) the basic harmony of faith, within the Hebraic-Christian tradition, with the functions and methods of the modern sciences.

Commitment and the Language of Faith

THE RESULTS OF COMMITMENT AND FAITH

What happens when religious commitment and faith, as matters of personal and ultimate concern, take hold of men? What are some distinctive characteristics of the religious response of man's whole being to that which has become his supreme object of devotion? What illustrations will serve to illuminate these?

However, as we discuss these questions, we need to face an important issue: Is Christianity just one more religion among others? Or is it in some sense unique? Is there any such thing as religion in general? Or do we always move within given historical and cultural contexts?

If the latter is the case, then we must be exceedingly careful when we speak of religion. For religion is not necessarily a "cure" for what ails men and nations. It depends on what religion; what level of maturity is attained; what content of belief, emotional tone, and pattern of action is involved. Christianity does not demand commitment to itself or devotion to religion or faith in faith. It is not a tool to be used consciously and deliberately to attain release from tension and anxiety. It does not guarantee "peace of mind," success in living, complete knowledge of all mysteries, or even a workable system of values. If these come, they come as consequences of a self-giving devotion that asks for nothing in return. For commitment is to be given utterly and completely to none of these but only to God, who is the ultimate ground of all nature, history, and personal existence. Devotion to anything less than this is to make relativities into absolutes and, in the end, brings further disruption of human selfhood and of community within which selves live.

The religious response, then, is specific and personal. And we prefer to use the adjective *religious*, rather than the noun *religion*. For religion is not a thing or an entity. It is nothing in itself. It is a word we use to describe what happens within and among persons in the midst of day-by-day experiences. Religion comes alive in the whole personality of men and women. It does not transport them into another world. Rather they remain within this world, on the plane of human history where they earn their bread; fall in love; marry; beget, conceive, and bear children; create their social, economic, and political institutions; devote themselves to the sciences, literature, arts; and finally worship their God. But as they make religious response, persons in utter commitment to the ultimate ground of everything begin simply to see all these things of everyday concern in a new light. Theirs is a new and creative dimension of depth where meaning is illuminated and made relevant to the whole of human existence.

Moreover, religion is not a mere system of forms, dogmas, or theories. To know about religion and to formulate beliefs in rational and coherent order, as in systems of theology, are essential to the development of mature religion. But theological systems and formalized modes of practice originate in the experiences and insights of men and groups of men sharing these in common. *If you want to know what a man's religion in itself is, then discover what it is outside himself to which, in total response of deep thought, feeling, and will, he has committed his entire destiny.*

John Buchan, in his novel *Mountain Meadow,* tells about a man who finally found the ultimate answer to his all-consuming quest, not in solitary contemplation, but in service to a tribe of ill and poverty-stricken Indians in the Canadian North. His own physical stamina was rapidly ebbing away as day by day he sought to bring healing and solace. Yet: "As his strength declined, he could speak only in a whisper. But his whisper had the authority of trumpets. For he succeeded in diffusing the impression of a man who had put all fear behind him and was ready for communion with something beyond our mortality."

The story is told how an honorary degree was once conferred upon the courageous Christian missionary, David Livingstone, by one of the Scottish universities. According to university custom, the students sat in the balcony and called out all sorts of names and

Commitment and the Language of Faith

raucous remarks. Livingstone stood before them with one arm hanging limp at one side, for his shoulder had been torn by a lion amid the jungles of Africa. What did the students do in the presence of such a person? They rose as one man and stood in absolute silence.

Here stands a vibrant personality whose commitment was made clear in an all-consuming purpose that took him to the edge of civilization. And youth and age alike respond, at least in respect. This response is not to abstract systems of theology or philosophy, or to codified lists of moral rules. Men and women respond to a life, behind that life an experience, all through that life and experience a vibrant impulse of response, a whole self being taken hold of by that which gives ultimate meaning to human existence. That response, although deeply inward, is expressed in outward acts of worship and of devoted service for the welfare of other persons. These are the expression of thought, feeling, and action as a matter of personal and *ultimate concern.*

We have used the words ultimate concern several times in this characterization of the religious response. Paul Tillich has made this term central to his system of theology, and it is rapidly coming into wide usage on the contemporary scene. Tillich states:

Ultimate concern is the abstract translation of the great commandment: "The Lord, our God, the Lord is one; you shall love the Lord your God with all your heart, and with all your soul and with all your mind, and with all you strength" [Mark 12: 29, Revised Standard Version]. The religious concern is ultimate; it excludes all other concerns from ultimate significance; it makes them preliminary. The ultimate concern is unconditional, independent of any conditions of character, desire, or circumstance. The unconditional concern is total; no part of ourselves or of our world is excluded from it; there is no "place" to flee from it [Psalm 139]. The total concern is infinite: no moment of relaxation and rest is possible in the face of a religious concern which is ultimate, unconditional, total and infinite.[1]

[1] Paul Tillich, *Systematic Theology,* Chicago, University of Chicago Press, 1951, Vol. 1, pp. 11-12.

Essentials in Christian Faith

THE CHARACTERISTIC LANGUAGE OF RELIGIOUS FAITH

This perspective on the nature of religious response leads us to ask: What sort of *language* can express this concern that reaches beyond the levels of ordinary human experience, a concern that is ultimate, unconditional, total, and infinite? Obviously, the language of exact scientific description, as we have characterized it in the preceding chapter, cannot convey what he has encountered within the depths of his own personal being when he makes religious response to his world.

We have discussed what contemporary logical empiricists would do with the language of religion and the "realities" to which it purports to refer. So much the worse for the words and sentences which religion uses, they would say; for they are neither formal nor factual statements of mathematics, logic, or the sciences. They are therefore pseudo-concepts employed within pseudo-sentences which have no cognitive meaning but only subjective, emotive meaning. They are neither true nor false, but they may at their best provide those who use them with inner emotional satisfaction, peace of mind, or a sense of security. Or, at their dangerous worst, religious utterances may become the tools of persuasion and social control over the lives and conduct of ignorant people.

Aside from logical empiricism's positive contributions and drawbacks, which we have indicated in Chapter IV, we would now acknowledge a debt of which all contemporary students of religion and philosophy ought to be aware. The logical empiricists have raised with challenging vigor the whole question of the nature of language. This means for our purposes that we have an important task before us, in which some of the greatest scholars are taking the lead: that of discovering in fresh ways the nature and significance of religious language. By way of contrast to the exact, mathematical language of the scientists, what kinds of utterance take place in prayers, worship, Scripture, hymns, sermons, or theological writings?

Commitment and the Language of Faith

Here involved is a distinctive form of symbol making, as men attempt to express their religious concern of ultimate, unconditional, and total commitment. There is no other mode of expression fitted to communicate such concern. For if men would convey any insights at all as to their grasp of man's ultimate destiny, they must do so in terms of symbols which are rich in imagery and vivid in their suggestive power.

The reader will recall the point of view developed in Chapter IV about the metaphysical quest for the understanding of the nature of the universe. We stated then that the way in which a metaphysical system is developed lies closer to the imaginative creativity of the poet, novelist, or artist than to the precise experimentation of the chemist or physicist. In our metaphysical quest, we employ world hypotheses, expressed in analogies or root metaphors, as significant keys or clues suggestive of the nature of the whole of reality. Thus a selected segment of human experience comes to be employed as a symbol for that which it represents. Metaphysics in this sense is not a demonstrative science but an analogical art. In this process, such a symbolically expressed world hypothesis must be tested, not as scientific hypotheses are verified, but by the method of dialectical experiment. We test them for their consistency and adequacy. We ask: Do they enable us to make sense of as wide ranges of experience as possible with depth of insight and courageous action?

We have said also that men of Christian conviction may develop a philosophy. This will be one of unique perspective, throwing light on all the wider ranges of the universe, nature, history, man, and his values. But it begins with direct, personal encounter between an "I" and a "Thou" where there takes place moral demand, ontological insight, and religious commitment. Christian philosophy takes its clues and draws its analogies and significant symbols from this deeply intimate life of individual persons, within which God and man meet, and also from the broad ranges of history where God moves and acts dynamically. Of these analogies also we must ask:

Have they breadth, inclusiveness, depth of insight, and momentum enough to embrace all things of concern to man?

Thus, what of our attempt to communicate the significance of this encounter and response? How shall man express what he can understand of that ground of his being that transcends and yet is dynamically related to everything in space and time? What symbols can he use? What root metaphors or analogies taken from this finite world of things, persons, and events can possibly grasp the nature of God?

J. V. Langmead Casserley stresses the seriousness for contemporary thought of this problem of language and communication. "Can human speech," he asks, "express the most profound elements in human experience? If not, are these apparent experiences, which seem to elude speech, genuine experiences? Must we not conclude that what cannot be lucidly spoken cannot be clearly thought, so that for us the real world must be taken to be the clear-cut world of scientific definition and accurate observation and experiment, all else being dismissed as no more than a world of shadows, a land of subjectivity and all-pervading imprecision?" [2]

It is a paradox. For, till our dying day, the full nature of God remains a mystery beyond human apprehension. And yet man, the symbol-making animal who himself in part transcends nature, never rests satisfied until he has attempted to say of God, whom he can never understand, something of what He is. Selecting actual objects all around him, the man of faith tries to find adequate symbols with which to speak of God: light, rock, high tower, eternal goodness, judge, father. In the moving cadences of music and poetic utterance, he uses the language of faith to express the inexpressible, to convey in rich imagery how God discloses Himself in events of history and personal experiences and what meaningful insights are involved in man's response of utter commitment to the God who confronts him.

[2] J. V. Langmead Casserley, *The Christian in Philosophy*, New York, Charles Scribner's Sons, 1951, p. 80.

Commitment and the Language of Faith

What we are saying here partly anticipates discussion of the next chapter on the nature of revelation, or the self-disclosure of God's own Being to finite selves. Revelation is not identical with the words of language themselves, considered as "information about otherwise hidden truth." [3] God discloses himself, not through propositions or items of information, but in and through *events* in nature, history, and the inner experience of men. These events are the revelation of God. The words which men use to describe the significance of these revelatory events become then the medium of revelation. Religious symbolism is thus the vehicle through which men try to convey to other men what has happened in that personal, I-Thou encounter of man's whole being with God. For now, our concern is with the language through which the meaning of divine-human encounter, response, and commitment, is expressed. When this that we call religious response occurs within men and women, they must have at hand an appropriate language through which to say where they have been and what they have seen.

When we discussed in a previous chapter the nature of man and his personal predicament, we were confronted by contrast between the Greek-classical and the Hebraic-biblical views. Throughout the entire development of western culture, the way of Greek Platonic and Neo-platonic search for ultimate reality stands as a challenge to the way of Hebraic faith and commitment. For the Hebrew, this means utter devotion to the Will of God who is at once Creator of the universe and also Purpose disclosing Himself specifically and personally in events of history. The Greek quest, as it culminates in the mysticism of Plotinus, for example, is a long journey from this unreliable world of things experienced by the senses up through the realm of rational understanding to union with the One, which is the absolute and final reality. Once the mystic has attained this union, then all that belongs to sense and to intellect is sloughed off and left behind. What then can logical

[3] Tillich, *op. cit.*, p. 124.

99

reasoning or even interpretive experiment with materials of sense say in words and sentences about such an unknowable reality as this transcendant One? Only one method and one language mode seemed possible for the Neoplatonist: the "way of negation." That is, man can look all about him at objects of ordinary experience and then proceed to state what the One Real Being is *not*. For, said Plotinus of the One:

It is not a thing, it is not quality, it is not quantity, it is not Intelligence nor Soul. It does not move, and yet it is not at rest, either in space or in time. . . . He that would speak exactly must not name it by this name or that; we can but circle, as it were, about its circumference seeking to interpret in speech our experience of it, now shooting near the mark, and again disappointed of our aim by reason of the antinomies we find in it.

The greatest antinomy abides in this, that our understanding of it is not by way of scientific knowledge nor of intellection, as our understanding of other intelligible objects, but by a presence higher than all knowing. In making knowledge of an object, the soul suffers defect of unity and is not wholly one; for knowledge is an account of things, and an account is manifold, and so our soul lapses into number and multiplicity, and misses the One. Wherefore she must travel beyond knowledge, and refuse all departure from her unity; she must withdraw herself from knowing and the knowable, and from every alien contemplation, be it never so fair; for all Beauty is consequent upon the One and has its origin from thence, as all the light of days is from the sun.[4]

Professor Casserley helpfully reminds us that thought such as this out of the Greek tradition "confronts the Christianity of the Bible with a fundamental challenge. The God of the Bible is not an ineffable One, a remote and lofty Absolute, who is searched out by philosophical method which inevitably falls short of Him, and is found only rarely in the bliss of mystical absorption and ecstasy." For the Hebraic-Christian tradition, rather, God moves, acts, and discloses Himself in events of history "as Person, Purpose and Will." Here the response of faith is not negation but affirmation. For this

---

4 Plotinus, *Enneads*, VI, ix, 3, 4.

is the language of Scripture, telling positively of "His Purpose, His Providence, His Justice, His Wrath, His Love. He has shown Himself to us in Jesus, so that 'whoever has seen Jesus has seen the Father,' because Jesus is 'the image of the invisible God.' Again," adds Professor Casserley, "we seem to have reached a point at which it would appear that Greek thought and the Gospel can make no sense of each other." [5]

Early Christian thinkers, under the influence of both Greek and Hebraic perspectives, found themselves committed to these two ways: the way of *affirmation,* which in Biblical language asserts a positive knowledge of God; and the philosophical way of *negation,* which tells us that the full nature of the Creator-Father-God ever exceeds our attempt to know Him or to express in ordinary language what He is like. Combining the ways of affirmation and negation, such men as Augustine make statements that involve striking paradox concerning the God who is known and yet never completely known:

It becomes our duty to envisage God, if we can and so far as we can, as good without quality, great without quantity, creator without necessity, foremost without relations, comprehending all things but possessing no mode of existence, everywhere present but without location, eternal without subjection to time, capable of action without submitting to the changes of mutable things, and of feeling without passion. Whoever thinks thus of God, although he is by no means able to discover Him, nevertheless takes such precautions as are possible against entertaining false notions regarding Him.[6]

Professor Casserley comments that such passages as these indicate the possibility of another approach to this problem of language about God. This is a third way called "the way of paradox, in which we speak affirmatively and negatively of God at the same time, asserting the image as genuinely revealing while denying the limitations which our experience of it inevitably suggests. From this point

[5] Casserley, *op. cit.*, p. 38.
[6] Augustine, *De Trinitate*, V, 1, 3.

of view," states Casserley, "the ways of affirmation and negation would appear to be not two ways at all, but twin aspects of a single movement of the mind, which we shall call the way of paradox." [7]

Those who employ the language of faith, taking a firm hold on this method of paradox, thus express themselves through the symbolism of sacrament and myth. Sacrament involves investing with symbolic significance commonplace acts or objects, such as eating, drinking, washing. As Suzanne Langer indicates, these actions take on symbolic meanings and they become rites or sacraments. Myth is rooted deeply in man's inner world of dreams and fancies. Myth, however, is vastly different from fairy tales or imaginative fiction related simply for entertainment. Myths deal with man's serious attempt to portray, in highly imaginative words, significant insights about this real world and man's relationship to it. These metaphorical world pictures deal sometimes with cosmologies, God's creation of the world and man. They are attempts at portraying the ultimate meaning of human existence and of the ways man is oriented to this meaning. Poetic figures, images, stories become the vehicles of insights which the accurately descriptive and objective language of the sciences simply cannot convey. This is not the literal language of direct report which Wheelwright calls "stenolanguage." [8] Rather it is expressive language or "depth language" through which men would penetrate into the mystery of their own being and that of the universe around them. If "depth meanings" are the concern of myth, then men employing this language move beyond the fictional or false, as popular thought would have it. "Myth, then, is not in the first instance a fiction imposed on one's already given world, but a way of apprehending that world. Genuine myth is a matter of perspective first, invention second." [9]

[7] Casserley, *op. cit.*, p. 41.
[8] See Philip Wheelwright, *The Burning Fountain,* Indiana University Press, 1954, pp. 52-75.
[9] *Ibid.*, p. 159.

Commitment and the Language of Faith

Mythic thought begins thus with the colors and shapes which impinge upon our visual awareness, immediate data of consciousness or images. *Imagination* works freely on these images, interpreting them, moving freely with them out into all sorts of envisioned possibilities. Of course, free imagination is the creative source of new knowledge and insight in the sciences as well as the arts, philosophy, and religion. But there are significant differences between these modes of imaginative relation to the world. John Hutchison expresses it this way:

Rational or critical thought consists in bringing images into responsible relation to facts. Thus, for example, once a new idea comes into being in science, it is deliberately tested on facts. The measure of its truth is its adequacy to the facts. This is true, in varying ways and measures, in all thinking; the life of reason is a quest for adequacy.

The mode of religious or mythical thinking consists in the occurrence in the mind of the religious person of compelling or authoritative images. Where in art the mind contemplatively enjoys images evoked by the work of art, in religion these images possess authority or force over a person's whole life. Indeed the essence of religious experience is just such an experience of the authority of an image. Religion is thus poetry by which men live. The reference to action makes clear why religion entails morality and poetry does not.[10]

Moving now within the context of the Hebraic-Christian perspective, the Bible uses imagic myth to portray the significance of events through which God discloses his Being, power, justice, and love to men and groups of men. From the account of creation ("In the beginning God created . . .") to that of the final fulfillment in the Book of Revelation ("The grace of our Lord Jesus Christ be with you all . . ."), there is portrayed the dramatic sweep of God's impact upon those who, as actual participants, felt the full force of that impact. For these men, simply being persons, active, purposing, dynamic, is the most luminous experience of all. For being a person is unique. It is a vivid, dramatic affair. It is unre-

[10] John Hutchison, *Faith, Reason and Existence,* New York, Oxford University Press, 1956, pp. 56-57.

peatable. Especially as encounter with God takes place, he realizes he is somehow different as a consequence of this encounter, and commitment of the whole person in response of faith is the only adequate answer. Such events are singular: once occurring yet indicative, so the man of Christian conviction believes, of all of God and the world of nature, history, and persons that stretches out beyond his sure grasp of understanding. The only adequate way of expressing their significance is the richly imagic language of myth.

THE BASIC HARMONY OF FAITH AND THE SCIENCES

We conclude this chapter by brief reference to the basic harmony of faith, within the Hebraic-Christian tradition, with the functions and methods of the modern sciences. This perspective on the nature of expressive, mythic language as the medium of religious insight is a difficult one for modern-minded men and women to comprehend. We live, as has been said, in a "post-mythical age." No longer do the vivid expressions of Christian faith, as celebrated traditionally in rite, poem, picture, doctrine, appeal to men so imbued with the "scientific" outlook that they view myth as prescientific fiction or story which simply is not so.

Reinhold Niebuhr makes helpful suggestion at this point of tension between modern scientism and Christian faith within this post-mythical age of ours. In order to point up what is perennially valid in the Christian affirmation, he distinguishes between *primitive myth* and *permanent myth*.[11] The first consists of elemental, prescientific interpretations of the world and man, as in early accounts of the creation and other natural phenomena. But permanent myth concerns man's relation to that which is ultimate. In the vivid language of poetic images, it has to do with perennial concerns of total commitment and insight into human destiny. Thus, mythical

[11] Reinhold Niebuhr, "The Truth of Myths," cited in Eugene G. Bewkes (ed.), *The Nature of Religious Experience*, New York, Harper & Brothers, 1937, Chap. VI, pp. 117 f. See also Hutchison, *op. cit.*, p. 54.

thinking, says Niebuhr, "tells many little lies in the interest of one great truth." These "many little lies" may be mythical falsification of what actually occurs among natural phenomena, but the "one great truth" is man's relation to a meaningful order of things and ultimately to the God "in Whom he lives and moves and has his being." We are therefore, according to Niebuhr, to "take myth seriously but not literally." Some among biblical interpreters insist on reading myth as if it were scientific description, thus taking it literally. Often the modern-minded critic looks at myth as pre-scientific illusion, thus refusing to take it seriously. Niebuhr disagrees with both these perspectives in the interest of the depiction of ultimate depth meanings and man's personal and ultimate concern, which only imaginative mythic language can convey to men of this or any age.

For biblical religion, the sciences, and faith, far from conflicting, actually form a working partnership. What myth in the Bible conveys is a sweeping story of divine action within history and man's response. This self-disclosure of God occurs in and through specific events and hence these events themselves become revelation to men who receive and respond. Thus this world of detailed fact, time, space, matter, and action is a real world. For the Hebraic-Christian perspective, it is a world within which things of significance and purposive direction happen. Yet we do not know in advance nature's entire pattern and structure, for these are hidden from us. As John Baillie points out, this is the case not only for Biblical religion but for modern science as well.[12]

It is for the rationalistic Greek mind, says Professor Baillie, that the universe is conceived as an eternally fixed pattern. All men had to do, therefore, was to discover this "ideal pattern of nature and deduce from that the details of its processes." But actually this point of view blocked rather than encouraged the development of experimental science. Modern scientists do not begin with the

[12] John Baillie, *Natural Science and the Spiritual Life*, New York, Charles Scribner's Sons, 1952.

claim to knowledge of an eternal structure from which actual detailed facts in nature can be deduced. What they say is "that the pattern is hidden from us, and that therefore we must begin from the other end. The method of science must be fundamentally inductive, working by observation and experiment." [13]

Nature is contingent, therefore, for the sciences, depending upon occurrences that are not absolutely certain. We must then begin with active experiment, with details at hand, and work our way forward to fuller and fuller understanding. Baillie makes the emphatic point that this active and experimental method of the modern sciences is utterly impossible for the Greek mind:

It is quite clear to me, then, that modern science could not have come into being until the ancient pagan conception of the natural world had given place to the Christian. . . . Hardly was any Greek scientist able to rid himself of his pagan preconceptions concerning the course which the world-process must inevitably follow. It would follow, they all believed, a cyclical course. . . . The spectacle of nature was like a continuous performance at a cinema show. Within so many thousand years from now everything in nature would again be exactly as it is today, and so on, times without number, to all eternity. Nor was this merely because the same or similar things would periodically recur within the stream of time, but because, as Aristotle expressly says, the movement of time is itself circular. What Christianity did was, as it were, to roll the circle of time out flat. The rectilinear conception of time, which we all now take for granted, was introduced into Western thought by Christianity.[14]

This world of detailed fact, time, space, matter, and action is a real world. Its nature must be discovered piecemeal. "Modern science, as Hutchison states it, "is *active*." That is, it progresses through actual experimentation and it places in men's hands instruments of control over natural processes. This mastery of nature also never could have occurred to a Greek scientist. It is the Hebraic-Christian viewpoint which reminds us that man is made in God's

[13] *Ibid.*, p. 19.
[14] *Ibid.*, pp. 25-26.

image and has been given "dominion . . . over all the earth, and over every creeping thing that creepeth upon the earth" (Genesis 1:26-28).

This means that if man's commitment to God is to be complete and total, his science is an important part of that devotion. The enterprise of the sciences thus becomes one of the phases of man's response to God: a *calling,* or *vocation.* Its task is that of grasping and controlling all those forces of nature, including man's own organic, psychic, and social nature, within which human selfhood comes to fulfillment of response and commitment in God. This is to take seriously what von Hügel calls "the *thing*-element in religion." [15] For the life of faith requires coming to grips with the natural world as it actually is.

Not only does faith need science but, from the Christian perspective, science also needs faith to provide directions and purposes toward which the resources of the sciences must move as means to the end of man's life in God. Thus Christian commitment and scientific understanding and control of the forces of nature are essential to each other within a world of dynamic events through which God reveals Himself to men waiting to respond in faith.

[15] *Ibid.,* p. 32.

Chapter VIII

The Bible and History

Christianity takes history seriously. History in the Hebraic-Christian perspective is that sphere of dynamic events within which and through which God discloses Himself to persons as those persons respond in total commitment. Christianity is often called a historical religion and biblical faith a historical faith. But the special significance of this term *historical* as used in this connection is difficult for modern-minded students to grasp. The Hebraic-Christian tradition has a history. But so do all the religions of the world. The historian may study how these various religions began, the biographies of founders, the contributions of seers and teachers, the cultic practices, the systems of belief and social consequences. But biblical faith is itself a series of events. It therefore does not simply *have* a history. It *is* a history.[1]

Unlike the cyclical time of the Greeks, time in the biblical view flows purposively in a straight line. Here time is the sphere of action. As one writer states it: "For the Christian, the Bible is a mirror of both personality and history. . . ." It is the real world of persons in all the unique detail of their individual and social living. For it is not abstract, mathematical time but man's time which is the dynamic context of biblical faith. The events of man's

[1] See Will Herberg, "Biblical Faith as *Heilsgeschichte*," *The Christian Scholar*, March, 1956, p. 25.

time are singular, unrepeatable, vivid, dramatic. They do not move as the monotonous reflections of a static, eternal pattern. Rather, man's time is a series of crises, of person-to-person encounter, decision, response. Each moment, then, is a moment for wonder and opportunity.

But in the midst of the crises of birth, marriage, daily work, joys, sickness, loss, death, there are some events of more momentous significance than others and which illuminate all these others. For the man of faith holds that in and through certain events God speaks, acts, and discloses Himself in such a way as to require response and responsible decision. Thus man's history, although real, is not ultimate. It belongs to and finds its significance in relation to the transcendent God who is source, ground, and goal of all time and history. It is with this encounter that the Old and New Testaments are concerned. This is their main theme: God, man, man's rebellions, God wooing man to Himself, man responding in faith, consummation, deliverance, salvation. These themes are not treated abstractly, but vividly and concretely. The Bible is not a textbook of argument about ideas, but exciting drama of living personalities.

It is our purpose in this chapter to help the reader understand more fully and vividly for our own day, first, the central role of the Bible in Christian belief and practice; second, the significance of the sweep of historical events which the Bible records. In the following chapter, we shall consider in more detail that term which keeps recurring in our discussion, *revelation* as God's self-disclosure, and the meaning of the response to God's self-disclosure that we call *faith* in its relation to reason.

If God discloses Himself in and through events of history, of which the Bible is the record, and men in years gone by have responded in faith, then men and women of the twentieth century may also participate in those selfsame events. For as these events are remembered, folk living today become dynamically involved in the events which are our own contemporary history in a fresh and decisive way. For us, and to us also, God discloses Himself and men are called to act responsibly. Thus what happened centuries ago is continuous with what is happening today and will happen all down through men's tomorrows. But the future is not simply being thrown together in a heap. History is moving with purpose and direction.

CENTRAL ROLE OF THE BIBLE IN HISTORICAL RELIGION

As for the central role of the Bible in Christian belief and practice, there is no adequate substitute for actually reading and pondering its written pages. The "cover-to-cover" Bible-reading practices of our grandfathers appear useless and irrelevant to the down-to-earth needs of our fast-moving age. Yet from every quarter there are indications that, out of the midst of the human predicament as experienced in our time, people are going back to the Bible with new seriousness and expectation. As one writer reminds us, this cannot really be a "going back" to the Bible because in a genuine sense we have not ever been able to get away from the Bible. It is inextricably bound up with our western heritage in language, literature, democratic institutions, sense of private morality, and public justice. Yet ours is in large measure a generation characterized by biblical illiteracy. The reasons for this situation probably lie in the all-pervading influence of that perspective discussed especially in Chapter V, the classical-humanist world view within modern America, serving as substitute for biblical faith. Self-sufficient man, living progressively and reasonably by the resources of his natural and social environment, has no need of a transcendent God who is the Lord of all history. He does not need renewal or faith so much as the overcoming of his ignorance by the effective methods of the natural and social sciences. Or so he believes.

But, at least on the European scene, confidence in progress and optimistic estimates of man's rational abilities have given way to pessimism, disillusionment, and despair. Men like the theologian

The Bible and History

Karl Barth, amid the rubble and shattered hopes which were war's aftermath, began to question the futility of preaching a gospel of human progress under the pretext that this is the basic message of the Bible. He thus began to probe the Scriptures for their bearing on the lostness and aloneness of modern men involved in the perennial predicament of human existence. Week by week he sought to unfold the drama and strength of the Bible to his congregation. He later wrote of this experience: "As a minister, I wanted to speak to the people in the infinite contradiction of their life, but to speak the no less infinite message of the *Bible* which was as much a riddle as life." [2]

This happened about 30 to 35 years ago. The waves of influence which originated in Barth's biblical preaching to his own parishioners have spread all across the world, in Europe, England, and America. It seemed as though a new Protestant Reformation was in the making. And, in a profound sense, it is just that—as men and women listen eagerly for the speaking of God's Word in and through the words of the Scriptures.

I am the Lord your God, who brought
you out of the land of Egypt, out of the
house of bondage.—Exodus 20:2

God is our refuge and strength,
a very present help in trouble.
Therefore we will not fear though
the earth should change,
though the mountains shake in
the heart of the sea;
though its waters roar and foam,
though the mountains tremble
with its tumult.—Psalm 46:1-3 [3]

[2] Quoted in Bernhard W. Anderson, *Rediscovering the Bible*, New York, Association Press, 1951, p. 4.

[3] Reprinted from *The Holy Bible, Revised Standard Version*, by permission of the National Council of the Churches of Christ in the U.S.A. Copyright 1946 and 1952 by the Division of Christian Education of the National Council of Churches in the U.S.A. Hereafter references from the Revised Standard Version (R.S.V.) will be so designated.

111

Some would say that this reaching out to the Bible for resource and renewal in our day is just "failure of nerve." This is an interpretation of our predicament and seeking which cannot be dismissed with an indifferent shrug of the shoulder. But any statement which would disparage the world view expressed through the Bible is itself based upon the assumptions of a rival world view. This is thus fundamentally the philosophical predicament of man returning now in a new guise. We do not have a choice of faith or no faith, world view of a specific sort or none at all. It is rather a choice between biblical faith and some other. Biblical faith makes the affirmation that all time and all history find their significance in dynamic relation to the transcendent God who is their source, ground, and goal. Other rival viewpoints must hold that some other reality is ultimate whether that ultimate be matter, nature, or man himself. Somewhere in the process of day-to-day living, commitment to some object taken as ultimate must take place within us all.

The Bible in our day, if read searchingly and seriously, thus sooner or later confronts men and women with this God who moves creatively through the events recorded in its pages. As Joshua put it to the Israelites centuries ago: "Choose ye this day whom ye will serve." Or as Martin Luther was later to say: "Trust and faith of the heart alone make both God and idol. . . . Whatever then thy heart clings to and relies upon, that is properly thy God." Therefore, those who would read the Bible cannot do so casually or out of indifferent curiosity; it involves risk. For to read is to enter a world of events, perhaps unwittingly to be caught up in them and become participant in them. As modern readers make the experiences of ancient men their own, encounter between God and themselves takes place. This means to be swept up in an ultimate concern. And the final issue of the process is commitment to the God who lives and speaks in events of history and experiences of persons today as well as long ago.

It may be that this is the only meaningful way the Bible can be read: as men and women approach its pages, not as objective observers or literary critics, but as eager searchers and active participants. As a companion of Barth's said, the Bible was read under that preacher's guidance "with the eyes of shipwrecked people whose everything had gone overboard." For on its pages modern men, as have men of every age, may see the mirrored image of themselves. But they may also be confronted by the God who moves in and through the days and years of man's time toward resolution and reconciliation.

HISTORY IN THE BIBLE

We look briefly then at the sweep of history which tells the story of the Hebraic-Christian tradition. These unique peoples lived out their days in the midst of the mighty powers of the Fertile Crescent, that arch of land stretching from the Tigris and Euphrates valleys to the Nile. Over three thousand years ago tribes of Hebrews came to Canaan, later to be called Palestine, and after a struggle possessed the land. Egypt took them captive. But under the leadership of Moses came freedom from slavery, the Exodus, and wilderness wanderings (1290-1250 B.C.). It is here that their real history begins; for down through the centuries, this creative act of deliverance became the focal point for prophets and psalmists as they persistently reminded Israel of her destiny and mission among the nations. Then came slow and difficult "conquest" of the land of Canaan (1225-1004 B.C.) About 1020 B.C., a new unifying force emerged in the person of Saul, who, together with his son Jonathan, waged successful war against the Philistines. After dramatic events, among the most stirring in the Bible, David became king and centered his rule in Jerusalem, forever after to be a city of political and religious significance.

Sometime after the death of Solomon (scholars believe, about 850 B.C.), an unknown writer or writers set down the records of David's life and a cluster of stories around his career (e.g., I Samuel 8 ff). Other records were added to these, and then the stories concerning Elijah were written, now included in I Kings. Although the accounts about David were recorded first, obviously they do not deal with the earliest times. For in the meantime men asked what had happened before this, and always it was more than a recital of historical "facts" and ordered sequences of events which concerned them. They wanted to know about Israel's living relation to their God, Jahweh, whose past promises of deliverance comprised their assurance in their present and hope for their future.

Thus, about Elijah's time, another writer began to gather the ancient traditions which had come down through the generations by word of mouth: songs, ballads, stories of the great figures of history and legend. These an unknown writer wove into a continuous narrative: the Garden of Eden, Abraham, Isaac, Jacob, Joseph, Moses, Joshua. This earliest document composed in the Southern Kingdom has been designated by the symbol "J." For biblical scholars are able to discern the strands of another document written in the Northern Kingdom about a century later, 750 B.C., and called "E." After the Northern Kingdom had fallen in 722 B.C., a Judean editor combined these two documents so as to preserve the basic materials of each of them. Still another strand was composed about the middle of the seventh century, this time a code of law used for purposes of reform by King Josiah in Judah in 621 B.C. This is designated "D," and forms the nucleus of the Book of Deuteronomy.

This literary activity took place against a background of pressing and critical historical events. For in the meantime, division between the Northern and Southern Kingdoms had shattered the unity these people had enjoyed for a brief period. And furthermore, each succeeding century brought more serious crises in international relations. In the eighth century, when the prophets Amos, Hosea, Micah, and Isaiah did their work, Assyria (722 B.C.) threatened and took the Northern Kingdom, Israel, into captivity. The Southern Kingdom, Judah, lasted until 586 B.C., when it was pulled into exile under the Babylonians. After the Judeans' return to Jerusalem, they rebuilt their walls and their temple to preserve purity of practice within a religious community set in the midst of a turbulent outside world governed by power politics. Here, about 500 B.C., the priestly code known as "P" was composed. Then, about 400 B.C., the document "P" was blended with both "JE" and "D" to bring the Pentateuch, or the first five books of the Bible, to completion. All this was an expression of an intense sense of corporate unity among Jews both at home and abroad. They believed they were God's chosen people, bound to God and to one another in a distinctively intimate way, supporting each other as neighbors and brothers in mutual loyalty, sympathy, and service. The following phrases may thus be used to summarize the perspective of this particular people: God-given law, God-controlled history, pure worship, mutual relations among their own brothers.

But much as the heirs of God's promises might have wished to live as a particular people, forces of universal significance would not permit them to pursue the even tenor of their ways. For two centuries (538-333 B.C.) Persia's power surrounded them and her cultural patterns profoundly influenced Jewish belief and practice. Then in 333 B.C., Greek pressures moved all across the Mediterranean world and Hellenistic influence made itself felt among the Jewish people. From 165 to 63 B.C., a succession of local high priest-kings tried to reëstablish the fabled days of "Jewish" supremacy which had been enjoyed under David and Solomon nearly a thousand years before. Turbulent years of rebellion and counter-rebellion finally gave way to the conquest of Pompey, who entered Jerusalem as a Roman general in 63 B.C. and destroyed what semblance of independence the Jewish people had enjoyed.

But the point is this: How did all these series of events look to the Hebrews? How did they interpret their history? The events of their history they believed somehow to be unique. For, as has been indicated, it is central to Hebraic-Christian faith that God does not simply act in all human history. Rather He acts in and through these singular events which unfold throughout the biblical drama *in such a way as to illuminate all history*. Thus the unity of theme which knits the Old Testament (and, as we shall see, the New Testament also) into a continuity is God's special revelation through a people specifically chosen and called, and the working out of His purpose of redemption in a series of unique events.

Conceived in this way, the Bible is often called the "History of Redemption," "Sacred History," or, in the German, *Heilsgeschichte*. It is a mistake, however, to think that biblical history is entirely different from the course of events in which all the nations and peoples were involved. Rather, biblical history is the same history lived and interpreted from a unique perspective through the eyes of faith. Will Herberg writes vividly of what it means to understand our human existence in terms of history and to think of our faith as *Heilsgeschichte:*

Examining the structure of our existence, we see that each of us has—or rather *is*—many partial histories, reflecting the many concerns and interests of life. We are Americans, members of a particular family and ethnic group, intimately associated with particular social institutions and movements. Each of these concerns, allegiances and associations has its own special history through which it is expressed and made explicit. But most of these histories, we ourselves realize, are merely partial histories; they define only fragments of our being and do not tell us who we "really" are. Underlying and including the partial histories of life, there must be some "total" history, in some way fundamental and comprehensive, some really ultimate history. Such a history, the history which one affirms in a total and ultimate manner, is one's *redemptive history (Heilsgeschichte)*, for it is the history in terms of which the final meaning of life is established and the self redeemed from meaninglessness and nonbeing. This is the history that defines, and is defined, by one's faith; it is, indeed, the history that *is* one's faith. "To be a self," H. Richard Niebuhr has said, "is to have a god; to have a god is to have a history." If we reverse this—"To have a history is to have a god; to have a god is to be a self"—we get a glimpse of the full significance of the relation of faith and history.[4]

[4] Herberg, *op. cit.*, p. 28.

The Bible and History

The unique perspective of faith by which the Hebrew people saw their history is defined most sharply as the "covenant relation." Israel, and the Christian community which grew out of Israel, are both conceived as people of the Covenant. This is indicated when we speak of the Bible as the book of the two covenants, the Old Covenant and the New Covenant.

A covenant between parties is an agreement entered into voluntarily by an act of moral decision. Such a relationship, once decided, is exclusive and demands absolute loyalty. As between human parties, this relationship finds its origin in early patriarchal and nomadic societies in which individuals or groups entered into legal arrangements to preserve peaceful relations.

George E. Mendenhall, in a study of the covenant conception as employed in international treaties of biblical times, distinguishes two kinds of covenants, *parity* and *suzerainty* covenants. In a parity covenant, equal parties come to reciprocal agreement, for here obligations are binding on both. A suzerainty covenant is more strictly unilateral, as a king, for example, binds his vassal. Here the ruler in authority gives or grants the covenant guaranteeing security and protection, in return for which the inferior party is obligated to obey the rules and commands stated by the one in authority.[5]

Helpful comment on this view of the covenant relation is made by Bernhard W. Anderson: "The most striking aspect of the suzerainty covenant is the great attention given to the king's deeds of benevolence on behalf of the vassal. The vassal is obligated to obey his sovereign, but motivation for obligation is that of *gratitude* for the deeds of benevolence done on his behalf. Obedience is the expression of a personal relationship."[6]

This suzerainty covenant is the political form which Israel appro-

---

[5] See George E. Mendenhall, *Law and Covenant in Israel and the Ancient Near East*, Pittsburgh, Biblical Colloquium, 1955. Reprinted from the *Biblical Archaeologist*, May, 1954, pp. 26-46, and September, 1954, pp. 49-76.

[6] Bernhard W. Anderson, "The Biblical Ethic of Obedience," *The Christian Scholar*, March, 1956, p. 68.

priated to express her relationship with God. For, as Professor Anderson states it, "Clearly, Israel's covenant was not a parity covenant, a bargain or commercial contract between equals. Rather it was a covenant *given* by God, a relationship conferred upon the people by the Sovereign. Hence it was a covenant that required obedience."

The terms of the covenant relationship are clearly and dramatically set forth in the Book of Exodus (20 ff.), beginning with the statement of the Ten Commandments. Here it is God who addresses man directly in I-thou, person-to-person terms: "I am the Lord, thy God, who brought thee up out of the land of Egypt, *thou* shalt have no other gods before me." These words of command are addressed not to individuals but to the entire community. The God who speaks is the same God who through many years has guided their historical destiny and now has performed His "mighty acts" of deliverance. He is the God upon whose sovereign power all the meaning of their life depends. Thus to Him they would now express their gratitude in willing obedience. Two principles are involved in their obedient obligation to God's Will: *absolute and exclusive allegiance to God Himself, and concern for their fellowmen within the covenanted community.* For this is the theme which runs all through the Bible: God's persistent love and creative action in history to bring into being the community of the Old Covenant (Israel) and then the community of the New Covenant (the Christian Church). But men's resolves to utter obedience in matters of worship and social justice often become rebellion, rejection, and hence the disobedience of pride and sin. Their filial relation to God is broken when the people turn to strange cultic practices in the ceremonial worship of false gods or forget the demand for social justice.

The Bible records a recurrent pattern through the centuries of Hebraic history: a pattern of loss and recovery. For the community may begin in utter obedience to God, and at first prosperity results, as all goes well within the context of this relationship. But then complacency sets in and out of arrogant pride are born cultic impurity and moral laxity. As sensitive men interpreted what happened as a result of their rebellion against God, they thus saw misfortune come to Israel, destruction, famine, invasion, captivity. Especially this became the burden of the Prophets' message; for only one other alternative was possible for them now, short of catastrophe, that is, repentance and obedience to God once more.

It is thus the distinctive function of the prophet of God to use this pattern of experience to remind the people of the terms of the covenant in order to restore meaning and direction to their disrupted life. More and more insistently, Amos, Hosea, Micah, Isaiah of the eighth century, for example, spoke God's Word of judgment and hope, telling the people that ritual alone is not a sufficient fulfillment of covenant obedience, especially when ritual keeps borrowing pagan practices from neighbors. Still more serious was the religious pretension of men who thought they had fulfilled their covenant obligations simply by the mechanical observance of ceremonies while they had left undone freely chosen acts of social justice.

But the voice of the prophets did not speak simply a word of judgment. For throughout the writings of these interpreters of God's actions in history, there occur many passages which point to a new age which was to come. This is a message of forgiveness, mercy, promise, and hope. It was not God's purpose utterly to destroy those who deliberately broke the covenant relation, but only to chasten human pride so that men might respond in loving and faithful obedience to God.

This word of hope found expression in Isaiah, for instance, as he spoke of a remnant of Israel whom God would preserve as a gracious token of a new beginning (Isaiah 10:20-23). Thus emerged more and more clearly a distinction between the outward Israel and the true Israel which would remain faithful to the covenant. Here also occur intimations of a coming Messiah, an "anointed One," who would bring God's reign to consummation in an Israel completely restored and made over (Isaiah 9:2-7, 11:1-9). But most significant is the affirmation, like that of Jeremiah speaking out of the depths of outward tragedy that had come to the nation, that beyond God's judgment against man's sin lies the living reality of a "New Covenant." There would come a day, he said, when a merely formal, legal relationship between man and God would give way to an inward and direct knowledge of God Himself.

". . . But this is the covenant which I will make with the house of Israel after those days, says the Lord: I will put my law within them, and I will write it upon their hearts, and I will be their God, and they shall be my people. And no longer shall each man teach his neighbor and each his brother, saying, 'Know the Lord,' for they shall all know me, from the least of them to the greatest, says the Lord; for I will forgive their iniquity and I will remember their sin no more." [7]

It is a mistake to regard this utterance of Jeremiah as an affirmation of sheer individualism as against a so-called collectivism of an earlier age. Rather the New Covenant is a reaffirmation of the solidarity of a whole people and the inwardness of God's relationship with Israel which had linked them together from the very beginning. But, still more specifically, the age of the New Covenant would bring God's loving forgiveness, in which all divisions and alienations would give way to reconciliation and renewal. It should not be forgotten that this new age could never be ushered in through the moral or political efforts of men. Only God, acting in wrath and love, judgment and renewal, can bring to fulfillment the redemption of all men and all history according to His good will and purpose.

This forward look into the future, according to Christian conviction, was never to find complete fulfillment until God's love was embodied in the judgment and forgiveness of the Cross of Jesus Christ. For here the prophetic expectation of a Messiah and the perfect uniting of God and men in a New Covenant found consummate expression. Students of religion often ask: What then

[7] Jeremiah 31:33-34, R.S.V.

is the difference between the Hebraic tradition and Christianity? Christianity is built on to the continuous tradition of Hebrew life, practice, and hope. It came about with the formation of a new religious community, whose faith is centered in Jesus Christ, after His life, death, and resurrection had been completed.

This new community consisted at first of men and women who also were members of the Jewish community. They were convinced that as members of the new fellowship they were now heirs to the promises God had made to the Hebrews many centuries before. Thus, in place of the Old Covenant, they now lived under a New Covenant—a new agreement established in power and love through the life, death, resurrection, and continuing presence of this unique person, Jesus Christ. Christians therefore continued the Hebrew covenant tradition and yet added to it significant elements in the ways in which they understood the terms of the Covenant. For them, *God had now acted decisively in human history through a unique event or series of events in which through their own commitment of faith they themselves shared.* Here also, as in the whole movement of Hebrew life, history is concretely significant because God has acted in a divine-human event in such a way as to require response on the part of men and out of person-to-person encounter to demand responsible decision. This is the event which now illuminates all other events and in which the very significance of human existence in relation to God stands disclosed. Here, so the Christian believes, an encounter takes place between God and man to which man must either respond by rejecting God's claims upon him or by complete and utter devotion as a matter of personal and ultimate concern.

Chapter IX

Revelation and Response

It is the purpose of this chapter (1) to reëxamine the meaning of a word that is the source of a great deal of misunderstanding in its connection with reading and understanding the Bible. That word is revelation. (2) In the light of the significance of biblical revelation, we shall discuss the kind of response required of men of faith. (3) We need to consider the relation of faith to reason for thoughtful persons in our own day.

THE MEANING OF REVELATION IN HISTORICAL RELIGION

We turn from this brief account of the sweep of history, which the Bible records as the arena of God's mighty acts, to the question: What do we mean when we say the Bible is inspired? This involves summarizing now the significance of a term already used in our discussions of mythic language and also of the Bible. But now we are in a position to see its meaning more clearly. It is the term *revelation*. We have stated that revelation is not identical with the literal words of language themselves, as though God communicated directly to men through specific propositions or items of information necessary for man's salvation. Such a view, of course, is normative for Roman Catholicism and Protestant fundamentalism, involving belief in verbal infallibility or inerrancy of revealed Scriptures. But this perspective has brought, through the centuries, terrific strain between the claims of the sciences and those of faith. From the controversies precipitated by the Copernican revolution in astronomy to the Darwinian revolution in biological theory, battles have been joined over the issue as to which is "right," "religion," or "science."

If we now recall what has been said in preceding chapters concerning the methods and role of the sciences, and the functions of mythic as against descriptive language, we may appreciate the course of these intellectual struggles. For, on the basis of appeal to fact, the sciences were bound to win. Taking this victory of the sciences for granted, scholars within the theological movement called modernism began the laborious task of examining the various books of the Bible as to authenticity of text and authorship. But these textual analysts scarcely bothered to ask about what the Bible has to say as to its content. What we have been attempting to reflect is an entirely different trend which has been taking place in recent years. The term revelation itself thus assumes new and fresh meanings out of the concrete, historical context of the Scriptures themselves. For, as we have indicated, the "word of God" is not identical with the words of the Bible. Rather God's "word" is a term borrowed by analogy from the sphere of person-to-person human relationships. Just as you and I use words to convey to others who we are and what we are, so does God disclose Himself. And the Bible is the medium of that process of self-disclosure. Barth speaks of this process of divine self-disclosure as threefold: (1) God encounters and speaks to man; (2) man tells where he has been and what he has heard by proclaiming God's word to others; (3) somebody writes down the record of these events.

As we today read the record of these events, we can but create the conditions under which the same kind of encounter may take place in our own experience. The Bible is thus inspired, but in the sense in which Alan Richardson, for example, uses the term when he writes:

Essentials in Christian Faith

When we speak of inspiration of the Scriptures we ought primarily to mean the inspiration of the men who wrote them, if it is men who are inspired and not books or words, except in a figurative sense. In this way a new theory of inspiration was reached. . . . One might speak about the inspiration of the Bible only because the Bible was the record of the religious experience of inspired men. Its power to evoke a similar experience in us was the pragmatic test of its inspiration, and when judged by this test it was found to be authoritative and normative; it stood in a class by itself amongst the religious literature of the world. . . . The degree of inspiration of the Bible . . . was to be measured by the level of truth which it contained and by its power to awaken in us a genuine experience of God.[1]

With this dynamic conception of inspiration, it becomes possible to deal with such questions about the Bible as these: Is it "true"? What of the accounts of creation and of the "last things"? How may we understand the miracles? To answer questions such as these, we must keep in mind once more the historical character of the biblical drama. Time, flowing purposively in a straight line, is the sphere of action in and through the singular events in which God discloses Himself to the covenanted people as these folk understand themselves to be a nation, then a holy Jewish community, and finally a community of faith. But this drama of God's mighty acts of redemption has both a prologue and an epilogue, as Bernhard W. Anderson suggests in his *Rediscovering the Bible:* "The prologue begins with an account of the creation of the world and the 'fall' of man; the epilogue gives an imaginative description of the Last Judgment and the New Creation. Thus the whole drama is set within a vast and baffling time-span. The biblical pageant moves from the beginning of history to the end of history, from creation to consummation, from the book of Genesis to the Revelation of St. John."

The Hebraic-Christian view of history and the creative use of mythic language to express the significance of man's response to

[1] Alan Richardson, *A Preface to Bible Study*, Philadelphia, Westminster Press, 1944, pp. 3-5.

Revelation and Response

his encounter with God now come into clearer focus. Such singular events, in which God acts and man responds in commitment, are unique and yet indicative of God and the world of nature and history that stretches beyond man's understanding. The only adequate way of expressing their significance, we have said, is the richly imagic language of myth. But the uses of symbols in biblical religion differ in important ways from those of the mystical tradition. To be sure, for both of these kinds of religion, symbols indicate something of the metaphysical nature of reality. Yet the mystical view denies the reality of this world of space and time; for men seek to extricate themselves from the actual world of history and achieve union with a transtemporal Reality. However, for men of biblical faith, symbols are actual historical events which stand for and point to other historical events, both past and future. For it is in time that God acts and men respond.

It is precisely the case also with myths, especially those primitive myths which tell of the beginning and end of history. As Professor Cherbonnier states it, such myth is "an extrapolation into past or future based upon what God has already done within recorded history. It describes how the world *must* have begun, and what the outcome of history will have to be, consistently with God's experienced character and purpose." [2] It is thus on the basis of a unique interpretation of history that the myths of beginning and end are significant. The writers of such myths were not misled scientists trying to give an accurate (though mistaken) description of the evolution of nature or its dissolution at the end of time. Rather, in imaginative language they were giving voice not to scientific accounts but to religious utterance concerning the ultimate relation of nature, history, and man to the everlasting God. Their convictions were these: God is Creator, for all things have their source and ground in Him. God is Final Judge, for all history moves for consummation toward a goal which is assigned by God. Not merely

[2] E. La B. Cherbonnier, "Mystical vs. Biblical Symbolism," *Christian Scholar,* March, 1956, p. 42.

ınan's time but also the whole of creation is embraced within God's purpose of redemption which He is even now bringing to pass.

If the student will turn to these accounts in the Bible with sharpened imagination and an expectant attitude, he will read more than literal words. Rather, he will himself become participant in events which are organic parts of the unfolding drama of God's redemption. As God thus speaks in I-thou terms, revelation takes place.

The same principle of historical interpretation holds true with respect to our understanding of the recorded miracles of the Bible. Some would dismiss them as the mistaken utterances of a pre-scientific age. For, from the viewpoint of modern science, miracles, as supernatural intervention into the natural order, simply do not happen. We would then be well advised, we are told, to ignore the "miraculous" accounts written by men who could not have known any better and concentrate on the "spiritual truths" they contain.

But this perspective completely ignores the historical context within which these events were recorded. We cannot possibly know what actually happened. We are not dealing in the Scriptures with a photographic record of all the details of past events, for recorded history is interpreted history. All events therefore must be seen in the light of central affirmations of faith which are the themes of the Bible. At the heart of these is the conviction of God's call to Israel and later to the Christian community. Miracle stories cannot be detached from this basic belief and its living context of response.

Anderson helps our understanding at this point when he writes concerning the miracle accounts of the Old Testament in their relation to God's call to Israel:

The deliverance of the infant Moses from the pharaoh's massacre, the plagues in Egypt, the crossing of the Marsh Sea, the pillar of cloud and fire, the sending of the manna and quails, the striking of the rock to obtain water, the defeat of Amalek—each one of these incidents, viewed from the standpoint of faith, was an assurance or sign of the saving activity of God in the history of his people, Israel. We could go so far as to say that even though any one of these stories could be shown on historical grounds to be an inaccurate or legendary account of the actual situation, the truth of the miracle tradition as a whole would not be affected in the slightest. For it is precisely the central element of the tradition, namely the call of Israel, which lies beyond the scope of historical or scientific inquiry. Israel's faith did not rest merely upon the Exodus and accompanying incidents, which are open to historical or archaeological study; rather, Israel's faith rested upon an experience that the Exodus was God's *redemptive act*. A people had been created by God's sovereign activity in history! This was the miracle that "happened." [3]

Even if with Professor Anderson we insist on pressing the question as to whether a particular episode illustrative of this central truth actually took place, the main contention still holds. To be sure, the many detailed stories must be discussed in terms of historical criticism. Some are evidences of the "folk mind," such as the infant Moses floating down the Nile or the rod that worked wonders. Or other stories greatly exaggerate certain occurrences in nature, such as those about the plagues which visited the Egyptians or the crossing of the Red Sea. It is difficult to move back through the welter of details involved in long years of oral tradition before these accounts were ever written down. Nobody knows how to discern the "facts" apart from the interpretive context in which they come to life. For, as again Anderson expresses it:

These stories were remembered not because men were interested in nature as such, but because nature also manifested the glory of the God of history. We find it difficult to understand the Bible on this matter because today nature is something we look at "out there," something we control by means of our science, something which is indifferent to the history in which men are involved. According to the Bible, however, nature is involved in history because God is Lord of both nature and history. Nature is, as it were, a mirror which reflects the meaning of man's life in history. [4]

[3] Bernhard W. Anderson, *Rediscovering the Bible*, New York, Association Press, 1951, pp. 59-60.
[4] *Ibid.*, pp. 61-62.

127

In bringing our understanding of the concept of revelation to summation, we find among the most helpful suggestions those expressed by H. Richard Niebuhr in his book *The Meaning of Revelation.* Niebuhr clearly distinguishes, as we have tried to do in other words, "history as lived" in contrast to "history as seen," between participant and objective observer. Niebuhr illustrates this difference by comparing the abstract, external, objective, factual account as described in the *Cambridge Modern History* with the way that same event was viewed by a participant in a living tradition. The first begins: "On July 4, 1776, Congress passed the resolution which made the colonies independent communities, issuing at the same time the well-known Declaration of Independence. If we regard the Declaration as the assertion of an abstract political theory, criticism and condemnation are easy. It sets out with a general proposition so vague as to be practically useless. The doctrine of the equality of men, unless it be qualified and conditioned by reference to special circumstance, is either a barren truism or a delusion." But Lincoln's Gettysburg Address speaks in moving cadences of the same event: "Fourscore and seven years ago our fathers brought forth upon this continent a new nation, conceived in liberty and dedicated to the proposition that all men are created free and equal." [5]

Taking this distinction between "history as lived" and "history as seen," Niebuhr then states a clear definition of revelation:

Revelation means for us that part of our inner history which illuminates the rest of it and which is itself intelligible. Sometimes when we read a difficult book, seeking to follow a complicated argument, we come across a luminous sentence from which we can go forward and backward and so attain some understanding of the whole. Revelation is like that. In his *Religion in the Making*, Professor Whitehead has written such illuminating sentences and one of them is this: "Rational religion appeals to the direct intuition of special occasions and to the elucidatory

[5] See H. Richard Niebuhr, *The Meaning of Revelation,* New York, The Macmillan Company, 1941, p. 60.

power of its concepts for all occasions." The special occasion to which we appeal in the Christian Church is called Jesus Christ, in whom we see the righteousness of God, his power and wisdom. But from that special occasion we also derive the concepts which make possible the elucidation of all the events in our history. Revelation means this intelligible event which makes all other events intelligible.[6]

RESPONSE OF MEN OF FAITH

But revelation, as God's self-disclosure in and through certain intelligible and luminous events of history, requires *response* on the part of men. In biblical religious life this response is faith. It is a truism to say that everyone in his everyday affairs has "faith" or else none of us would venture beyond present achievement into creative adventure in science, industry, government, education, or personal concerns. In this sense, faith is thrust out from what is known to what is not known.

But we would hasten to say what faith is not. At the outset, *faith is not hostile to reason or intellect or intelligence.* The small boy said: "Faith is believing a lot of things that just ain't true." But this view of faith is a caricature. Nor is faith a kind of "spiritual pill" or special kind of "moral exercise" which will bolster our flagging energies when the demands of practical life become unbearable. There are composers of songs, writers of books, and speakers on the air in our day who tell us simply to believe. But they do not state very clearly in what men and women are to believe. In a previous chapter we said that Christianity does not demand commitment to itself, devotion to religion or faith in faith. It is not an instrument to be employed consciously or deliberately to attain release from tension and anxiety. It does not guarantee "peace of mind," or success in living, or knowledge of all mysteries, or even a workable system of values. The stress therefore cannot be on faith itself but on the object of faith: on nothing less than God, who

[6] *Ibid.*, p. 93.

discloses Himself and to whom response must be given, according to Christian conviction.

But to continue, neither is faith just intellectual assent to abstract truths stated in theological propositions. Some traditions have so understood religious faith: saying yes to specific doctrinal creeds or system of dogmas, such as "God exists," "God is all-powerful." "Jesus Christ combined in His person both human and divine qualities." The intellectual phase of the total religious response is a significant element. But it is derivative rather than primary. For assent with the mind is an abstraction if it does not involve the active and total commitment of the whole self. Therefore, just as revelation is not identical with the literal words or propositions communicating items of information from God, so the response of faith is not mere belief in abstract truths stated in propositions.

When does faith become religious? It does so when it engages the total person in ultimate concern. Faith is practical and moral in terms of personal faithfulness, loyalty, and trust. Faith means action. And although faith is not identical with intellectual assent, intellectual judgment or belief, on the basis of evidence, is an essential ingredient. But also, out of this kind of practical commitment and intellectual judgment, there may emerge insight and immediate awareness of God in terms of the I-thou relationship. We vary in background and experience. Thus some of us may begin with personal awareness and insight, which finally result in intellectual judgment of belief and practical commitment and action. The order depends on individual differences of temperament and opportunity. But whether we personally begin with action, commitment, belief, or awareness, all these elements in varying degrees are essential to the full life of faith. And, to be meaningful, faith always involves the total personality's response to the total life situation as centered in God, the object of ultimate concern. As one writer expresses it: "Faith is not blind assent to divine truths imparted to passive minds, but an affirmation arising out of experience and a commitment to the way of life required by those insights."

Revelation and Response

THE RELATION OF FAITH TO REASON

But a problem still remains. When thoughtful people discuss their religious convictions, they are confronted with the problem of deciding in more specific terms *what the relation of reason to faith is.* This, of course, has been the case ever since the Hebrew and Greek ways of approaching God flowed together into our western heritage. The classical Greeks had no such problem, for they did not accept the authority either of revelation through singular events or of sacred writings. But as soon as men avow a faith in a God who reveals Himself and at the same time these men wish to follow the lead of their reasoning minds, then the issue comes to focus. Some said, and still say, that Christianity is "sheer faith" in authoritatively revealed truth and therefore needs no intellectual support. But others see the importance of the work of their minds; for reason is itself a gift of God, and thus His revealed truth, grasped in faith, cannot be unreasonable. It is true that some Christian scholars of the second and third centuries did embrace pure irrationality. For example, Tertullian cried: "I believe because it is impossible." (*"Credo, quia impossible."*) But this extreme attitude did not prevail, and in the long run faith tended to seek the support of reason.

Bringing this issue into sharper focus, we can easily see, as John Hutchison expresses it, four possible combinations of these elements of the religious consciousness: (1) reason is primary and excludes faith, (2) reason is primary and includes faith, (3) faith is primary and excludes reason, (4) faith is primary and includes reason.[7]

The first way, which states that the claims of reason are primary in order of importance but faith is excluded, is usually in evidence,

[7] John Hutchison, *Faith, Reason and Existence,* New York, Oxford University Press, 1956, pp. 97 ff. I am indebted to Professor Hutchison for the suggestion of casting this age-old problem in this particular form and also for his clarification of the arguments for the existence of God, to be discussed in the next chapters. See his chapter, "The Significance of Rational Theology."

for example, in any campus discussion of religious beliefs. One student may state certain affirmations concerning God's existence based on faith, that is to say, from inside the Hebraic-Christian tradition. But other students, standing outside as observers, try to subject these statements to the running criticism of rational inquiry. The result is an impasse; for critics are often the skeptics who state that the question of God's being can be answered only by discursive reasoning of the logical mind, and that the answer the intellect gives is negative. In short, persons such as these (including the Greek Sophists, David Hume, and Bertrand Russell) say: "If you could rationally prove to us the existence of God, we would believe in Him, but there is no such proof; therefore, there are no good grounds for the conclusion that God exists." Thus rational proof is attempted and the attempt fails.

The second point of view states that, as reason is primary and includes faith, ultimately affirmations of faith and the conclusions of reason can never conflict. This position, so far as establishing the existence of God is concerned, is closest to that of Thomas Aquinas (1225?-1274) within the context of Roman Catholic thought. For him, some of the convictions we accept on faith can be supported also by reason. The existence of God is one of these. For Thomas, so long as ordinary men live in this world, they can have no intuitive knowledge of God. Thus God's existence must be established by inference from the evidence of His effects in the actual world of natural events.

This general point of view has always been a positive encouragement to scientists, especially to those who are also men of faith. They need have no hesitance in pursuing their independent investigations, for nothing they can confirm experimentally can possibly run counter to "true religion."

The third view affirms that faith is all important and excludes reason. This is the view of Tertullian, whom we mentioned earlier. Such a person would say that of course reason's attempt to prove the existence of God ends in skepticism. But why give intellect

Revelation and Response

final jurisdiction over such matters? Do not trust reason at all. Only through faith can men find God and hence the answers to their most pressing existential questions. In more recent years this perspective has found expression in Karl Barth's repudiation of natural theology. But to follow the lonely path of faith without the guidance of reason is difficult if not impossible. One main thesis of this book is that Christian faith can and must make relevant contact with all human experience. For even the attempt to say what he believes involves a man in the use of rational categories. To speak of his experiences at all is to interpret them, and to act is to attempt to verify them.

The fourth option places emphasis on the primacy of faith, but then asserts that reason is essential to the life of religion. Augustine, for example, attempted to evaluate fairly both faith and reason: "I believe that I may understand, and I understand that I may believe." This perspective is represented by a long line of Christian philosophers and theologians: Anselm, Bonaventura, Pascal, William Temple, John Baillie, and, perhaps with qualifications, of two of the leading thinkers of our own day, Reinhold Niebuhr and Paul Tillich. It is the view of faith we have been describing in this chapter. For faith is not just assent to truths expressed in propositions and grasped by the intellect. But faith is the response of the total person in commitment to God.

But does reason, in relation to faith, then have any useful function to perform? Indeed, the whole philosophical task in its relation to the life of the Christian is involved. As the Christian seriously undertakes rational inquiry, what he tries to do is honestly to become aware of the way human experience *looks* to such a committed person as himself. Such self-conscious awareness entails serious criticism of his own beliefs, for no religious beliefs are immune from honest criticism. But beyond this, the man of faith is faced with the responsibility of attempting to communicate to other persons what he holds as faith. This also involves clear and logically cogent utterance. And just as times change and cultures differ, so do the terms in which religions express themselves vary. Therefore the Christian must stay alive in and to the age within which he happens to be born in order to make effective application of his belief in God to the pressing personal and social needs of his own day. All these concerns of reason thus become ways of "testing" the affirmations men make when they say they believe in God and are committed to Him as the Source and Ground and Goal of their very existence.

This task performed by reason on behalf of faith is called in traditional terminology *natural* or *rational theology* in contrast to *revealed theology* or *revealed religion*. William Temple has summarized its function in this way: "Natural theology should be the criticism of actual Religion and of actual religious beliefs, irrespective of their supposed origin and therefore independently of any supposed act or word of Divine Revelation, conducted with full understanding of what is criticized, yet with complete relentlessness of scientific inquiry." [8]

Thus we would advocate the view of reason's function in relation to faith which frankly regards faith as prior to reason and yet assigns to reason an important role. A man may begin in utter commitment or encounter with God through sensitive awareness. Or he may find his starting place in forthright action on behalf of fuller justice for his fellow men. Or he may begin with belief, he knows not why, in the rootage of the justice and love he seeks to serve in the very nature of things. Our temperaments differ and our opportunities vary. But faith, for each of us, must seek understanding.

As Alan Richardson expresses it concerning the responsibility which thoughtful men and women of religious concern have today:

It is doubtless true that every man must be in some sense a philosopher; he must have *some* kind of view of man's place and purpose in the scheme of things. The choice, as it has been well said, is not between

8 William Temple, *Nature, Man and God,* New York, The Macmillan Company, 1934, p. 27.

being a good philosopher and a bad one. The important fact to be noticed here is that Christianity does not come to men in the twentieth century, any more than it came to men in the first century, as a fully-fledged metaphysic which they are asked to adopt as the basis of their own philosophy of life. It comes with the offer of the *possibility* of constructing a philosophy; it brings to thoughtful men a faith-principle which (though it is much more than this) is a master-key, opening the doors of rationality and understanding. Had Christianity come into the world originally as a philosophy, it would long ago have passed into the museum of the thought-systems of the past, or it would have been transmuted into many varieties of philosophical forms, combining and dissolving again in the various shapes which loom out of the mists of men's thought down the ages, as Platonism has done. It came, however, not as a philosophy but as a faith, as the belief that certain actual and historical events provide the key or clue to the understanding of human nature and destiny, and this clue it offers to the metaphysician as the category of interpretation by which he may "make sense" of the universe. As a faith it is compelled to seek in every century a philosophical expression, in which its insights may unify and interpret all the knowledge and experience which that age has garnered—scientific, historical, aesthetic, moral, social, and so on. The relation of Christianity to philosophy can hardly be better expressed than in Whitehead's luminous sentence: "Christianity . . . has always been a religion seeking a metaphysic, in contrast to Buddhism, which is a metaphysic generating a religion." [9]

[9] Alan Richardson, *Christian Apologetics*, Harper & Brothers, 1947, pp. 38-39.

Chapter X

The Being of God

"I no longer believe in God," said a student. He addressed these words authoritatively to his counselor. Wisely, the more experienced man did not reply with a barrage of arguments or dogmatic statements. Instead he listened and gently asked an occasional question: "Why? How did you get this way? What started you off in this direction? How long have you been thinking along these lines?" When the student had completely emptied himself of his complaint against God, his counselor made a statement which came as something of a surprise. For he did not exclaim: "You are entirely wrong! You are a heretic." Rather, he said, quietly, "The only trouble with you is that you are at least twenty years behind the times. I gave up believing in *that* kind of God twenty years ago myself." [1]

CHANGING IDEAS ABOUT GOD

The one who cites this incident adds that it has been written, "When the false gods go, the gods arrive," and comments that this is not necessarily true. Rather, when the gods have gone, demons may come to take their place—unless we are exceedingly careful.

[1] Based on an incident related by Albert W. Palmer, *The Light of Faith*, New York, The Macmillan Company, 1945, pp. 7-8.

The Being of God

But, in any case, we must understand that our ideas about God are constantly changing and that they should often change. The patterns of daily living are deeply influenced by what we think He is. Some of us advance in the knowledge of almost everything except our religion. We carry about with us immature pictures, symbols, analogies by which we attempt to grasp what God is like. We must attempt to change these. False and inadequate conceptions of God must go. For modern man's creative thinking and acting are often thwarted because he insists on retaining the God (or the image of God) of his childhood, either to go on believing in that God—perhaps to his later hurt and disillusionment—or to reject all belief on the grounds that if God is the kind of God he thinks He is, He is hardly believable.

"I no longer believe in God," says the student. Let the reader assess his own experience. In what sorts of gods do we believe and how many have we outgrown? Perhaps one of these gods in whom the student no longer believes is the Absentee God who resides in some remote "heaven," never breaking into the natural order of the world because, having once set the universe in operation like a huge machine, He no longer needs to be concerned with natural or historical events. This is the God of deism, for example. Or there is the glorified Policeman God standing with his big club poised at a moment's notice to crack down on bad little men for some minor infraction of conventional mores. Then, too, some modern-minded persons find themselves violently rejecting what they call the Big-Momma-and-Poppa-in-the-Sky God, whom weak and anxious men project as the object of their wish for security, refuge, and escape from life's responsibilities. Others carry about with them the Errandboy God, eagerly poised and ready to jump in answer to the buzzer so as to fulfill men's every little selfish desire. Finally, there is the cruel and terrible Tribal God, armed to the teeth, even in these modern days, to do battle for our side, redress the right—as we see it—and avenge the wrong, acting, of course, against our enemies.

Essentials in Christian Faith

This is the problem of religious language, discussed in a previous chapter, recurring now in new and pressing form. For inevitably, in our understanding of the being and nature of God, we employ the way of paradox or analogy, in which we must speak both affirmatively and negatively of God at the same time. Deliberately we choose from elements within human experience those images or symbols through which to express most adequately the nature of God. The full character of God ever remains a mystery beyond human apprehension. And yet man, the symbol-making animal, never rests satisfied until he has attempted to say of the God, whom he can never fully understand, something of what He is. Thus, employing the language of faith to express the inexpressible, we seek to convey through rich imagery how God discloses Himself in events of history and personal experiences, and what meaningful insights are involved in man's response to the God who confronts him. Within the Hebraic-Christian tradition, the most adequate analogies are found in the personal and the historical: creator, judge, father, love, goodness, justice, everlasting presence.

Many a thoughtful person today can say with the skeptical student: "I no longer believe in God. Not the Absentee God, the Policeman God, Momma-and-Poppa-in-the-Sky God, Errandboy God, or the Tribal God." But such a person may hasten to add, in the suggestive language of mythic utterance: "I do believe in the God who is that transcendent source, ground, and goal of all time and history and who yet keeps disclosing Himself within human affairs. This God I do not discover from the outside as impersonal, objective observer but from the inside by becoming dynamically involved as participant in those selfsame events. From this center I find all other events illuminated. I do not 'prove' God by exact calculations of logic or experimental science. Rather, God finds me in and through an act of faith involving action and commitment, out of which may emerge a deepening of belief and intensification of awareness. I believe thus in the God who is that central meaning which gives significance to everything else, including my own personal existence. He is the Being in whom is gathered up all the perfect realization of values. He is the power which makes possible the embodiment of these values of truth, beauty, justice, and love in the actual life of human society. He is the energy that moves the world. He is the mind that directs it. He is the truth that gives it order. He is the goodness that enriches it." As we have stated, He is the object of personal and ultimate concern, a concern that is not only ultimate but also unconditional, total, and infinite.

"Until a man has found God and been found by God," H. G. Wells has written, "he begins at no beginning, he works to no end. He may have his friendships, his partial loyalties, his scraps of honor. But all these things fall into place only with God. God, Who fights through men against Blind Force and Might and Non-Existence; Who is the end, who is meaning; He is the only King."

And William E. Hocking of Harvard has stated: "Without God, meaning is simply a human specialty, the vast universe devoid of meaning. With God, the world has sense, perhaps a direction. And the wide frame of meaning returns upon our small lives to lend them significance."

This is a way of stating the central Christian affirmation of faith. We do not belong to ourselves. We do not create our own life. We do not "integrate" ourselves by ourselves. We do not find the great Reality simply by reading our own little thoughts, as if God were simply shut up within the tiny boxes of our own individual minds. Our true being, so the Christian affirms, comes to fulfillment as we are linked in utter commitment with the God who is Ultimate Power, Creative Intelligence, Perfect Will, Just and Loving Father, Source and Goal of all our striving, seeking men with even deeper concern than ever men seek Him. He is active, present, accessible in the midst of our common, everyday experience, able to help us because He is more than a glorification of ourselves.

But here a basic point may occur to students. We might grant that we must talk about God through the use of symbolic images, thus extending elements of ordinary experience to convey ultimate meanings. But how do we select these images? Can we find and develop any standards by which to gauge the adequacy of the symbols we employ? For we have seen that men and women do persistently understand God in terms of elemental and immature images either in their acceptance or their rejection. But what is to be said about these other more "adequate" images just suggested? Are these simply selected arbitrarily? Why should we choose these rather than the others?

For reply to these questions we have but to recall what has been stated in Chapter IV concerning metaphysical world hypotheses and Christian philosophy drawing its analogies from the broad sphere of human history and the life of individual persons. This is not to claim absolute proof. Rather, the question is: How well does the evidence converge around this hypothesis as against other alternative world views? The claim of the Christian philosopher is expressed in terms of a confession of his own conviction and a winsome invitation: to see life steadily and see it whole, come and look at it from this vantage point. Every fact which fits into such a hypothesis may be regarded as positive evidence. All those facts of human experience which are left dangling in unexplained fashion, incoherent, inconsistent with this perspective, may be regarded as negative evidence. But also the Christian world view employing these images must become a dynamic center for dealing with practical everyday responsibilities. Does it enable us to solve and handle our problems of human relations and to thrust forward creatively into new areas of concern? Is this perspective trivial or profound? Is it relevant or irrelevant? These are some of the tests to apply rigorously to various world views and the images that cluster around them as we attempt to distinguish the adequate from the inadequate among the symbols we use to understand and deal with our relations to God, the world, men, and ourselves.

Moreover, these are tests which apply to the "arguments" for the existence of God themselves. Many of the commonly held arguments, some of which we shall discuss in this chapter, are not so many "proofs" supported by logical and factual evidence. Rather, they are basically personal affirmations of faith in the living God of the biblical heritage. But these affirmations by personally committed men are then objectified into forms of rational thought, and thus the traditional arguments become ways of stating the analogies and root metaphors through which Christians interpret their faith. Just as *faith is prior to reason,* so those who would "argue" for God's being must begin with prelogical assumptions. In this chapter we shall examine four of the commonly held traditional "arguments" for the being of God. In the next chapter, we shall consider perhaps the severest obstacle to belief in God among concerned persons, the problem of evil; and also we shall make some attempt at reinterpreting the traditional arguments in terms of the demands of personal existence in our own day.

TRADITIONAL ARGUMENTS FOR THE BEING OF GOD

Despite the ordered language in which traditional arguments for the being of God are cast, we would understand them, then, not as logically or factually supported "proofs," but as affirmations of faith expressed in forms of rational thought. Each of them becomes a specific way of stating in the imagic language of analogy some aspect or aspects of God's boundless being. In turn each must be subjected to the kinds of "testing" we have indicated. These four arguments are (1) cosmological, (2) teleological, (3) ontological, (4) moral.

1. The first argument, the *cosmological,* is perhaps a line of reasoning of longest standing, dating back to the philosophies of Socrates, Plato, and Aristotle, finding classic expression in Thomas Aquinas, and reformulation in contemporary times. Its advocates are generally opposed to the position of men such as Augustine and those who employ the ontological argument to be discussed below. In fact, throughout the course of medieval thought and

down into modern times, two ways stand in contrast to each other. One is the Augustinian, which begins with inner experience and finds within human consciousness itself evidences for the being of God. The second is the Aristotelian tradition, carried on by Thomas. Here the stress is not so much on the inner life of the individual. Rather, God's being is inferred from outward facts in the order of nature, such as motion, change, and development. Thus the human soul is no disembodied, angelic intelligence. Man is a rational being who requires sensation and experience of actual, observable phenomena in nature as the material for his logical thought. As you look about you, Thomas says in effect, you observe that everything seems to be dependent for its existence upon other things, and these on still other things, and on and on, until you finally reach one thing above all others which is not dependent upon anything else but is the very condition of all the rest.

Throughout the complete argument, Thomas cites five types of phenomena which point back and back to God as the first cause of all the world. They are (1) change or motion in the natural world as evidence for an unchangeable first mover; (2) efficient causation among actual phenomena as evidence for a first cause; (3) the fact of the contingent or the accidental in natural events as evidence for a being, behind all these shifts and changes, which is a completely necessary being; (4) the occurrence of gradation or degrees of excellence to be found in things in ordinary experience as evidence for a perfect being through a knowledge of whom we are enabled to recognize various degrees of imperfection; (5) the factor of harmony in nature, design, or adaptation as evidence for an intelligence which lies behind and is the ground for accord and purposiveness that pervade all things. The last of these phases of argument is actually the second in our list, the teleological argument, in which everything in the natural universe is interpreted as ordered and moving toward ends or goals.

The logical form of the first three is identical. We shall therefore cite the second, for this is generally regarded as the typical statement of the cosmological argument. Every event that occurs in nature has a condition which precedes it in time. This is called its efficient cause. This cause has a cause. The cause of the cause has a cause, and so on. Such an endless regress is intolerable, for to keep pushing causal explanation back and back is never really to "explain."

The words of Thomas speak for themselves.

The second way is from the nature of the efficient cause. In the world of sense we find there is an order of efficient causes. There is no case known (neither is it, indeed, possible) in which a thing is found to be the efficient cause of itself; for so it would be prior to itself, which is impossible. Now in efficient causes it is not possible to go on to infinity, because in all efficient causes following in order, the first is the cause of the intermediate cause, and the intermediate is the cause of the ultimate cause, whether the intermediate cause be several, or only one. Now to take away the cause is to take away the effect. Therefore, if there be no first cause among efficient causes, there will be no ultimate, nor any intermediate cause. But, if in efficient causes it is possible to go on to infinity, there will be no first efficient cause, neither will there be an ultimate effect, nor any intermediate efficient causes; all of which is plainly false. Therefore it is necessary to admit a first efficient cause to which every one gives the name of God.[2]

Thomas's language falls strangely upon our modern ears. He made several assumptions against the background of his thirteenth-century understanding of Aristotle to demonstrate the rational truth of orthodox Christian doctrines. Thomas presupposed views of cause and of motion which he adopted from Aristotle. For him, a cause is understood as a real productive force which makes things happen everywhere throughout the universe. Ever since David Hume in the eighteenth century made his critical analysis of the traditional notion of causation, moderns have taken a different view. To trace causal connections between events today

---

[2] St. Thomas Aquinas, *Summa Theologica* (trans. English Dominican Fathers), New York, Benziger Brothers, Inc., 1924, Part I, p. 25. Translation published and copyrighted by Benziger Brothers, Inc.

means to correlate observed regularities in sequences of natural phenomena. Thus the notion of necessary, productive power no longer is a useful concept in scientific investigation. Present-day followers of Thomas insist that the Aristotelian-Thomist notion of cause was never intended to be taken as science but as philosophy. And, as such, this conception of cause is a valid idea when applied in the search for metaphysical reality.

But Thomas had an entirely different view of motion from that used in modern common-sense and scientific thought. He did not mean by motion simply mechanical shifting of *things* from one place to another, as in the case of a billiard ball that is moved when another one strikes it. Rather, he took his cue from Aristotle and had in mind *development*, as when organisms become in actuality what they are potentially. Acorns change into that which fulfills their proper end; they become oaks. Embryos within chicken eggs realize their goal and become chickens. Motion, for the Aristotolean-Thomist view, thus means development from potentiality to actuality. Strangely, what is last in order of time is first in order of importance; for it is the end, the goal, which determines what a thing, an organism, or a person is essentially. The end thus coexists with what it now is.

If this is the case, then the First Cause or God is not simply the first member of a whole series of causes. In fact, God is not a member of a series of events at all. Rather, He is entirely outside the whole series; for He is the ground upon which the whole series of events depends. Thus God, as unmoved mover, is the very source of all motions whatsoever, whether past, present, or future. He is timeless and thus not Himself involved in any processes of development, but He is that eternal Being who is pure actuality. Everything in the natural order is contingent and dependent on God, for God alone is necessary.

2. The traditional *teleological* argument begins with the way things and processes in nature seem to be designed for some purpose, end, *telos,* and then reasons to the existence of an intelligent

designer. Here are the words of Thomas, as he discusses the fifth of the types of phenomena which point to God as the ground of the universe:

> The fifth way is taken from the governance of the world. We see that things which lack intelligence, such as natural bodies, act for an end, and this is evident from their acting always, or nearly always, in the same way, so as to obtain the best results. Hence it is plain that not fortuitously, but designedly, do they achieve their end. Now whatever lacks intelligence cannot move towards an end, unless it be directed by some being endowed with knowledge and intelligence; as the arrow is shot to the mark by the archer. Therefore some intelligent being exists by whom all natural things are directed to their end; and this being we call God.[3]

The teleological argument in this elementary form again indicates Thomas's assumptions, common to the Greek and medieval world view, concerning nature and man. Even inorganic phenomena in the natural order operate in terms of ends. These things cannot behave this way by mere chance but because of some sort of deliberate intention. But inorganic things are not themselves conscious. Therefore, if they are to act toward ends, they must be directed by an intelligence who is endowed with knowledge. These rather naïve assumptions seem to say that man's own well-being is the goal for which natural objects exist: vegetables to eat, air to breathe, mountains to look upon. But the impersonal world view of modern physics, astronomy, and finally biology rendered this elemental teleological explanation untenable. The teleological argument has undergone refutation and reformulation and qualification several times throughout the course of western theological and philosophical thought. The contemporary student must ask himself about the significance of this argument as restated in the light of a modern world view.

3. The *ontological* argument, which Thomas rejected, belongs distinctively to that other way of apprehending the being of God

[3] *Ibid.*, Part I, pp. 26-27.

within the human consciousness itself. It found its inception in Augustine and classic expression in Anselm (1033-1109). The statement of this "proof" of God's existence sounds like a logical argument. God is by definition that than which no greater can be conceived. If he were nonexistent, a greater could be conceived (i.e., a God who did exist). Thus the greatest conceivable being must exist. For a nonexistent being could not qualify as the greatest conceivable being because, if it had existence, it would be still greater. Stated in a single sentence: Greatness or perfection implies existence, and God is by definition perfect. Descartes (1596-1650) later on employed the ontological argument by drawing an analogy between the properties of a triangle and the properties of perfection belonging to God. Certain characteristics belong by definition to a triangle (assuming Euclidian geometry), without which it simply would not be a triangle: the sum of its angles equals two right angles, the greatest angle is opposite the greatest side, etc. Just so, said Descartes, existence is a property which belongs to that perfect being, God.

Classical criticisms of the ontological argument were given by a monk named Gaunilon, in Anselm's own time, and later by Kant (1724-1804). The former cited the instance of "the fool" who has no knowledge of the Augustinian way of inner experience and proceeds to deny God's existence. He might indeed have a picture in his mind of a perfect island, but this could hardly prove the existence of such a delightful place. Just so, Anselm's conception of a perfect being does not establish his existence. Anselm could but reply that his argument applied to one unique being, and not to a physically existent object such as an island. Kant pinned down the same basic criticism by saying that "existence" is not a logical predicate at all. We cannot state that "God is existent," for the *is* or *existence* is a copula or connective which links a subject to a predicate. And the assertion of existence must be based on a genuine experience. For instance, a hundred real dollars contains no more

The Being of God

coins than an imaginary hundred dollars, and only sense experience will tell us which is actual.

Kant rejected all three of the traditional arguments which we have discussed so far. In each case, he asserted that we can, with equal logical cogency, prove or disprove the existence of God. There is no way, therefore, by which traditional rational theology can lead the human mind to absolute certainty of God's existence. The cosmological argument, he said, tries in vain to establish a first cause; for causation applies only within the world of space, time, and sense experience and not to some "world" beyond it. The teleological argument, Kant believed, deserved respect, but cannot prove conclusively the being of a world creator. These two arguments reduce to the *ontological;* for, in each case, we are confronted with the question of the *being* and *nature* of the first cause or the cosmic artificer. And, as we have seen, the ontological argument itself is not convincing because existence is not a predicate.

4. Kant has led the way for modern men in developing another approach to the being of God: through the *moral experience.* For what he denied as rational knowledge Kant proposed to establish as faith. In his moral philosophy, Kant developed what he believed to be universal and necessary foundations for the ethical life. Absolute devotion to duty is the obligation of every rational man. Ask of every act you intend to do what would happen if everyone in your position followed the same procedure. Would it involve self-contradiction? Universalize the rule by which you intend to act. Then act always, Kant would say, so as to treat human beings as ends and never as means. But how is moral experience, based on absolute demand, to be possible? Can man alone attain this highest good? Three postulates are necessary, in Kant's view, if this moral obligation is to be intelligible: freedom, immortality, and God. Freedom must be presupposed if man is to choose the service of the highest good. The perfect union of obligation and happiness cannot be effected in this life—hence, immortality. The only agency which can render actual this pursuit of this absolute

moral demand is a moral governor of the universe, God. Moral man must therefore assume as an act of faith that God, the guarantor and ground of morality, exists.

This moral argument, like the other three, has been subjected to criticism and restatement many times. In the following chapter, we shall attempt to discuss the bearing of these arguments and their possible meaning as analogical statements of Christian faith. As such, they are of positive value for those who would clarify what they believe both for themselves and for their generation. But before proceeding to this evaluation, we must face prevalent arguments against the being of God, principally, that argument known as the problem of evil.

Chapter XI

God, Evil, and Personal Existence

The problem of evil stands for many thoughtful persons as a main obstacle to belief in God. It is our purpose in this chapter, first, to discuss the significance of this problem for Christian faith, and, second, the bearings of the traditional arguments for the being of God as affirmation of faith in spite of the fact of evil in human experience. Our orientation throughout this discussion will be God in His living relation to persons and their existence in the midst of day-to-day affairs.

THE PROBLEM OF EVIL

The term *problem of evil* is an abstract way of stating concrete difficulties which emerge out of everyday, personal human experience. In fact, it is within the context, not of theoretical discussion, but of moral decision and action that solution may be found for men of Christian faith. This practical bearing of the problem of evil was vividly illustrated one evening during a student discussion around the fireplace. One of the group, a veteran of the Korean conflict, and hence older than most of the others, had been expressing his own Christian convictions centered in the being of God. "But," exclaimed younger, eager, but more skeptical friends, "how can you assert the existence of God? Why, just look at all the wars, pain, cruelty, and suffering in the world!" "Yes," replied the older student quietly, "I often wondered about that when I wallowed in mud and filth in Korea and saw men shot and all the pain and the dying." To this young man's critics the "problem of evil" appeared to be a neat, logical rebuttal—not that they were any the less sincere than he. But nonetheless they conveyed the impression that the "evil" they used to score a logical point was remote and secondhand. But he spoke of the evil he had seen and known in his own experience, including, as he expressed it, his own bestiality and cold indifference to the pain and loss which war's system enforced within him.

Yet the striking point for Christian conviction is that despite the fact of evil, seen and participated in, the man of faith still believes in God as the ground of all good and commits his whole self to the practical cause of seeking solutions to individual and social ills. It is precisely this apparently irrational holding together of three affirmations that comprises the problem of evil: (1) belief in God as the source and ground of all things, (2) a God who is at once the all-sufficient creator and sustainer of the universe and also a God of love and justice, (3) frank acknowledgment of the fact of evil, both physical and moral, in human experience. The dilemma can be eliminated by denying the being of God as at once all-powerful and the God of love and justice (or, in the case of some thinkers, limiting God's power) or denying the actuality of evil in the world. If God's being is denied completely, then, instead of the "problem of evil," we have on our hands the "problem of good." If the fact of evil is denied, we are faced with the problem of constructing some form of monistic, pantheistic, or idealistic world view in which evil simply is regarded as illusory or as a part necessary to the whole.

Among several proposed solutions to the problem of evil, the suggestion that evil is illusory is prevalent in the Orient, in forms, for example, of philosophic Hinduism; or in the West, in Christian

Science. Also, within our western tradition, this perspective has found expression in those varieties of philosophical idealism which make sharp distinction between an ultimate absolute and appearance. The limerick about the faith-healer of Deal expresses it:

> There once was a faith-healer of Deal
> Who said, "Although pain isn't real,
> When I sit on a pin,
> And it punctures my skin,
> I dislike what I fancy I feel." [1]

Common sense simply acknowledges the brute reality of pain, suffering, injustice, and brutality within human experience; for the whole universe just does not seem to be all good. It hardly relieves the darkness we sense hovering over human existence to dismiss it as a delusion of our own minds because the very existence of such minds still clamors for explanation. Nor does it seem to bring solution any closer to say that evil is *necessary* to the good of the whole universe. Yet some would insist that evil is analogous to the blot in the picture, painted in deliberately by the artist, or to the crashing dissonance which by force of contrast enhances the whole symphony. But this kind of explanation is poor comfort to the incurably sick man wracked in real pain or to the widowed mother desperately trying to feed and clothe her children. Moreover, on this view, God Himself would seem to be author of the evil which he deliberately creates in order that good may be the final outcome. This is to assign to God an expediency we would hardly condone in men: ends justifying the means. Even more serious is the objection that, on this supposition, it would be wrong for men to try to eliminate pain, suffering, want, degradation, cruelty, and injustice from the world scene; for such action would

[1] John S. Whale, *The Christian Answer to the Problem of Evil*, New York, Abingdon-Cokesbury Press, 1936, p. 21. This little book is a clear presentation of the problem of evil from the perspective of Christian faith. For some years now, I have been indebted to him for help in stating the terms of this human dilemma and for grasp of insight concerning what persons of Christian conviction ought to do about it.

only diminish the good of the whole. For Christian faith, these evils are grimly real and must be dealt with by responsible and forthright action. They are thus not delusions of the mind or discord put here for the sake of harmony for the whole.

Another proposed solution to the problem of evil is a thoroughgoing determinism which makes the God who is the author and creator of all things completely responsible for evil also. But if the sin of men, their prides, rebellions, hatreds, and acts of violence to their fellows, are all God's doing, what happens to human freedom and responsibility? It is the Christian conviction concerning man, as we have seen, that he is partly free and partly bound, made in the gracious image of God, constantly tempted to deface that image, but never able completely to destroy it. What is evil in this view? It is separation from God. What is good? It is reconciliation and commitment which leads to fellowship with God. Such restored fellowship cannot come into being through coercion or mechanical manipulation, as if men were puppets on a string. Hence it is a basic Christian belief that, while the all-sufficiency of God is central, so also is the responsible freedom of men.

Nels F. S. Ferré makes the imaginative suggestion that evil is like the barbs on the fence on which rebellious men get caught when they try to climb away from the goodness of God. On this interpretation, God does not deliberately create evil by direct act of will. Rather it is a consequence of human freedom, for to choose good is of no significance whatsoever unless I am able also to choose evil. God thus permits evil only in the sense that it is a derivative of the responsible freedom of His children. No matter what the outcome for rationalistic logic, it is thus essential to Christian faith to hold within a single affirmation the all-sufficiency and the goodness of God together with man's moral responsibility, freedom, and creative action.

This perspective involves an important distinction. The evils which beset men are of two kinds: *moral* evils for which free men are responsible and *physical* evils for which we are not wholly responsible. Inadequate housing, bombing cities, and the like are within human control, providing we are willing to work at creating the conditions of their elimination. At present, earthquakes, volcanoes, hurricanes seem to be beyond human control. This distinction leads to another. Moral evils are intimately bound up with the problem of sin as men in pride and arrogance constantly put themselves at the center of concern. Physical evils constitute the persistent problem of human suffering. Of course, these distinctions are not absolute, because some evils belong to both kinds, such as poverty and disease. Men may not be responsible for the varieties of virus which cause poliomyelitis, but, as we are now witnessing, they do have within their power the control of this dread disease through the discovery, distribution, and dispensing of vaccines.

It is a dangerous fallacy to claim that there is an exact moral requital whereby the sinful are visited with physical and spiritual disaster and the good are duly rewarded. But although this is a fallacy, John S. Whale states that "we have to add at once that human selfishness and sin, *collectively considered,* will explain much if not most of human woe. . . . If we could eliminate from the problem of evil man's inhumanity to man—itself the outcome of his greed, fear and ignorance—and of the fact that sinful lives interlock to form a vast and organized system of evil—would not the problem have dwindled to relatively trifling proportions?" [2]

There are other proposed solutions to the problem of evil, such as that of a cosmic dualism, which would ascribe evil to the work of an equal and opposite force forever pitted against God. But this explanation, which blames a Devil for the world's evil, only pushes the problem one stage further back. It is no more satisfactory than the other solutions. Each proposal we have discussed makes a one-sided emphasis which turns out finally to be a falsification of the full divine-human situation. The Christian holds at

[2] *Ibid.,* pp. 34-35.

one and the same time to the three affirmations stated above: (1) God as source and ground of all that is, (2) God as loving goodness, (3) the fact of evil within God's universe. So long as we hold to these convictions, we have a problem on our hands as baffling and as mysterious as life itself. Of course, we could eliminate the problem simply by refusing to believe in God at all and substitute some other world view. But this is the very issue with which we are concerned in this chapter and, in fact, our whole concern as Christians. If there is no God, then we are obligated, as thoughtful and concerned men and women, to suggest another world hypothesis and fearlessly to follow out the consequences for action which it entails.

It would be comforting to a generation perhaps already too heavily burdened with problems to suggest some logical solution to the dilemma of evil. But, as Whale writes from the perspective of Christian faith:

There is no neat reasoning whereby the heavy and the weary weight of all this unintelligible world may be lifted and taken away. Rachel weeping for her children, Job cursing his day, Socrates drinking the hemlock, Saint Paul dying daily, Saint Joan crying, "My voices have deceived me"—Christianity itself has no formula explaining these things. Intellectually considered, the mystery remains a mystery. Neither theism nor atheism, neither the philosophies nor the sciences can solve this, the deepest problem for humanity. We do not understand why this child is blind; nor why that mother, for whom life already has been one long discipline, now loses her only son. If she herself understands (and she probably does), it is because the true and sufficient answer comes only out of life itself, life with Christ's cross towering in triumph over it. The real issue of life can be solved only in terms of life's experience, and not of any intellectual theory. It is when the problem of evil is deliberately shifted from the purely intellectual to the practical plane—out of philosophers' classrooms into the street, the hospital ward or the sanctuary—that it becomes its own answer. The very belief in God which creates and constitutes the intellectual riddle is turned to truth by the test of life.[3]

[3] *Ibid.*, pp. 52-54.

God, Evil, and Personal Existence

These solutions to life's problems in terms of life's personal experience will return to us in discussion of the divine-human event in history and in the specific problem of the significance of Christ's cross, for now we reaffirm that it is belief in God which creates our problem. The Christian faith holds to the being of God in spite of the fact of evil in human experience: a God who is all-great and all-loving.

BEARINGS OF THE ARGUMENTS FOR THE BEING OF GOD

But, bringing discussion of these two chapters on God to summation, what are the bearings of the traditional arguments for the being of God as externalized symbolic expressions of inner conviction? They are based in personal affirmations of faith in the living God of the biblical heritage. But although faith is prior to reason, Christian conviction must find cogent and clear utterance in and for the present age, involving utter commitment, creative action, and deepening awareness. The theistic arguments for God's being are thus attempts to state in the form of analogies what this unique I-thou relationship between man and God means.

Furthermore, the point of view we are expressing would regard the ontological argument as basic to the others. This means that the cosmological, teleological, and moral arguments are formulations of the ontological. Anselm, standing in the Augustinian tradition, realized that Christian affirmation begins with inner experience which finds within human consciousness itself evidences for the being of the God who is the transcendent ground of man's personal and historical existence. The ontological argument does not fit the Greek point of view, for the cosmological and teleological lines of reasoning were sufficient for men who put stress on the rational structure of the cosmic order. But men of biblical faith affirm *a God who discloses Himself from beyond history in and through events within history, of nature, and of personal existence.* Of the bearing of this biblical perspective on deity, John Hutchison states:

155

It is this view of deity which is formulated in the ontological argument, and the significance of the argument is that it communicates to the philosophic consciousness of the Western world the impact of this understanding of God. Thus in so far as the other arguments formulate and communicate this understanding of God, they may be regarded as special cases of the ontological argument. And, again, the ontological is not an argument but a formulation of man's apprehension of the transcendent-immanent God; it is a statement in the language of philosophy of the particular kind of apprehension of finitude and infinity which characterizes the Hebrew-Christian tradition.[4]

In effect, the ontological argument is not an argument in the strict sense at all, and those who would state it as such, together with those who attempt to criticize it, miss the point. For it is not appropriate to speak of God as merely existing, since He is the ground of all existence. As Paul Tillich expresses it, the very "question of God is possible because an awareness of God is present in the question of God. This awareness precedes the question. It is not the result of the argument but its presupposition. This certainly means that the 'argument' is no argument at all. The so-called ontological argument points to the ontological structure of finitude. It shows that an awareness of the infinite is included in man's awareness of finitude. Man knows that he is finite, that he is excluded from an infinity which nevertheless belongs to him."[5]

With this perspective as background, it becomes possible to translate the ontological argument into terms we can understand today. Let each of us ask himself what is involved in the very fact that man can *think* about the universe. Consider all the thinking that is going on at any given moment all over the world: in the sciences, education, business, industry, statesmanship, literature, the arts, philosophy, and personal affairs. What must we presuppose in order to do all this thinking? Is the world basically intelligible

4 John Hutchison, *Faith, Reason and Existence,* New York, Oxford University Press, 1956, p. 153.
5 Paul Tillich, *Systematic Theology,* Chicago, University of Chicago Press, 1951, Vol. I, p. 206.

and manageable? Does all this thinking go on without any parallel or kinship between man's thought and the universe thought about? Is there any structure there, any uniformity? Do we imagine we find something that is not there? How do we read the world's signs, interpret them, understand them in ordered sequences and systems? That the universe is ordered and hence lends itself to understanding is not a testable hypothesis. Rather, it is a collateral hypothesis belonging to every family of working hypotheses.[6]

But if we assume that the universe lends itself to understanding, then there would seem to be some close kinship between our minds that think and the reality that is all around us. In short, *thought is congruent with existence.* Or do we prefer another alternative? Perhaps the minds of men are just isolated accidents without any counterpart elsewhere in the scheme of things. If God is not the source and ground of all essence and existence, this would seem to be the case. But if He is the ground that holds all things together in an intelligible wholeness, then the world, in all its systematic detail, makes sense. This presupposition, this belief, thus is one which makes all thought possible. To know anything at all then is to think the thoughts of God after Him, man's being meeting God's Being.

Moving on now to the significance of the cosmological and teleological arguments, it is important to note that these are more specific applications of the ontological argument. God is not simply found among the ordered and teleological processes of nature as if He were one more datum alongside the myriad phenomena of the cosmos. You do not stand gazing off toward the distant horizons at the snow-capped mountains and discover God within their signs of sublimity and beauty. But men of biblical faith encounter God within the personal and the historical first and then affirm their belief that that same God is also the God of the stars, the planets, the mountains, and the seas. The creation accounts in the Old

---

[6] See Chapter VI on the role of hypotheses in the sciences.

Testament, for example, emerged as a result of the intermingling of Hebrew and Babylonian peoples and the appropriation of Babylonian myths to express Hebrew faith. The myths of creation thus affirm the utter dependence of all of nature upon this same God who is experienced as the God of history. The cosmological argument especially is then the translation into the language of philosophy and theology of the creation myths of the Bible. Once again, the affirmations of the cosmological argument are not conclusions but presuppositions in terms of which it is believed the world makes sense.

Standing in the midst of all the phenomena which make up this richly intricate universe, many modern men believe they live in a cosmos that is ordered. Out of their faith emerges the following more detailed interpretation. Running through the whole scheme of things, so they affirm, there is apparently some kind of purposive direction from simpler to more complex forms. Thus they employ a reformulation of the teleological argument. It is not the mass of details in which we are interested here but signs of forward and upward movement. Out of inorganic materials arose life in its earliest and simplest forms, leading in ascending scale of variety and complexity to living organisms making up invertebrates, fishes, amphibians, reptiles, birds, mammals, and man.

Many scholars draw from this pageant of living forms, with its specialized organs and functions interacting with their environments, the impression that working through all this process is a purposiveness, a movement toward ends, that is not merely mechanical. Inferred also are the elements of continuity, progression, and emergence of the new and different at crucial stages in the process. Lloyd Morgan has pictured this. At every stage is to be found some principle of organization or directive factor, thrusting up through the levels of matter, life, and mind. To explain this development, there seems a choice of two alternatives: either the cause of all this is material and mechanical or it is more like a directive intelligence, mind, will. To many, this force looks like

God: intelligent, creative, purposive, rich in being and power, using this long complex process of development for the working out of universal ends and goals.

J. A. Thomson says, "The evolutionary momentum is with man at his best. It finds expression in some of the fibres of his being and in the social system which he has developed. When we think over the intelligibility, the order, the beauty, the advance and the progressiveness of nature, we feel that the world is more divine than demonic, that it is not unlike a great thought, that it is congruent with the concept of a Creator." [7]

Similarly, the traditional moral argument has its modern counterpart. Man is rooted in nature and he is the product of nature. This is true of his biological functions and also of his values. He is a creature who drives after goals and is enabled by nature to contrive instruments to overcome obstacles. Thus mobility and sight have emerged as special functions in the process of the development of organisms. In the same way, intelligence has emerged, and ideas of right and wrong, good and bad. Out of the pressures of the environment developed the sense of obligation and the ability to act in terms of ideal ends of goodness, truth, justice, beauty. Although men's conception of the ways in which these values may be expressed may differ, the fact of moral obligation remains constant. Whatever he conceives to be the good, man says: "I must embody it and realize it. I ought to live up to the best I know."

Does this sense of obligation mean that we obey God or nature? Some would answer that perhaps it makes no difference which you call it. The results are the same. Psychology shows us that thoughtlessness, anxiety, self-centeredness, fear, carry their own consequences as evidenced in functional disorders. To deny moral claims with your mind is to have them spring up out of your body. Everything has a law of its own being, including humans. The very structure of things is made for truth and love. Tell the truth and

---

[7] J. A. Thomson, *Science and Religion*, New York, Charles Scribner's Sons, 1925, p. 206.

the universe itself is for you; lie and it is against you. The law of love is written into the very constitution of ourselves and the universe; to deny it is to take the consequences of self-disruption and social chaos. Wars, hatred, suffering wrought by man, far from proof that moral law does not exist, are rather indications that moral law exists in the very nature of things.

Following this line of argument, some are led to ask: Is this science or religion, God or nature? If the order of the universe is a moral order, then our sense of *oughtness* has some secure foundation; for the laws of Nature, we believe, are the Laws of God— including moral laws. To obey these is to obey the existence of moral law, and value indicates the existence of God.

G. W. Cunningham says:

> Moral values are objective in the sense that they are essential qualities of human nature; they are therefore, real parts of the world-order in so far as human nature is a real part of the world-order; now man cannot but hold . . . that he and his values are real: the world-order must consequently be in some sense a moral order, in the sense, namely, that there is room in it for man and the ideal of goodness which is basal to his nature; and this could not be unless the world-order is directed by a conscious, rational Being who wills the final triumph of goodness; God exists, therefore, as the necessary implication of the objectivity of moral values.[8]

As expressions of a point of view concerning the nature of the physical, organic, and moral orders, these lines of argument are convincing to the man of biblical faith. Certainly they are more consistent with Christian affirmation than the strict mechanism of materialism or the limited perspective of logical empiricism. But the fact of evil and the evidence of *dysteleology*, or dispurpose in the universe, stand as counterarguments and, logically, the contest ends in a draw. These arguments, as we have seen, are special cases of the ontological argument, as they state in rational form the

[8] G. W. Cunningham, *Problems of Philosophy*, New York, Henry Holt and Company, 1924, p. 418.

prior commitment of the man of faith. For here again such a man intends to affirm the perspective that all of nature and human existence is meaningful and dependent upon the transcendent God who discloses Himself within this finite order.

In the final analysis, it is the existence of persons in their individual and sociohistorical contexts which is most significant for Christian faith concerning God. As was stated toward the end of Chapter IV, we must make a choice as to what kind of universe we believe we have on our hands. What sort of universe could have brought persons into being with capacity for fellowship with each other and God?

This is the crux of the entire matter for the Christian. Persons have emerged, new and unique, out of a world of inorganic matter, and have become capable of thought and the realization of value. Persons, as we have said, are more than things. If persons exist, then the universe must be a person-producing universe, not just a thing-producing universe. Man is at home in that universe. He fits. Man belongs. There must therefore be some power at the heart of things that is capable of producing and sustaining persons. That power must be equal to the task—certainly higher and not lower. For can a stream flow uphill? The Reality that creates persons is not less than persons; for if it is less, then we have simply arisen out of a subpersonal world of atoms and physical forces, and that is a return to nontheistic materialism. That Reality which has created us must therefore be much more than personal. God, then, is a person-producing power, capable of so doing, and must be greater than His creation.

The most convincing indication of God's existence and power is to be found in the kind of life which flowers from those who believe in Him and seek to serve Him. Not all great spirits are Christian, but the noblest of all ages have rooted their lives in religious faith—not in dogmas and doctrines about God, but in living relationship to Him and as a consequence a relationship of creative good will toward fellow men.

Essentials in Christian Faith

A man named Dr. Parker gave his life and professional career in caring for a colony of lepers in New England. A dying sailor asked to be confessed before a priest. When the priest asked, "Do you believe in God?" the sailor said, "I don't know whether I believe in God or not, but I believe in Dr. Parker."

The Christian affirms this. You may not know all about God or the mysteries of existence, but to live each day on the basis of creative good will toward your fellow men is to come into vital relationship with God. Creative good will is not an abstract theory; it comes alive in persons. Behind the kind of life Dr. Parker demonstrates stands the dynamic power of God. When that personal power surges with creative energy in us, too, that is to know God—and, perhaps, all we need to know.

One night in 1924, Roland Hayes, the American Negro singer, was scheduled for a concert in Berlin at a time when the French occupying the Rhine were policing it with Negro troops. In the face of mounting indignation and against the advice of friends, Roland Hayes insisted on keeping his engagement and entered the concert hall at eight o'clock exactly, only to be greeted by a barrage of hisses and stamping of feet. It is this artist's wont to recall to himself that he is only an instrument through which his mission is being fulfilled. So on this critical night he stood there with hands clasped, praying that Roland Hayes might be entirely blotted out of the picture; that the people there might feel only the spirit of God flowing through melody and rhythm; that racial and national hatred might be forgotten. Usually audiences sense what he is doing, but this night was different. Yet, with absolute trust, he stepped to the curve of the piano and stood there with head up, eyes closed, letting the spirit do its work, waiting for the hissing to die down. Two minutes, three, four, five, ten interminable minutes. Suddenly the hissing and stamping of feet stopped.

Hayes tells us that he spoke to his accompanist and asked him to play Schubert's "Thou Art My Peace." This composition begins

God, Evil, and Personal Existence

very softly, almost in a whisper. As the notes sang out, the hostile people became silent. Hayes tells us that it was not a personal victory but rather the victory of a power greater than himself that was able to overcome hatred and fear. The Christian would affirm that it is the Power of the Living God.

God is not a museum piece to be studied by archaeologists. God is not simply a projection of man's wishful thinking—a human fiction to be studied by psychologists. God is not just deified humanity—a social phenomenon to be studied by sociologists. But with the help of scientists, scholars, artists, engineers, doctors, lawyers, religious leaders, politicians, businessmen, housewives, workers—men and women, all striving, learning, laboring, praying—God, the great dynamic Reality, can come alive in human experience. For God is a loving, creative Will to goodness actively at work in wooing the world of men to Himself. And that means that we, for our part, must become God's instruments, dedicated to working all our moments, hours, days, months, years—all of time—for an everlasting purpose of truth, justice, and love until someday all human history becomes, in fact, *His* Story. In Him, says Paul, we live, and move, and have our being!

Chapter XII

Jesus Christ: Divine-Human Event

Lloyd C. Douglas paints a word picture in his book, *The Robe*. All the world was on its way that day to Jerusalem to celebrate the feast of the Passover. Caught within the press of the crowd was the Greek slave, Demetrius. In Douglas' own words:

Suddenly, for no reason at all that Demetrius could observe, there was a wave of excitement. It swept down over the sluggish swollen stream of zealots like a sharp breeze. . . . Far up ahead the shouts were increasing in volume, spontaneously organizing into a concerted reiterated cry; a single magic word that drove the multitude into a frenzy. . . .

Wedged tight against his arm, and grinning up into his face, was another Greek, older but smaller than himself, a slave, easily recognizable as such by the slit in his earlobe. Impudently the ill-scented little fellow bent about for a glimpse of Demetrius' ear; and, having assured himself of their social equality, laughed fraternally.

"Athens," he announced, by way of introduction.

"Corinth," returned Demetrius, crisply. "Do you know what is going on?"

"They're yelling something about a king. That's all I can make of it. . . ."

"You think they've got somebody up front who wants to be their king? Is that it?"

"Looks like it. They keep howling another word that I don't know— Messiah. The man's name, maybe. . . ."

164

Jesus Christ: Divine-Human Event

Standing on tiptoe for an instant in the swaying crowd, Demetrius caught a fleeting glimpse of the obvious center of interest, a brown-haired, bare-headed, well-favored Jew. . . . He was clad in a simple brown mantle with no decorations of any kind, and the handful of men—his intimate friends, no doubt—who tried to shield him from the pressure of the throng, wore the commonest sort of country garb. . . .

"Can you see him?" called the little Athenian, who had stuck fast in the sticky-hot pack an arm's length away.

Demetrius nodded without turning his head.

"Old man?"

"No—not very," answered Demetrius, candidly remote.

"What does he look like?" shouted the Athenian, impatiently.

Demetrius shook his head—and his hand, too—signaling that he couldn't be bothered now, especially with questions as hard as this one.

"Look like a king?" yelled the Greek, guffawing boisterously.

Demetrius did not reply. Tugging at his impounded garments, he crushed his way forward. The surging mass, pushing hard from the rear, now carried him on until he was borne almost into the very hub of the procession that edged along, step by step, keeping pace with the plodding donkey. . . .

Everyone was shouting, shouting—all but the Corinthian slave, whose throat was so dry he couldn't have shouted, who had no inclination to shout, who wished they would all be quiet, quiet! It wasn't the time or place for shouting. Quiet! This man wasn't the sort of person one shouted at, or shouted for. Quiet! That was what this moment called for—Quiet!

Gradually the brooding eyes moved over the crowd until they came to rest on the stained, bewildered face of Demetrius. Perhaps, he wondered, the man's gaze halted there because he alone—in all the welter of hysteria—refrained from shouting. His silence singled him out. The eyes calmly appraised Demetrius. They neither widened nor smiled; but, in some indefinable manner, they held Demetrius in a grip so firm it was almost a physical compulsion. The message they communicated was something other than sympathy, something more vital than friendly concern; a sort of stabilizing power that swept away all such negations as slavery, poverty, or any other afflicting circumstance. Demetrius was suffused with the glow of this curious kinship. Blind with sudden tears, he elbowed through the throng and reached the roadside. The uncouth Athenian, bursting with curiosity, inopportunely accosted him.

"See him—close up?" he asked.

Demetrius nodded; and turning away, began to retrace his steps toward his abandoned duty.

"Crazy?" persisted the Athenian, trudging alongside.

"No."

"King?"

"No," muttered Demetrius soberly—"not a king."

"What is he, then?" demanded the Athenian, piqued by the Corinthian's aloofness.

"I don't know," mumbled Demetrius, in a puzzled voice, "but—he is something more important than a king." [1]

After nearly two thousand years we look back. We also are puzzled. We seem to have come face to face with a mystery. We do not know exactly what to make of this One called Jesus, the Christ. He obviously was a magnetic leader of men. Yet men and women aplenty in his own day thought he was crazy. His own family considered him a harmless madman. Others believed he was a religious crank who ought to have been locked up for his own good. The religious authorities took a more serious attitude. For this man Jesus was a definite threat to their own established power. And, in the end, Jesus' road led through a garden of decision, betrayal, and a trial, to death on a cross.

Yet, as we read the course of history since his time, these events clustered about his dynamic personality seem somehow to illuminate all other events even down to the present moment. At least, this is the stupendous claim of Christian faith. In Jesus Christ, God now acts decisively in human history in a revelatory event that brings to climax all other events through which He discloses Himself. According to Christian affirmation, Jesus was not simply a moral reformer or a teacher of a new ethical code. He does not merely add the note of love to the old Hebraic refrain of justice, as some in our day insist. Neither does the man of Christian faith begin with some beliefs about God and add to these some beliefs about Jesus Christ.

[1] Lloyd C. Douglas, *The Robe*, Boston, Houghton Mifflin Company, 1942, pp. 97-101.

Jesus Christ: Divine-Human Event

Rather, it is the basic claim of the Christian that in and through this new event, of which the person of Jesus Christ is the creative center, the very nature of both God Himself and man in relation to God stand disclosed.

The deeply personal or existential predicament, which we discussed in Chapter V, now reaches resolution. We need to recall briefly this perspective on man, his nature, and his needs. This curious being of contrasts and contradictions called man is yet a whole self which belongs essentially to the transcendent God. Man, the creature, is like God, is made in the image of God. In his freedom he distorts the divine image, but he can never utterly destroy it. Although man is like God in essential make-up, he is yet a free and responsible agent who is capable of accepting or rejecting God's claim of justice and love. This, then, is the dilemma which finds decisive answer through Christ. It is not just ignorance from which man needs to be cured. Neither is it merely a matter of control of natural forces or impulses within himself through scientific methods. Nor may he effect cure by fleeing the practical world into some "spiritual" refuge. Serious as these human concerns are, it is the Christian conviction that knowledge, science, and practical affairs themselves need redirection and revitalization. For even in his claims to knowledge, man forgets he is a creature and tries to become "god" in his pride, arrogance, and rebellion called sin. This means separation in his total person from the God to whom he really belongs. The solution to this basic personal or existential predicament, so the Christian believes, lies in an ultimate reconciliation between God and man who is created in God's own image, an image lost for awhile, and defaced, but never completely destroyed. To be found of and by the creatively loving God, as He discloses Himself in Jesus Christ, brings this genuine solution for the human predicament and ultimate reconciliation. Yet such reconciliation does not somehow magically lift men out of the everyday world of joy, sorrow, privileges, and demands. It does not create a Utopia where all personal or social problems are solved.

167

Rather men and women remain within the practical world to live and work. Yet they do so as dynamic and creative centers through whom God's purposes of justice and love may be realized. This, at any rate, is the radical claim of Christian faith as it drives to the roots of men's personal dilemma to heal and restore.

It is the purpose of this chapter, and the one following, to examine this claim more closely in the light of the views which we have developed on the meaning of faith, religious language, the Scriptures, and revelation through historical events. First, we shall discuss the person of Jesus Christ as the dynamic center of an event or series of events in history. Second, we shall inquire how this perspective helps us to understand more adequately who Jesus Christ is, what he did and said. In the following chapter, we shall be concerned with the problem of the miracles as signs of Jesus' messianic power and authority. Then our discussion will center in a summary of the central Christian affirmation that Jesus Christ is both divine and human. In Chapter XIV, we will consider the significance of the atonement as the climax of God's action in history.

Throughout this discussion of all these points, we shall be dealing with issues concerning which theologians have pondered for centuries and have contrived the most intricate doctrinal explanations. Necessarily our discussion must be brief and as free from technical terminology as possible. But the most serious difficulty which faces us is that through our theorizing we are always tempted to claim too much or too little. As men and women are confronted by God in Jesus Christ, they are face to face with an ultimate mystery which religious language can never fully express. Yet if humans are to speak at all of their convictions, they must rely on the utterance of words. For it is through words, of the Scriptures and of Christian witnesses down through the ages, that the eternal *Word* of God is conveyed from generation to generation. So in each age men and women read the Scriptures in order to be confronted by the God who moves throughout the history recorded there, to become participants in the unfolding drama of God's redemptive action in the world, and to speak of what these things mean to their own generation. Thus, perhaps through such words used in this generation, we shall be led into the very center of the mystery that men can never fully understand, where encounter and response of faith and commitment may occur. This is to know from the inside as participant and experiencer in a way that is never possible for the objective observer looking in from the outside. It is only fair to admit that this is the case. For, as in the employment of the traditional arguments for the being of God, evidence for Christ's divinity cannot be adduced as for a scientific hypothesis.

Statements about Christ are externalized symbolic expression of inner conviction. They are based in personal affirmations of faith in the living God of the biblical heritage who has now acted within history in a once-and-for-all way. Here also faith is prior to reason, but Christian conviction must find cogent and clear utterance in and for the present age, as men and women who thus speak find themselves involved in utter commitment, creative action, and deepening awareness.

CHRIST AS CENTER OF HISTORICAL EVENTS

As to Jesus Christ as the dynamic center of a series of events, we recall that throughout the entire Bible moves a single theme: the covenant relation between God and a people. God has called these folk in a special way to assume unique responsibility among the nations of the world. Here recorded then is the moving drama, beginning with God's summons to Israel and moving dynamically forward to the establishment of the Christian community, the Church. Thus in terms of the New Covenant, the Christian way and life are built on to the continuous tradition of Hebrew life, practice, and hope.

We have touched briefly on this perspective in a previous chapter. But its force now comes to bear in a crucial way for Christian belief. At the living center of the new agreement is the unique event or series of events: the life, death, resurrection, and continuing presence of Jesus Christ, together with the formation of the Christian community. It was through Him that the earliest Christians believed themselves to have become heirs to the promises made to the Hebrews many centuries before. Here also, as in the case of the Old Covenant, God had acted in such a way as to require response and commitment. Out of person-to-person encounter, men made decision of faith and, as they did so, became themselves, as members of the believing Christian community, part of the event or series of events through which God disclosed Himself. Thus in theological thought today there is the trend we have been stressing: toward insisting that historical facts, interpretation of facts, and faith are inextricably bound up together. As John Knox states in his book *Christ, the Lord,* our Gospel record shows how Jesus was "remembered, was known still, and was interpreted."

The announcement that God had now disclosed himself in a new and decisive way is called *euangelion* in the Greek. In our language we use a word of old English origin, *Gospel,* which means "God story" or "good story." Basically the Gospel is thus the good news itself: how God has acted in history through the person of Jesus Christ. In a derivative sense, the term is applied to the written records concerning this good news.

But it is important, as in the case of the Old Testament records, to note that the living actuality of persons, responding in community to God's self-disclosure, *precedes* written literature. During the thirty years or so (A.D. 30-60) of life in the Christian community there were no written Gospels; for the only scripture the earliest Christians possessed was the Old Testament. But there was preaching among the communities of believers. This is the *kerygma,* or preached message, which scholars can now reconstruct. A. M. Hunter, in his little book *Introducing the New Testament,* summarizes this earliest form of the good news:

170

Jesus Christ: Divine-Human Event

God's promises made to His People in the Old
    Testament are now fulfilled.
The long-expected Messiah, born of David's
    line, has come.
He is Jesus of Nazareth, who
      went about doing good and wrought mighty
        works by God's power;
      was crucified according to the purpose of God;
      was raised by God from the dead and
        exalted to His right hand.
He will come again in glory for judgment.
Therefore let all who hear this message
    repent and be baptized for the for-
      giveness of their sins.[2]

It is significant that the earliest Christian message was not a list of moral precepts. For what these first believers took seriously as the essence of the Gospel did not consist in a statement of abstract ideas but rather in a dramatic story concerning a series of climactic events: a cross and an empty tomb as "mighty acts of God." Yet, as the years passed, believers filled in the outline of the *kerygma* with stories about Jesus himself: of the deeds he had performed in healing the sick, forgiving sinners, rebuking the religious authorities, feeding the crowds, breaking bread with his disciples. Scholars hold it probable that in each of the centers where Christians gathered for their common meals or worship—in Jerusalem, Antioch, Caesarea, or Rome—cycles of stories grew up which believers told and retold to one another. As yet no written records existed, but these people's memories were retentive and their faith was strong.

Yet they must also have asked about the things that Jesus had taught. And those who had known and heard him kept the memory of his sayings fresh and vivid, as his teaching was applied to the problems of life and practice within the community. After a time

---

[2] A. M. Hunter, *Introducing the Bible*, Philadelphia, Westminster Press, 1946, pp. 25-26.

these sayings of Jesus were collected and found their way into the Gospel record. However, during the time of this first generation, the materials which were later to be woven into the written Gospels were expressed by word of mouth. For this was the period of what is called the *oral tradition*.

The earliest writings contained within the 27 books of the New Testament were written during the decade A.D. 50-60. These are the letters of Paul, penned to meet practical situations which arose among the churches during the course of his wide missionary travels. But, beginning about forty years or so after Jesus' death, a strong need arose for a written account of his life and ministry. A second generation was now emerging to replace the first. New converts were joining the fellowship and these needed definitive instruction in the Christian faith. In A.D. 64-65 the Roman emperor Nero instigated the persecution of Christians. Tradition has it that Peter was among those martyred in Rome. And many other eyewitnesses like him were passing from the earthly scene. Thus, about A.D. 70, to meet the need for a written record of Jesus Christ, John Mark wrote the Gospel which bears his name. He was an associate of Paul and Barnabas and perhaps the one who had interpreted from Aramaic into Greek Peter's sermons to the congregation in Rome. He took the bare outline of Jesus' ministry contained in the *kerygma* and added to it what he had heard from Peter and others current among the Christian communities. In simple, straightforward language, Mark set forth the story of God's saving acts in Jesus Christ and bade everyone who would share in his victory to "take up his cross and follow."

Then about A.D. 85, a Jewish Christian writer set down the Gospel according to Matthew, stressing the continuity of the Christian movement with the history of Israel. He based his work on Mark, but he also used a hypothetical source called "Q" (from the German word *Quelle* meaning "source") as well as more than three hundred verses of his own which contain the stories of

Jesus Christ: Divine-Human Event

Jesus' birth, other narrative material, and sections of Jesus' teaching, such as large portions of the Sermon on the Mount.

During this same time another associate of Paul wrote the Gospel of Luke and then added to it a sequel, the Acts of the Apostles, dealing with the spread of the Christian movement throughout the Greco-Roman world. He also used as the basis of his Gospel both Mark and Q, but in addition he utilized special materials of his own, consisting of more than four hundred verses of narrative and teaching, such as the famous parables of the Good Samaritan and the Prodigal Son. It is conjectured that Luke might have gathered this material in the years A.D. 57-59 at Caesarea during Paul's imprisonment in that place.

These first three Gospels, Mark, Matthew, and Luke, are called the Synoptic Gospels because they are based on the same *synopsis* or common outline of the life and ministry of Jesus. But finally, a fourth writer at a much later date (ca. A.D. 90-110) composed the Gospel of John, which is sometimes called the "Spiritual Gospel." This term indicates a characteristic atmosphere which pervades the fourth Gospel. For this writer tells the story of the eternal God's unique act of self-disclosure in the world of men from an entirely different perspective and in distinctive style and treatment. The writer envisions the whole life and significance of Jesus as having begun in the very heavens. "In the beginning was the Word, and the Word was with God, and the Word was God." But here a word means "an uttered thought," spoken so men may hear and grasp. Thus for centuries God has been voicing His thought; but now, "when the fullness of time was come," God made His thought come alive in an actual man. "The Word became flesh and dwelt among us." The fourth Gospel expresses in a single sentence what might well have been said in all of the Gospels, despite the differences among them. They were written not to relate the biography of just another great man. Rather, their purpose was to bear witness that Jesus was the long-awaited Messiah. As the writer of John's Gospel said: "These are written that you may believe that Jesus is the Christ, the Son of God, and that believing you may have life in his name" (John 20:31). This is the utterance of a community remembering decisive events of a history in which they shared, interpreting what they had experienced, and speaking because they believed.

A MORE ADEQUATE UNDERSTANDING OF CHRIST

Who was Jesus Christ? What did he do and say? Can we recover the "historical Jesus?" Attempts have been made in recent years to explain just how the writers of the Synoptic Gospels drew from a common store of oral traditions which the Christian community had shaped into definite forms of preaching and teaching. This has been especially the concern of a group of New Testament scholars called the *form critics*. Form criticism states that Mark, for example, functioned as an editor who took from the oral tradition whole units of material, already shaped into definite form through years of oral repetition, and compiled them into his written Gospel. There were pronouncement stories in which Jesus uttered a climactic word in a conflict situation, teaching materials, miracle stories, legends concerning the power and spiritual stature of Jesus, and the account of Jesus' Passion. According to the form critics, then, these were the forms in which what Jesus did and said were *remembered* by the early Christian community as its members sought to meet the practical situations of their common life in the spirit of their Lord. Thus the written Gospels are the literary deposit of the cumulative experience, memory, and faith of the church, a record of decisive events of which the person of Jesus Christ is the center.

This is not the occasion for detailed, technical discussion of the issues which the form critics have raised among biblical theologians. The reader is referred to books in the field of New Testament criticism, some of which are listed in the Appendix. But for our purposes the crucial question is this: Is it possible to penetrate behind the interpretive faith of the Christian community and recover "Jesus as he actually was?" If we take the form critics seriously, it would appear that we cannot possibly reconstruct a "life of Jesus." By that we mean that no writer, even the Gospel writers, can set down Jesus' travels in day-to-day diary form, date his sayings, locate incidents with geographical accuracy. For even the order of events in Mark's Gospel is simply a reflection of his own interests and interpretation as he joined together sections of the oral tradition by artificially contrived devices (such as "that evening at sundown," "in the morning," "when he returned to Capernaum after some days," "as he was setting out on his journey," etc.). Can we recover, then, the actual "Jesus of history?"

At one stage in modern discussion, attempt was made to distinguish between the "Jesus of history" and the "Christ of faith." For there were those who wished to separate the Jesus who was ethical teacher from Christ, the divine Saviour who redeemed the whole world through His death on the cross. Here emphasis is placed on the *humanity* of Jesus. This perspective finds sympathetic response among many modern-minded folk in our own day. Here at least, many say, behind all the "mystifications" of theology, is something solid and practical for everyday living. Such a reaction against traditional Christological doctrine is understandable, since the language and concepts of the early Christian era sound strange to our modern ears. For the ancient creeds of the church make the paradoxical declaration that God and man are joined together in a unique way in Jesus, the Christ. Somehow divinity and humanity, two natures of utterly different origin and character, are contained in his person. The council at Chalcedon (A.D. 451) affirmed that Jesus Christ "is at once complete in Godhead and complete in manhood, truly God and truly man." Indeed he is "one and the same Christ, Son, Lord, Only-begotten recognized in two natures, without confusion, without change, without division, without separation . . . the characteristics of each nature preserved and coming together to form one person and subsistence."

The main trend of Christian belief has always insisted on this holding together in a single person both the divinity and humanity of Jesus, the Christ. Yet, as has been indicated, for twentieth-century men and women this fifth-century wording of the council, with its assumption of two separate worlds and two separate natures, seems to sacrifice the genuine humanity of Jesus. Hence, out of impatience with this ancient point of view, has been born in our day the "quest of the historical Jesus," to use a phrase popularized by Albert Schweitzer. This search would lead us eventually, so it is held, to a Jesus who was an actual man living in a particular place and time within a specifically conditioned cultural environment. Those who embark on this quest already have in their minds an assumption about the kind of Jesus they believe they will find. He is an altogether human Jesus. But if this is the case, how and in what sense can God disclose Himself through this Jesus in any unique way?

The form critics thus have served to show us how impossible it is to recover such a Jesus "as he actually was." For historical "facts" cannot be separated from interpretation held in faith. As John Knox in his *Christ the Lord* has written: "It was in Jesus *as known in the church* both before his death and afterwards, that the fresh activity of God among men which we afterward call the revelation in Christ first occurred."

But if we cannot penetrate behind the faith of the Church to a "Jesus as he actually was," we need not come to completely negative conclusions. In a significant passage in his *God Was in Christ,* D. M. Baillie insists that we must keep history and faith together. Yet, he says, it is absurd to say of the New Testament that it knows nothing of the human character and personality of Jesus Christ. In Baillie's words:

It seems to me that a good deal of confusion would be averted if we reminded ourselves that the phrase, "the Jesus of history," means simply and precisely: "Jesus as He really was in His life on earth," which includes of course what He did and said, what He intended and what He taught. . . . When we speak of "Jesus as He really was," we must not mean "Jesus as a figure which can be described and authenticated by a cold and detached criticism." For that would not be real history at all. I am sure that this is a fertile source of confusion in the whole matter: the habit of setting "history" and "faith" too sharply against each other. . . .[3]

Bernhard Anderson writes in evaluation of form criticism's contention that it is impossible to reach a "historical Jesus":

This does not mean that we are driven to skepticism about the historical Jesus, for we would face a similar problem in dealing with, say, Socrates, who left no writings and is known to us only by his impact on others. As a matter of fact, the fragments of the oral tradition are invaluable to us, for in many cases they give vivid glimpses of Jesus in action, small tableaux of various episodes in his ministry. Moreover within the limitations defined by the nature of the gospel tradition it is possible to reconstruct in outline the broad features of his career and the essential aspects of his message.[4]

The most meaningful way in which to catch the sweep of Jesus' career and impact on his followers, as remembered by the early Christian community, is to read in one sitting one of the Gospels, for instance, the Gospel of Mark with its blunt, straightforward language. The reader is advised to do this perhaps before reading the following brief outline of Jesus' ministry and teaching.

Jesus began his ministry of teaching and healing. He said: "The time is fulfilled, and the kingdom of God is at hand; repent, and believe in the gospel." [5] (Mark 1:15.) This is no message of doom; it is good news concerning the love of God. But what are the signs of the coming of God's kingdom, His reign of right relations among men? For God's kingdom is *already here* and yet it is *still to come*. The signs are twofold: first, Jesus astonished the people in the synagogue because he taught, not as their scribes,

[3] D. M. Baillie, *God Was in Christ*, New York, Charles Scribner's Sons, 1948, p 47.
[4] Bernhard W. Anderson, *Rediscovering the Bible*, New York, Association Press, 1951, pp. 184-185.
[5] Mark 1:15, Revised Standard Version.

but as one whose word had an authentic ring of authority. Second, he brought healing to the sick. In Jesus' time, many physical and mental disorders were believed to be caused by "evil spirits" or "demons." To drive these out meant to remove the cause of trouble. Now the Gospel affirmation is that this is God's work, the business of the Kingdom of God, a sign of the reign of God and its coming. Jesus staked his life on the conviction that God is at work in the world. They came to ask Jesus if he were the Messiah for whom they looked in expectation. He replied, in effect, that the signs were evident, not in the sudden overthrow of the world in spectacular power, but rather: "The blind receive their sight." "The lame walk." "The lepers are cleansed." "The deaf hear." "The dead are raised." These are the signs of the Reign of God—a kingdom of right relations among men and between God and men.

Luke's Gospel (4:16-30) records the story of how Jesus went to the synagogue in Nazareth, among his own people, read from the Scriptures, and gave his comment. He chose Isaiah 61:1-2:

> The Spirit of the Lord is upon me,
> Because he has
>   anointed me to preach
>   good news to the poor
> He has sent me to proclaim release to the captives,
> And recovering of sight to the blind;
> To set at liberty those who are oppressed,
> To proclaim the acceptable year of the Lord.

After closing the book, and as the eyes of all were fixed upon him, he said: "Today this scripture has been fulfilled in your hearing." [6]

[6] Luke 4:18-19, 21, R.S.V.

Chapter XIII

God in Christ

In the fifteenth year of the reign of Tiberius (A.D. 28-29), a prophet named John the Baptist suddenly appeared in the wild country east of Judea along the shores of the Dead Sea. In response to his demand for repentance and obedience to God, people streamed out to his camp meetings and asked John what they should do. He told them bluntly that they must reform and warned them that one greater than he was soon to come to institute judgment. Jesus also went out to listen to John and to be baptized. Jesus' own baptism must have meant to him a sign of his own resolve to fulfill the will of God through his own special call, for he heard a voice saying: "You are my son, my beloved. You are my chosen." After a period of solitary reflection on the problem of how he should carry out God's purpose, he gathered a group of chosen followers around him and set out on a ministry of teaching and healing.

Soon opposition on the part of the leading religious authorities grew up against Jesus; for he ate with hated tax collectors who served Roman power and associated with outcasts who did not observe the minutiae of the Law. He aroused the ire of each of the principal parties within Judaism: the Scribes and Pharisees for his disregard of the Law of Moses and their tradition of oral

179

interpretation; the Sadducees because of his threat to their vested interests in the Temple; the Zealots for his not joining in armed revolt against the political power of Rome. After a series of strategic withdrawals and returns to active work among the people, he took the offensive and started his fateful journey toward Jerusalem. Now, as he strode before his disciples, he was remote, absorbed, silent, austere in his determination to accomplish the Will of his Father.

Jesus entered the city in triumphant procession with the crowd shouting, "Hail! Hosanna!" He challenged the Sadducees for using the outer court of the Temple as a market place to sell goods for offerings by the general public. The Sadducees sought the collaboration of Rome in order to protect their Temple leadership. While the disciples fled in fear, Jesus was betrayed by Judas and led from the Garden of Gethsemane down across the brook Kidron into the sleeping city for trial. Finally he was brought to a skull-shaped hill called Golgotha and crucified like a criminal. No one party or group did Jesus to death, for both Jews and Gentiles contrived to get rid of him.

GOD ACTING IN HISTORY THROUGH CHRIST

In fulfillment of the hopes and expectations of Old Testament prophecy, so the Christian believes, Jesus came with an incisive message about God and God's realm of right relationships based on justice and love. God's Kingdom is already here and yet it is to come with a critical urgency which demands decision, repentance, and action. It is God who takes the initiative in seeking and saving those who are lost in order to bridge across all the separations between God and man. Those who would be reached by God's saving love need only to sense their own need to be forgiven. For Jesus had little patience with the respectably "good" folk of the day "who trusted in themselves that they were righteous." Men cannot solve their human dilemma of sin and separation by their own moral striving. Rather God Himself is active within human history in judgment and reconciliation to bring men into right relationship with Himself and with each other, to stir men out of complacency, and to transform. Thus, for the Christian community and as the central affirmation of its faith, Jesus' authority was that of the God whose decisive Word he had uttered and lived and to which they responded in utter commitment.[1]

But what is meant by the affirmation that "God was in Christ reconciling the world to Himself?" The creeds speak of the union in a single person of two natures, one divine and the other human. Support for this point of view usually takes the form of appeal to miracles, extraordinary powers, and supernatural signs. But the kind of historical approach we have been indicating demands a fresh understanding (1) of the miracles themselves, (2) of the doctrine of the Incarnation, and (3) of the doctrine of the Trinity. To these we now turn as the main concerns of this chapter. In the following chapter we will consider the meaning of the Atonement as the climax of God's action in history.

THE MIRACLES AS SIGNS OF GOD'S ACTION

As to the miracles, we would make it clear that, for the Christian, Jesus brought God's self-disclosure to fulfillment by what he did as much as by what he said and what he was. The general emphasis made in a previous chapter concerning the miracles of the Old Testament applies here as well. Miracles are regarded by some as superstitions of a prescientific age. This "modern" view, which

[1] For Jesus' teaching about the Law, see, for example, Matt. 5:17-18, 20; Mark 1:40-45, 10:17-20. The Sabbath: Mark 2:23-2:6; Luke 13:10-17. Divorce: Mark 10:2-12; Matt. 5:31-32; Luke 16:18. Vows: Mark 7:9-13, 3:31-35; Luke 14:25-26. Fulfilling the Law: Matt. 5:21-28, 33-37. For events in His career, see Mark 1:16-39; 2:13-14; 3:13-19; 6:7-13; 10:17-22; 32-35; 14:1-2, 10-11; 43:15-47. For examples of His parables, see Luke 15, 16; Matt. 24:43-25:46. For His conception of God, see Luke 2:49; Matt. 5:35, 18-23; Luke 16:13, 12:4-5; Matt. 4:5-7, 5:11, 43-48; Mark 2:1-12; Luke 7:36-50; Matt. 21:28-32; John 3:16, 14:9. Prayer: Mark 1:35, 6:46; Luke 3:21, 6:12, 9:28, 10:21; Matt. 9:37-38, 18:21-35. For His idea of the Kingdom of God, see Mark 1:14-15; Luke 14:25-35, 10:18, 7:11-17, 13:18-21; Matt. 8:11-12, 9:32-34, 12:43-45, 21:14.

is very much like that of the deists of the eighteenth century, is not based upon an understanding of historical study of the Scriptures but on a certain philosophical outlook, that of a naturalism which regards the methods of the sciences as the sole means of obtaining truth, and nature as the whole of reality. Referring now specifically to the problem of the miracle stories of the Gospels, we cite the judgment of Alan Richardson:

The skepticism of the modern mind concerning the Gospel miracles actually arises not from any historical understanding but from a garbled view of the "conclusions" of "science," and physical science at that. This means that for the unreflective mind of today historical questions can be answered by means of the study of physics and chemistry, since one of the conclusions established by research in those subjects is held to be that miracles do not and can not happen. A few moments' reflection, however, should suffice to show that the complicated questions of history cannot be settled in such a manner, and that whether or not the miracles of the Gospels really happened is not a question that can be even discussed with propriety from the standpoint of the physical sciences. If the Gospel miracles occurred, it is clear that they were not the result of the operation of any force which the physical sciences can measure or describe. The view that physical science can solve the problem of the miracles can be justified only by the assumption that the only forces in the universe are those which physical science can measure and describe, but that is a philosophical and not a scientific assumption.[2]

We are not dealing in the Scriptures with an exact, photographic record of all the details of past events. The form critics stress the point that the miracle story was one of the principal "forms" through which the Christian community gave voice to its messianic faith. The miracles are thus the *signs* of God's decisive work through Jesus Christ. Alan Richardson makes it clear that the earliest followers of Jesus, and those who opposed him as well, were con-

[2] Alan Richardson, *Christian Apologetics*, New York, Harper & Brothers, 1947, p. 174. See also his *The Miracle Stories of the Gospels*, New York, Harper & Brothers, 1942. For brief discussion, see Bernhard Anderson, *Rediscovering the Bible*, New York, Association Press, 1951, pp. 192 ff.; and William Manson, *Jesus, the Messiah*, Philadelphia, Westminster Press, 1946. I am indebted to these writers in the development of my own views.

vinced that he performed miracles. This is the burden of historical evidence.

There is no historical evidence to show that Jesus did not work miracles. It cannot be disputed upon historical grounds that all the people who came into contact with Jesus during His ministry in Galilee believed that He worked miracles; even His enemies believed it. If our judgment were to be decided by strictly historical considerations and nothing else, we could not avoid the conclusion that Jesus worked miracles. The evidence that Jesus worked miracles is just as strong, and is of precisely the same quality and texture, as that He taught that God is Father and that His disciples should forgive one another. We cannot on *historical grounds alone* accept the evidence for the one and reject that for the other.[3]

Just as we have pointed out in the case of Old Testament episodes, it is not necessary to accept literally the actual occurrence of each and every incident. Even if it were possible to decide whether or not a certain given incident took place, this evidence would be quite beside the point. It is upon *meaning* that the early Christians placed their emphasis from the very first. Theirs was the conviction that Jesus' miracles were signs of God's power among men. For it was through these signs that men of faith found themselves gripped by the saving love of God, who even now moved among them to conquer all demonic powers of evil.

Jesus clearly did not perform these deeds to prove his divine origin and status. The larger crowds apparently did not see or understand what any given miracle signified. Their basic faith was untouched. Even today, as for the earliest Christians, we cannot prove that Jesus was divine by citing the occurrence of miracles. It is quite the other way around. Those who look through the eyes of prior faith and commitment of the total self are the ones who see these occurrences as signs of the present power of God's Kingdom in their midst.

Professor Anderson underscores this emphasis when he states that the real miracle perceived by early followers of Jesus was the power

[3] Richardson, *Christian Apologetics*, p. 170.

of God's redemptive rule, the renewing and recreative power of his forgiveness manifested in the deeds of the Messiah. Each story was intended not as a proof compelling unwilling belief, but as a vehicle for communicating the discerned meaning of Jesus' actions. Jesus' exorcisms of demons was a sign of God's triumph over the forces of evil. His healings were not so much bodily cures as evidences of God's saving power. The resurrection of Lazarus from the dead was a sign of God's victory over death—not just the death of the body, but the more terrible spiritual death which may beset the living. Jesus' walking on water or his calming of the tempest signified that the Lord of history was also Lord over nature, even as we sing in the words of the Crusaders' Hymn: "Fairest Lord Jesus, Ruler of all nature . . ." Underlying all these miracle stories—the original nucleus as well as the expanded material— was the faith that "God was in Christ reconciling the world to himself." [4]

On one occasion (Mark 2:1-12), Jesus was preaching in a house so crowded that no more people could squeeze in. Four men carried a paralytic on a pallet and let him down through the roof. When Jesus saw their confident faith, he said simply to the paralytic: "My son, your sins are forgiven." The reaction this statement occasioned among the ecclesiastical authorities present is significant. Here is the strongest reason for Jesus' death: this claim in his own person that he was doing the very work of God Himself, particularly exercising the power to forgive sins. To those who were to bear part of the responsibility for bringing Jesus to the cross, this sort of claim was sheer blasphemy. But to those who believed, it was a sign of the love and just reign of God breaking into their midst. For Jesus said to the skeptics,

"Why do you question thus in your hearts? Which is easier to say to the paralytic, 'Your sins are forgiven,' or to say, 'Rise, take up your pallet and walk?' But that you may know that the Son of man has authority on earth to forgive sins"—he said to the paralytic—"I say to you, rise, take up your pallet and go home." And he rose, and immediately took up the pallet and went out before them all; so that all were amazed and glorified God, saying, "We never saw anything like this!" [5]

[4] Anderson, *op. cit.*, p. 197.
[5] Mark 2:8-12, Revised Standard Version.

God in Christ

THE DOCTRINE OF THE INCARNATION

What is meant by the belief that *Jesus Christ is both divine and human?* What is the significance of that belief known as the doctrine of the Incarnation? Two affirmations find their rootage in the message of the New Testament: (1) Jesus himself lived and died as an actual, historical person who brought to climax a whole series of events which have their beginning in Old Testament times; and (2) through Jesus as the center of this new event or series of events, God acts to confront men with His power, truth, and love. The world of nature and of human history reveals a great deal of the character and very being of God. But it is the Christian faith that He is disclosed most completely in and through the life, personality, teaching, deeds, death, resurrection, and continuing presence of Jesus Christ.

Often thoughtful people have difficulty grasping this abstract theological language and say: "I believe in God because there must be a Supreme Intelligence behind the order of the universe. But why did He not make Himself known more plainly? What evidence is there for His genuine concern for the world? Look at the hatred loose among men and naked power conquering goodness! And I also believe in Jesus," some go on to say. "He was a good man. He taught great and noble ideals. But what connection does he have with God? And, after all these centuries, what connection can he possibly have with me?"

The Christian affirmation in the face of questions such as these is straightforward. It says in effect: "You may not know all about the mysteries of the universe and of human existence. You may not grasp the fine distinctions of logic-chopping philosophers or shadings of doctrine contrived by theologians. You may not know all about God. You may not know about the future or the outcome of the pressing issues of good and evil in our time. But one thing you can do: you can let a power and a presence come alive within you. These are not your own invention. They come from beyond

185

you. But they move inside you and become through you a way of life: dynamic, contagious, creative enough to change a world."

What we are saying here is that in order to understand the crucial Christian belief that "God was in Christ," men and women must attempt to translate the formal into the personal. The link between the human and the divine, for which folk seek, is a matter of face-to-face encounter and response. Behind persons through the ages in whom this has taken place stands, so the Christian believes, the dynamic power of the *Person.* When that power comes alive in men and women in our age also, that is to know all they need to know of the Eternal God. This at any rate is the central affirmation of the Christian faith. In the words of Paul's Letter to the Colossians: "Now Christ is the visible expression of the invisible God. . . . It was through him that everything was made. . . . And now he is the head of the body which is composed of all Christian people. . . . It was in him that the full nature of God chose to live, and through him God planned to reconcile in his own person . . . everything on earth and everything in heaven by virtue of the sacrifice of his cross. . . . And you yourselves he has now reconciled. . . . This reconciliation assumes, of course, that you maintain a firm position in the faith. . . ." [6]

This affirmation, within the context of a continuing historic tradition, is thus more than intellectual assent. It involves commitment of the whole person in action based on insight. For the Christian believes himself, even today, to be an organic part of a continuing event, as God's power comes alive in persons through the person, Christ. If this is to know God, then consequences follow from this kind of knowledge. For some it begins with the insistent pressure of obligation to live in a distinctive way, to seek new directions for conduct, to feel more sensitively the needs of other people, to speak in different accents, to act in more constructive patterns of creative good will.

[6] J. B. Phillips, *Letters to the Young Churches,* New York, The Macmillan Company, 1948. Used by permission.

God in Christ

"But how do these things happen within men and women?" some ask in our day. "Just keep on trying," others would answer. "Try to be better." It is, however, the normative Christian conviction that trying to be good is like trying to lift ourselves by our own bootstraps. Many of us keep straining and tugging in energetic moral endeavor at our weighted-down selves. And the very trying itself becomes an added burden instead of an added power. Imaginatively the suggestion then occurs to the genuine seeker: "Supposing there *were* such a power and resource available for everyday living?" Then, as someone puts it, men and women like ourselves would not have to keep on carrying "the thing that ought to be carrying us." For what is needed, in answer to man's deeply personal, existential predicament, is not more and more attempts at dealing with the self, but resources from beyond the self. This same writer adds that the only kind of burden that will do for dynamic living is the kind of burden that sails are to a ship or that wings are to a bird. The Christian holds that what we humans need is not simply a sense of obligation, but rather a power that enables us to fulfill our obligations and leaves us with enough energy besides to be quiet, poised, and radiant. He then poses the searching, practical question: "Suppose folk in our day were able to find and appropriate that kind of power by living in the presence of a great personality who had faced everything that any human being has ever had to face and still had come out on top?" It is in effect the Christian's affirmation by way of response to his own question: "If a man found this, then he would move into the orbit of a deep contagion that kept gripping him more and more, leading him on by sheer attractiveness and quiet persuasiveness. He would then be living beyond himself, able to do what mere effort of his own could never make him do, just because he wanted to follow a new way of life more than anything else in the world." The Christian believes that there is such a great personality and that his influence is still alive through the continuing historical tradition of the Christian community. His name

187

is Jesus Christ. To find this power, affirmation, and faith so that it comes alive in ourselves also is to know all there is to know in answer to man's personal dilemma of separation and disruption. This is not abstract, hearsay knowledge about God but immediacy of encounter between a whole human self and God's. "Thou art the Christ, the Son of the Living God."

This historical-personal approach demands a new way of stating the doctrinal problem of Christ's divinity, or the *Incarnation*. The traditional creeds speak of the union in a single person of two natures, one divine and the other human, supported by appeal to miracles and extraordinary events. But a shift of perspective has taken place which Daniel Day Williams summarizes in the following way:

> It is not two "natures" which have to be related, but two "histories." There is the history of our human existence with its fate, its freedom, and its course of events. In this history stands the real person, Jesus of Nazareth, who is just as truly "historical" as any other. There is also the history of God's creative and redemptive dealing with men which has come to its climax in the history of Jesus. It is these two histories which we have to relate to each other. When we look for God's redemptive action it is not supernatural existence but personal meaning which concerns us. The emphasis on miracle gives way to that of personal faith. To use Richard Niebuhr's terms in *The Meaning of Revelation,* in Jesus Christ outer and objective history has come together with inner and personal history which is known by faith. It may well be that this shift in the terms of the Christological problem is more important for theology today than any of the particular solutions which have yet been put forth.[7]

Williams further reminds us that this perspective which puts emphasis on the historical and response of personal faith also has its difficulties. Just as the traditional views have trouble relating "two natures," this more recent view finds it difficult to relate "two histories." The older tradition seems to assert that Jesus Christ

[7] Daniel Day Williams, *What Present-Day Theologians Are Thinking*, New York, Harper & Brothers, 1952, pp. 102-103.

possessed a human nature, but that he was not quite actually human as you and I are. The newer doctrine appears to be saying that Jesus of Nazareth was really a historical person, but, because it is so difficult or impossible to recover "Jesus as he actually was," his "history and personality do not matter in the revelation of the word of God."

There are no easy, pat solutions to these problems. But gains are being made in contemporary theological thought at this point of greatest difficulty. Assertions of Christ's decisive disclosure of God are affirmations of the faith of the Christian community. But this is faith concerning real historical events of which the person of Jesus is the center; for he is an actual, finite human being who grew to maturity within a given cultural environment. Shall we regard his humanity as an embarrassment to the faith that claims his divinity?

In Williams' words:

Suppose now that rather than regard this finite element as an embarrassment to the Christian claim that God has spoken his decisive word in Christ we see it *as intrinsic to the revelation itself*. Could we say that the Christian faith claims final revelation in Christ just because it gives us the picture of a finite person who acknowledges his own limitation, and points beyond itself to God's truth which no finite structure can fully express? If this thesis can be cogently worked out, the reversal it brings to much traditional Christology is startling. We would now rest the case for the ultimately decisive character of the revelation in Christ, not upon miraculous signs that the limitations of existence have been set aside, but upon the discovery that there is a witness to God which comes through those limitations. We still have to say why it is that the revelation is given through Jesus. Not every finite person, but this One becomes an adequate vehicle for the revelation. But we are saying now that it is the very humility of Jesus and his trusting acceptance of the risks and uncertainties of our human lot that we find not a barrier to God's word, but the very means for the communication of that Word.[8]

[8] *Ibid.*, p. 108.

This point of view concerning Jesus' true humanity as the very medium of God's self-disclosure in history is not actually new. Contemporary historical understanding has helped us recover the central emphasis of the Bible itself. Here the Christian experiences a God who willingly becomes a human being with all the limitations and struggles which living within history involves. This is the meaning of the words quoted above: "the very humility of Jesus and his trusting acceptance of the risks and uncertainties of our human lot." His is apprehended as a love which saves men because it bears with them as they actually are in all their brokenness and bewilderment, as well as hope and joy. The series of events through which this redemptive love takes place in one sense has never ceased. It is still going on. As we have indicated, the Christian believes he himself even today has become a part of these events as they move on down into the tomorrows. He participates in them through his own human decision, commitment, and faith.

THE DOCTRINE OF THE TRINITY

Many men and women in our day have difficulty grasping the significance of the Trinity. In making the claim that Jesus Christ is fully divine and fully human, Christians do not give up their belief in *one* God. For it is "God in Christ" which becomes the supreme object of devotion and enabling power for the man of Christian faith. If this is understood, then we have the significant clue to the meaning of the doctrine of the Trinity: one God as Father, as Son, and as Holy Spirit. The word "Trinity" itself does not occur in the New Testament, although several passages form the background for later formulation of the doctrine (for example, Acts 2:33; II Corinthians 13:14; Ephesians 4:4-6). Those who formulated the creeds used the language of Greek philosophy. But they attempted to express this inexpressible Christian paradox concerning Jesus Christ the God-man: a completely human person in whom God moved and acted for man's salvation.

D. M. Baillie, in his *God Was in Christ,* points up the meaning

190

of the Trinity in a clear and interesting way. He pictures putting to a mixed group of theologians the question as to what distinctively new conception of God came into the world with the Christian movement. Two apparently different methods of answering would result. Some would elicit their answer from the Synoptic Gospels, citing especially Jesus' own distinctive teaching about God as compared with Old Testament prophets and wise men. Then they would add to this the development of this teaching in the rest of the New Testament and the kind of God in which such men as St. Paul and St. John believed. As a result there would "emerge an account of the 'character' of God as holy and loving beyond measure, taking the initiative in seeking men before they seek Him, infinitely merciful and redemptive." But others would take what appears to be an entirely different line. Their answer, writes Baillie, would be: " 'The new and distinctively Christian conception of God is the Trinitarian conception, Father, Son and Holy Spirit in one God.' " He concludes with a question about these two different approaches as to which is "the true answer." Baillie replies: "What I am suggesting is that the two are not really divergent but convergent and ultimately identical. The first needs to be crystallized into the second, and the second needs to absorb the first."

To understand this statement we need to recover in imagination the experience of the early Christian community. Baillie does so in terms of what he calls "the paradox of grace, expressed in the confession: 'I . . . yet not I, but the grace of God.' " The paradox under which the Christian of any age stands is that he ascribes any good in himself to the power and love of God from beyond himself, yet without implying any destruction of his freedom as a human personality. This is another way of stating what we have been saying in this chapter about a power and a presence that may come alive in persons through the person, Christ; for this is to know God in a way that has consequences for all of human existence. As Baillie expresses it:

. . . our actions are never more truly free and personal and human, they are never more truly our own, than when they are wrought in us by God. But the whole experience of this paradox, which covers only those fragments of our lives in which there is something good, has come into our lives through One in whom it covered the whole of His life, so that His life was the very life of God Himself, and yet was at the same time in the fullest sense the life of man. Jesus Christ is the One in whom human selfhood was wholly yielded to God, so that His whole life was the life of God. That was the one life which was wholly divine and wholly human. He lived His life in such a way that it was the life of God incarnate; but also, since the initiative is always with God, He lived it as He did *because* it was the life of God incarnate. And thus through Him there came to those who knew Him a new revelation of God.[9]

But, as Baillie further indicates, it is the Christian conviction that what took place through Jesus Christ did not cease when his earthly existence came to an end. The disciples, who at first thought He had been taken from them, soon made

two great discoveries. They discovered, first, that the divine Presence of which they had become aware while their master was with them in the flesh had come back to them, and was going to continue, in a far deeper and more marvelous way . . . now they know God for themselves and He has taken possession of them. And their second discovery was that this experience, which depended entirely on Jesus, need not be confined to those who had known Jesus in the flesh. It could come to anybody anywhere through the story of Jesus and their witness to its meaning. They went hither and thither and told the story; and the thing kept happening. It was a new experience of God, and it lifted people out of themselves, and above the moral struggle, into a spontaneous goodness which claimed no credit for itself but gave all the glory to God. This was something new in mankind's knowledge of God. It could not have come if Jesus had not lived. It all depended on Him. And yet it was different from the experience of knowing Jesus in the flesh—not less, but greater, deeper, more universal, more transforming. It was a further stage, which could not have come while Jesus was present in the flesh; so that it was actually

[9] D. M. Baillie, *God Was in Christ*, New York, Charles Scribner's Sons, 1948, p. 145.

"expedient" for His followers that His earthly life should end, in order that this might come.[10]

What was this that came to them and had to come in a new way because Jesus was no longer with them in person? They recalled, out of their Jewish tradition, prophecies of a coming age in which God would give His Spirit to ordinary folk. And they remembered Jesus' own promises that God would send His Spirit to help them in time of need. Once more Baillie writes imaginatively of what the early Christians must have said to themselves concerning *this* that was foretold by prophets and promised by Jesus:

This is the Holy Spirit, giving back to us for ever all that we thought we should lose, and much more; reminding us of all that Jesus taught us, helping us to understand it better, carrying us farther still, teaching us new truth, giving us the presence of Christ in a new and greater way, to dwell in our hearts and to do in us and for us what we could not do ourselves. Thus they could say, thenceforth, concerning any good that was in their lives: Not I, but the grace of God that was with me. Not I, but Christ that dwelleth in me. It is not we that speak, but the Spirit of our Father that speaketh in us.[11]

God the Father, God the Son, and God the Holy Spirit, three in one, is the Trinitarian affirmation stating this basic experience of Christian faith. Many controversies have been waged through the centuries over its meaning. Some think that it makes the one God into three gods in a kind of polytheism. Others object that it is too narrow a conception or a mathematical number trick that is rationally absurd. But each of these three "parts" does not purport to explain the *whole* nature of God. If this were the case, then Christianity would hold to three distinct and complete Gods. Neither are these three successive parts played by God, or three successive aspects of His being, or three separable functions. The full meaning of the Trinity seems impossible to summarize in a

[10] *Ibid.*, pp. 145-146.
[11] *Ibid.*, p. 146.

single rational formula. Nor does it make sense unless we keep in mind the historical situation and personal experiences out of which it sprang and then relate it to the demands and empowering grace of the Eternal God in and through Christians of every age. It is the same God in three of His many aspects, so the Christian believes, who discloses Himself as Creator-Father, as the Son, Christ the God-man, and as continuing presence through His Holy Spirit.

Once again it thus becomes essential to stress *the primacy of faith over reason.* Men and women in our own day cannot grasp the decisive significance of Jesus simply by objectively examining the historical evidence about his life and career within the social setting of the first century, or by turning doctrinal theories over and over. Rather, it is in an affirmation of faith that the Christian sees the Christ as the center of God's revealing event. But then he also claims that in the light of this climactic event all human existence is illuminated. It reveals the meaning of the believer's own life as creature and child of God, yet one who rebels and defaces God's image within him in assertion of his self-love and pride. But through Christ the Christian also believes that he is forgiven, restored, and reconciled with God, with himself, and with his neighbor in new life of responsibility and service. This reconciliation comes to climax, God's supreme act of love for mankind, through the Crucifixion-Resurrection events: Christ's cross, resurrection, and continuing presence to empower the Christian community.

Chapter XIV

Reconciliation Through the Cross

Several years ago we visited the University of the South in Sewanee, Tennessee. This place of picturesque beauty is located atop a high plateau, and on either side is a sharp drop to the flat country below. One scene is unforgettable. We entered a narrow, shaded lane with tall trees forming a continuous arch of green as far as the eye could see. As we rode through this leafy tunnel, we saw ahead, outlined against the blue sky at the far end, the huge figure of a cross. Finally we stood beneath it; and beyond was nothing, just a sheer drop-off into empty space. We could go no farther. At the end of the road stood a cross.

There is another road that began among the towns and villages of Galilee. It led toward Jerusalem, triumphal entry, an upper room, a garden of decisive struggle, betrayal, and arrest. This road which Jesus traveled brought him to the crowded court of a Roman governor and then wound its slow, tortuous way to a skull-shaped hill. For at the end of this road also stood a Cross.

This original Cross was no smooth object of metal or stone intended merely as a symbol of worship. It was a cruel, ugly thing which criminals were forced to carry on their sweating backs to the assigned place of execution. By the side of the road, on the day of Jesus' Passion, crowds of people stood watching the procession go toiling its way to death. Yet, amid the bustle of the city engaged in preparation for the feast of the Passover, most were probably unconcerned. It was hardly any business of theirs that another disturber of the peace was carrying a cross up the hill to Golgotha. Yet perhaps some remembered the man from Galilee for whom the crowds had cheered, just a few days before, "Hosanna in the Highest!" But now it did not seem to matter. "He's no Messiah. Crucify him!"

By this time Judas, who had betrayed his Master into the hands of the religious authorities with a kiss, had thrown down his bribe money and killed himself. The other disciples had fled in fear, even Peter who had lingered long enough during the trial to deny that he even knew his Lord. Now all that apparently remained of a former hope was a poor, beaten man trudging toward the Place of the Skull to be crucified between two thieves.

The strange paradox for Christian faith is that a Cross which stood at the end of the road was also a *beginning*. It is the Christian faith that, through this climactic event of the crucifixion of Jesus, the Christ, God acted to reconcile a whole world of men with Himself. In this chapter it is our purpose (1) to speak in this historical setting of the Cross as standing "at the end of the road" for man, for Christ, and for God. (2) We must discuss traditional theories of the Atonement which theologians through the centuries have used to explain the significance of the Cross. (3) We shall attempt to suggest some ways of translating these theories into terms which have meaning for the existential situation in which man stands today. The language we use may have value for the reader only as it stimulates him to express meanings for himself. It is important to remember as we approach this task that we are face to face with a mystery which we can only partially understand. Yet we stand under the constraint of a job which must be accomplished if we are to make clear to ourselves this basic Christian belief. It is that of using religious language to set forth a faith that has made a profound difference in the midst of society for nearly 2000 years. Necessarily, we must employ the figures and symbols of imagic utterance to express as clearly as we can the ultimate meaning of an act of God in human history that quite is beyond us. For in the Cross, even here, "God was in Christ reconciling the world unto Himself."

THE CROSS FOR MAN, CHRIST, AND GOD

The Cross as an act in history stands "at the end of the road" for man, for Jesus Christ, and for God. At the outset, then, according to Christian faith, in that event so long ago all the evil ever conceived by man was drawn into sharp focus. Jesus met his death on that day because there were men exactly like ourselves expressing what they deemed right at the time. Self-righteousness drove Him to the Cross. Ambition, untempered by sober judgment, put Jesus to death, as well as greed, jealousy, desire for power, fear, disillusionment, and indifference. This listing of human sins is not intended as an exclusive indictment of any group or groups of men. For the words of the Negro spiritual stand as insistent reminder that in a sense *all* men of every age must assume due share of responsibility for those grim events. Human evil and degradation had gone as far as it could go when Jesus died.

> Were you there when they crucified my Lord? . . .
> O, sometimes it causes me to tremble, tremble,
>   tremble.
> Were you there when they crucified my Lord?

What this facet of the Christian faith is attempting to state is that, given man's sin, the Cross is necessary to the fulfillment of God's redemptive purpose in history. For the early Christians, the Cross did not signify the death of just another martyr. Rather, it was conceived somehow as that decisive point at which God invaded the circle of man's self-centered life to do something which man could never do for himself. God took the initiative and in

197

His love and justice sought to break down the tragic separation of man from Himself. It is man's estrangement from God and from himself which makes reconciliation or atonement necessary. This solution to man's basic dilemmas presupposes, therefore, the analysis we followed in Chapter V, "Man and His Self." According to Christian perspective, we stated there, man's central predicament is *separation, in his total person,* from God. This separation man has brought upon himself because of his pride and arrogance; he makes all sorts of futile attempts to solve this predicament even to the extent of putting himself in the place of God as his own center of meaning and significance. From these attempts there develop tension, conflict, anxiety, longing, even for the God man would deny as inaccessible or unnecessary. But the solution, so the Christian believes, lies in an ultimate reconciliation between God and man who is created in God's own image, an image lost for a while, and defaced, but never completely destroyed. This takes place as one is found of and by the creatively loving God as disclosed through Jesus Christ who gave his life on the Cross. Thus the Cross in the Christian tradition always is focused upon forgiveness of the sin of man.

But in a far different sense the Cross stands "at the end of the road" for Jesus Christ. He was not tricked into ignominious death. He faced it and deliberately chose his course from the very beginning. Jesus recognized the necessity of sacrificial death if his God-given purpose were to be accomplished. "Verily, verily I say unto you, except a grain of wheat fall into the ground and die, it abideth alone; but if it die, it bringeth forth much fruit" (John 12:24). "Behold, we go to Jerusalem," he told his disciples, "and the son of man shall be delivered unto the chief priests and the scribes; and they shall condemn him to death, and shall deliver him unto the Gentiles, and they shall mock him, and shall spit upon him, and shall kill him, and after three days he shall rise again" (Matt. 20:18-19).

Bernhard Anderson holds that a critical study of the Gospel

materials leads to the plausible conclusion that this early interpretive faith centered in the Passion "was no afterthought." Rather he agrees with William Manson in the view that Jesus himself conceived his role as that of the Suffering Servant sent by God to bring about, through his vicarious death, a New Covenant between God and man.[1]

Throughout the Gospels of Mark and Luke there occur passages telling how Jesus himself said: "The Son of Man [the Christ] must suffer many things." Several of these passages include specific details concerning the actual events of that final week of Jesus' ministry which had not yet occurred, such as those just quoted: how He would be rejected by the elders and chief priests and scribes, condemned, mocked, scourged, and killed. It is clear that the Gospel writers themselves must have projected back into this earlier period their knowledge as to how the story actually ended. But, as Manson indicates, it is not historically impossible for Jesus himself to have said these things about his own sacrificial death. And there is every positive indication, by the words He uttered, the deeds He performed, and the signs and tokens He employed, that He did think of himself from the very beginning of his career as the one who should suffer vicariously for the salvation of God's people.

The impetuous Peter challenged his Master for teaching that "the Son of Man must suffer many things"; for Jewish traditions held that it was not in suffering but in triumph that the Messiah would come. Jesus turned on Peter with the words: "Get behind me, Satan! For you are not on the side of God, but of men." [2]

Again the Lord's Supper, or Communion, embodies a tradition which goes back to the events of Jesus' final night before his death as he gathered his disciples around him for a farewell meal

[1] See Bernhard Anderson, *Rediscovering the Bible*, New York, Association Press, 1951, pp. 199-203; and William Manson, *Jesus, the Messiah*, Philadelphia, Westminster Press, 1946, Chap. VII.

[2] Mark 8:31-33, Revised Standard Version.

in observance of the Jewish Passover Feast. Jesus himself, by word and act, transformed the significance of ordinary unleavened bread and a cup of wine. He took bread, gave thanks, broke it, and gave the broken pieces to his disciples saying, "This is my body." And likewise He gave them the cup with the words, "This cup is the new covenant in my blood." Thus it is evident that Jesus, through these symbolic words and acts, linked his own sacrifice to that of the Suffering Servant whom God would send to give himself on behalf of men. And thereby would be effected a new covenant between God and men based on love and forgiveness. It is strange and mysterious, and yet this is what the Christian believes, that through the God-man suffering on the Cross, God discloses Himself most significantly as love and justice. "Even while we were yet sinners, Christ died for us."

But there is another road. This is the road of God Himself, and there also stands a Cross. Here again is an entirely different view of this cosmic event of the crucifixion: different from man's and different from Jesus Christ's. In the classic book about boyhood, *Bevis,* by Richard Jeffries, there appear these words: "The crucifixion hurt his feelings very much: the cruel nails, the unfeeling spear: he looked at the picture a long time, and then turned over the page saying, 'If God had been there, He would not have let them do it.'"[3]

It is the Christian conviction that God *was* there. In and through that same event which brought human evil to its sharpest focus and where Jesus Christ willingly laid down his life, there also was disclosed the power and love of God. All these roads meet at Golgotha: man's sin, Jesus Christ's utter devotion, and God's love. In effect, evil was drawn to the Cross so that something decisive could be done about it. Christ was there as mediator between God and man to take it upon Himself. The all-powerful love of God was there to do the doing. The Cross is cosmic. It is the mightiest

[3] Quoted in J. S. Whale, *The Christian Answer to the Problem of Evil,* New York, Abingdon-Cokesbury Press, 1936, p. 66.

of the mighty acts of God. J. S. Whale writes of the Christian affirmation that the Cross is the ultimate fact in human history: ". . . beyond it there is and can be nothing. God Himself can do nothing more; greater love is impossible; the uttermost even of the infinite grace of God is there. The cross is not only a scandalous fact of history; it is the triumphant act of God." [4]

George Buttrick in his *Jesus Came Preaching* reminds us that there is a famous painting which tries to depict this insight concerning God's own involvement of love in and through the Cross. It shows, behind the figure of Jesus on the Cross, another figure, shadowy and vast. The nail that pierces the hand of Jesus goes through to the hand of God. Also, the spear that was thrust into His side is thrust into God's side. Men and women say sometimes, "If God were only good, the sin of the earth would break his heart." Using the imaginative language of religious utterance, the Christian is the man who points to the Cross and replies, "See, there, God's own breaking heart." "But if God were really good," comes the retort, "He would at least share the pains of the world with us." Christian affirmation then turns to that strange God-man on the Cross and says, "See, there, God Himself, sharing man's pains." Again some would state, "If God were so good, then He would assume the burden of our weaknesses and sin." The Christian faith replies, "Behold Him bearing man's sins." The words may vary from age to age and person to person, but we are bound to use what analogies and figures of speech we can muster to express the inexpressible. It is the ultimate Christian belief that God is in Jesus Christ—in his life, in his death—beckoning, wooing the human race in love to Himself.

How can God Himself suffer? For we have said, concerning the Incarnation, that Jesus' very humanity, with its struggles and limitations, is the medium of God's self-disclosure. And now *suffering* of the most terrible kind seems to become the strategic point at

[4] *Ibid.*, p. 69.

which God makes Himself known most significantly. Daniel Day Williams leads us to an insight as he writes:

We miss what is involved in the question about God's suffering if we think primarily of physical pain, mental torment, or death. These are forms of human suffering, to be sure. In Christ God has in some way experienced them. But "suffering" has a broader meaning. It signifies to undergo, to be acted upon, to live in a give and take with others. To say that God suffers means that he is actively engaged in dealing with a history which is real to him. What happens makes a difference to him. He wins an actual victory over the world through a love which endures and forgives. It means that the world's sorrow and agony are real for God, indeed in one way more real to him than to us, for only an infinite love can enter completely into sympathetic union with all life.[5]

This insight that God Himself suffered in the very act of giving Himself in love on the Cross involves the meaning of the Atonement, which we shall discuss below. For now, it is sufficient to say that theologians by no means agree that God suffered. But those who say God did not suffer support their view by the claim that it was just the human nature of Christ, and not his divine nature, that underwent agony and deep involvement in the struggles of men on the Cross. However, as has been indicated in discussion of the Incarnation, thought concerning Christ now tends away from speaking of his natures. It is rather two *histories* with which we are concerned—as much in the events of the crucifixion as anywhere else in Jesus' life and career. Here on a skull-shaped hill two histories cross: man's history and God's. At least this seems to be the very center of the faith of the early Church. The form critics indicate that the story of the Passion clearly took on definite, permanent form earlier than any others during the period of the oral formulation of the Gospel. Indeed, this was the burden of the early Christian message: God's power and love made manifest to redeem and forgive man's sin through the suffering, death, and

[5] Daniel Day Williams, *What Present-Day Theologians Are Thinking*, New York, Harper & Brothers, 1952, p. 113.

resurrection of Jesus Christ. These three meet dramatically at the Cross: man, Jesus Christ, and God.

THEORIES OF THE ATONEMENT

How have Christian scholars tried to capture this mystery in rational terms? Traditional theology through the centuries has attempted to interpret this central affirmation through the formal doctrinal statements of the *Atonement*. We cite here four major interpretations which are persistent in the thought of various branches of the Christian Church. Throughout all of these theories runs a common theme: the attempt to describe in theological words how God took the initiative and sought to overcome man's estrangement. This therefore is Atonement between God and man established in and through love. Each of the theories is rooted in the experiential faith of the Christian community. Each then uses an analogy or set of analogies from a given context of practical life to illuminate this unique relationship between God and man.

The first major interpretation turns to the court of law for its significant clue and is called the *legalistic, judicial,* or *Latin* theory of the Atonement. This view of the meaning of the Cross was advocated strongly by Anselm, who insisted that man by his sin has incurred a debt to God that is so great that no mere man could ever repay it. But Jesus Christ, by his death, earned an excess of merit. By offering his life, Christ made payment to God as satisfaction or compensation for the sin of man. What man cannot therefore do for himself God must do. Thus God became a man in Jesus Christ, through whose death God's own justice is satisfied.

The second theory is similar to the Latin view and is called the *sacrificial* theory of Christ's death on the Cross. As enunciated in the Epistle to the Hebrews, this perspective also presupposes that man cannot release himself from his own evil ways, but that still God's demand for justice must be satisfied. In this theory, it is God's wrath that has to be appeased and Jesus becomes a vicarious sacrifice offered as propitiation for man's sin. When this is done,

God's anger is assuaged, justice is established, and God's love is disclosed once more to mankind.

The third view of the Atonement, variously called the *subjective* or *moral* theory, was developed by Abelard in the early twelfth century and such men as Schleiermacher, Ritschl, and Rashdall in the nineteenth century. It centers not on the sheer justice or the wrath but on the gracious concern of God, who "commendeth His love unto us in that, while we were yet sinners, Christ died for us." No compensation or vicarious sacrifice is required. Rather Christ, by his perfect devotion to God's purpose, has revealed his Father's love in such great measure that men's hearts are stirred to follow his example. When we look at the Cross and meditate on the meaning of Christ's heroic deed, we too are moved to make our sacrifices and to follow the way of love to ever new moral achievements.

The fourth perspective on the significance of the crucifixion is called the *classical* or *dramatic* theory of the Atonement and is represented by such men as Paul, Irenaeus, and Luther. Here the clue is found in the empowering love in Christ through which God fought evil to the death and has broken its power over every man. Sometimes stress is placed on a picture of mankind in the clutches of the devil until God through Christ's death paid the ransom which secured our release. "For the Son of man also came not to be ministered unto, but to minister, and to give his life a ransom for many" (Mark 10:45). Paul said, "Ye were bought with a price" (I Corinthians 6:20, 7:23). However, this ransom notion, with its mechanical artificiality, belies the genuine intent of this general view. If we take the words of Jesus and Paul seriously, what emerges here is the concept of God's conquering power and love which do not so much appease as vanquish the forces of evil. This can never mean that *actual* evils of everyday existence somehow magically vanish. Rather, it is an expression of confidence that we live in a fundamentally moral universe; that evil is overcome in principle through a love that triumphs over even the worst of cruelty and ignominy that men can contrive. In the end, it is not the flame and sword of the militant hero that win out, the advocates of this view are saying, but the servant who gives his very life in sacrificial ministry. God does not force men into conformity to goodness. Rather, He demonstrates His power over all of human existence by evoking the free and willing response of men to a love that is contagious and all-consuming. When this occurs, God and man are reconciled; there is *at-one-ment*.

TRANSLATION OF THEORIES FOR TODAY

We now move to the third concern of this chapter, that of trying to suggest ways of translating these theories into terms which have meaning for man's situation today. It is evident that each of these interpretations of the crucifixion grows out of the cultural context of particular times and places. All address themselves to the question: Why did God act decisively in human history through this series of events centered in the life, death, and continuing presence of Jesus Christ?

At the center of each of these theories is the attempt to answer this basic question in terms of God's all-embracing love for man. But each of them in turn focuses attention on other more specific types of questions. One employs legal language to tackle the problem of reconciliation between a just God and sinful man. Anselm, stanch advocate of this view, insisted on the primacy of the law of justice over all other moral principles, even that of divine forgiveness. But this exclusive emphasis on God as the coldly impersonal judge whose claims to divine justice must be satisfied is artificial and unconvincing to our modern minds. Here, as Canon O. C. Quick points out in his *Doctrines of the Creeds,* there is confusion between two different conceptions of Christ's death: suffering a legal penalty *instead of us* as against suffering a voluntary sacrifice *on our behalf.* Moreover, in this legal theory, stress is placed not so much on reconciliation into togetherness as simply upon redress or making up for errors and detailed sins. In this view, God seems to be pictured as a coldly impersonal king or judge. Yet one can sympathize with the early Christians who tried to explain the significance of the Atonement to Romans steeped in concern for law or to legalistic followers of the Hebraic tradition.

The point is that if we abstract any of these interpretations of the Atonement from the original cultural context and insist on rendering religious language into literal descriptions that have authority for all times, then we destroy their significance and twist and distort them until they become meaningless. But if we move imaginatively with each of these clues or analogies, trying to understand them, letting go some elements and retaining others, we will be led into significant insights. Of course, reconciliation between God and man cannot be achieved by a money transaction or doled out by an arbitrary and vengeful king, or somehow magically attained by offering in sacrifice a "scapegoat." Neither will the too simple rendering of the moral-influence theory do; men and women *are* inspired by Christ's heroic sacrifice into following the way of creative good will. But, as we indicated in a previous chapter, trying to be like *Jesus* is not sufficient motivation in itself. This places a burden of effort on men and women themselves that often ends in disillusionment and self-defeat. If Jesus were only a heroic man and a noble example to our moral striving, then a man like Socrates would serve as well for inspiration.

For the Christian, the doctrine of the Atonement is organically bound up with his belief in the Incarnation. It is the God-man who suffered and died sacrificially on the Cross for the sake of man, to restore and reconcile. Every theory must somehow point beyond its own abstractions to this event in which God's history crosses man's in power and love to effect a creative togetherness. It is in the midst of this consummate self-disclosure that encounter and response between God and man plumb to the very roots of man's being. Here the most radical decision of acceptance or rejection is required on his part. As God gave Himself to the uttermost in this mightiest of His mighty acts, so man also may discover new freedom day by day. "He that loseth his life . . . shall find it" (Matt. 10:39). This is the Christian faith and way.

We, with our rational minds, do not know why forgiviness and reconciliation should always come at such cost. But we catch a glimpse of this law of divine economy if we look searchingly at the course of history and our own personal experience. Some years ago Dr. George Buttrick spoke of this in an unforgettable way in his contribution to the Yale Lectures on Preaching.[6] If human pride, arrogance, and pretension are so widespread and so deep-rooted, how shall sin be overcome? asks Dr. Buttrick. How shall it be forgiven? "By the red law and strange sacrifice of suffering." For by this law somebody always pays the price for others. That is how man's frontiers are pushed out as pioneers are lost on the ocean, in the arctic wastes, on the slopes of high mountains. Health is won by doctors and nurses who study disease and care for the sick. Human liberties are purchased by men and women who give themselves for the sake of fuller freedom of opportunity and equity in social, economic, and political human relations. Human ignorance is liquidated by scholars and teachers consecrated to truth. The mother dies every day for the life of the child.

Thus men live out this red law of sacrifice in every aspect of personal and social experience: pioneer, doctor, nurse, liberator, scholar, teacher, mother, father, wife, husband, son, daughter. Writes Dr. Buttrick: "We can fulfill that law for one another, and we must. But that fulfillment is not enough." All these human beings constantly atone for others. But who will meet the bitter cost for the whole of mankind? Who will not fall from sheer exhaustion, as humans do with their limited strength and narrow perspectives? Who is big enough, altogether good enough, for this larger task? It is the Christian conviction, however it may be expressed, that only God Himself is good enough, loving enough, powerful enough. "Is there sign of such a God, a *living* sign, a *functional* sign? Yes,

[6] See George Buttrick, *Jesus Came Preaching*, New York, Charles Scribner's Sons, 1931, Chap. Eight, especially pp. 212-218.

on Calvary! There is the red heart of the Christian gospel! A Man was found good enough to need no remission for Himself, compassionate enough to gather a world in love into the arms of a Cross. That Man is now the Saviour of mankind." [7]

Every attempt to catch the significance of this central Christian affirmation in words and figures of speech has value only as it points beyond itself to the ultimate mystery of God's relation to the whole of human history and to each individual in his unique personal situation. We may not care for the language either of traditional creeds or of contemporary attempts to understand those creeds. If this is the case, we are obligated to make our own attempt—each for himself—not in words only but in commitment and action which are the expressions of faith. If it is not this faith, it must be some other by which men and women live.

[7] *Ibid.*, p. 217.

Chapter XV

Resurrection and Fulfillment

Anatole France describes an incident which might well have taken place in the first century of our Christian era. A character named Lamia is speaking: "I knew a Jewess. . . . Some months after I lost sight of her, I learned by chance that she had attached herself to a small company of men and women who were followers of a young Galilean. . . . His name was Jesus; he came from Nazareth, and he was crucified for some crime, I don't know quite what. Pontius," continued this speaker, "Pontius, do you remember anything about the man?" Pontius Pilate contracted his brows, and his hand rose to his forehead in the attitude of one who was trying desperately to remember. Then after a silence of some seconds, "Jesus?" he murmured, "Jesus—of Nazareth? I cannot call him to mind." [1]

Pontius Pilate, under whose sanction Jesus Christ was tried and condemned, had forgotten. It may be that Pilate pretended to forget. Perhaps his sense of outraged justice still smarted under the stringing rebuke of the prisoner who had turned judge. Or perhaps he really did forget. There had been so many through the years like this Jesus, revolutionaries in all those minor provinces

---

[1] Anatole France, *Mother of Pearl* (translation by Frederic Chapman), New York, John Lane Company, 1917, pp. 25-26.

of the sprawling Roman Empire. And who could remember all of them? There is a tendency even among modern Christians sometimes to forget this Jesus standing there a failure, on his way to a Cross to suffer and die. Our philosophy of success makes an absurdity of failure. At any rate, many in this twentieth century feel they do not need any such grim picture of Jesus' death, and certainly they do not understand it. That men do not understand the Cross is natural. As we have suggested, sometimes abstract theologies have lifted the Cross out of practical life and set it in the midst of doctrinal argument. But the meaning of the Cross is quite beyond us. We cannot fully grasp the seemingly impenetrable mystery of one named Jesus Christ giving his life and somehow saving a whole world.

In the face of this kind of bewilderment, many a modern shrugs off the whole confusing business and concentrates on what he takes to be "essential" Christian teaching. This may be interpreted as a code of ethics or a system of philosophy or a challenging set of ideals for the betterment of the social order. Thus we are urged to take seriously, as basic Christian teaching, the Sermon on the Mount and the injunction to love our neighbor under the demand of the doctrine of the "Fatherhood of God and the brotherhood of man."

These ethical demands to love and justice are, of course, important. But they are not rooted simply in themselves; they are the fruits of men's encounter with God and their response of faith. At least this is the perspective in which the earliest Christians saw these ethical matters. For they *did* remember their crucified Master as one sent by God to accomplish a mighty act of deliverance and reconciliation. This was their basic affirmation and all else followed.

In this chapter we shall discuss, first, the intimate relation between the crucifixion and Resurrection as rooted in the Hebraic, historical tradition. Second, we shall be concerned with the scriptural accounts of the Resurrection and their significance for Christian belief. Third, our discussion will center briefly on the implications of the Resurrection for that doctrine called "justification by faith."

CRUCIFIXION-RESURRECTION IN HEBRAIC TRADITION

The early Christians remembered, but they might have forgotten if this divine-human event had not moved on beyond death into renewal of life, beyond crucifixion into Resurrection. These two phases of the total event are therefore inseparable: the crucifixion-Resurrection. Taken together, they comprise the center of gravity of Christian life and belief. For this was the dynamic point of contact with the unique act of God in history of which the personality of Jesus Christ is the very heart. And we need constantly to recall that, for Christian faith, this act is a *total* event which includes not only the life, career, teaching, and work of Jesus Christ but also his death, resurrection, and continuing presence as the creation of the conditions under which the Christian community could grow. Thus the Christ to whom they committed themselves was the triumphant Messiah, conqueror of sin and death, an everlasting presence in their midst even now. And the God they worshiped was the God who had raised Jesus Christ from the dead. All the words and work of their Lord were seen and told in the light of the Resurrection. From this climax of belief and worship the Christian community proclaimed the good news of the Reign of God, of which the New Testament is the record.

But, as A. Michael Ramsey suggests, there is a tension within the thought of the early community, a tension created by violent contrast between the crucifixion and Resurrection. When the hour of darkness came, Jesus' disciples fled in fear and disillusionment. Jesus had warned them that the Cross must come. But they did not believe him. Perhaps, even up to the last moment, they expected a miracle, but none came. Instead the darkness deepened. They had been mistaken. Such a one as this, dying in shame and disgrace, could never be the Messiah of their hopes. This was Friday.

Essentials in Christian Faith

Within three days these same men were transformed. Lost confidence returned. Boldness conquered fear. The disciples began to gather in their old haunts and resume their former customs. Messages were sent to absent friends about a strange experience. They whispered the good news in secret. After a time they were to shout it from the housetops. He who was dead had come back to life. Their faith was vindicated.

Men and women of our age ask what actually happened to bring about this change? Why is it so important to believe that Jesus was raised from the dead? What difference does it make? What did it mean to the disciples? It seems strange that this issue should be the turning point of the entire Christian faith. But this is the case so far as the earliest followers of Christ were concerned. It meant to them the reversal of their opinion of Good Friday. His death had said to them in the cruel language of the Cross that this man whom they had followed could never be God's Messiah. The Resurrection convinced them that they had been wrong. His coming back, according to their faith, was God's way of saying that the crucified Jesus was in fact what they had begun to believe him to be and what they now affirmed with all their beings: God's appointed Saviour.

But it is too simple a comparison between these two phases of the divine-human event to say that the Cross is a symbol of stark tragedy, evil, and despair while the Resurrection is a symbol of hope and deliverance. For, as we have emphasized, the crucifixion itself was the very medium of God's power and love. A. Michael Ramsey writes: "We discover as we read the New Testament that the two events, seen first as opposites, are found increasingly to be like two sides of a single coin." It is especially "in the narratives of the Passion in the Gospels," continues Ramsey, "that the drawing together of the two events is most significantly to be seen." Even in the austere loneliness of the Cross the "scene is not one of pathos, or tragedy or defeat." It is, however, only the Resurrection which could have brought about this transformation of darkness into light. This is the way Mark depicts it. And Luke, suggests Ramsey, goes even further in drawing Cross and Resurrection together. He shows even on the Cross "the serenity and mastery of love whereby the Son of Man reaches out in sympathy and tenderness to those around Him. It is they and not He whose need and plight are pitiable." In the Gospel of John the Cross becomes a symbol of "glory." All through the story of the Passion runs this theme of triumph. It is Jesus who is master of the situation, carrying his own Cross, freely giving his own life. "The Crucifixion is not a defeat needing the Resurrection to reverse it, but a victory which the Resurrection quickly follows and seals." [2]

The Resurrection, however our modern minds are led to interpret it, was for the early Christians the dramatic climax of a long series of "God's mighty acts" in human history. This is Hebraic thinking and not Greek perspective. For the Greek, body and soul belong to two utterly different worlds: the body to this world of flux and decay, and the soul to the world of the immortal or the deathless. But the first Christians did not believe in this kind of other-wordly immortality, but in a *resurrection* from the dead. This perspective out of Hebrew tradition implies not only a view of history but also a certain view of man, both of which we have been describing throughout these chapters. For, first, this event in which God raised Jesus from the dead "was not a mere signpost pointing the way toward eternity; rather, this was the transfiguration of history itself. It was the lightning thrust of God's truth in the light of which the whole landscape of human existence was brilliantly illumined. It was the assurance of God's triumph in history." [3] This view of history was a part of Jewish messianic expectations, pointing toward a fulfillment when history itself would issue in establishment of

[2] A. Michael Ramsey, *The Resurrection of Christ*, Philadelphia, Westminster Press, 1946, pp. 18-20, *passim*. I am indebted to Ramsey for his treatment of the significance of the Resurrection, as also to suggestions of Bernhard W. Anderson, *Rediscovering the Bible*, New York, Association Press, 1951, Chap. 9, "The Power of His Resurrection."

[3] Anderson, *op. cit.*, p. 211.

God's rule over the whole creation. It was in that climactic period that God would raise the dead so that all generations might participate in His final victory. The reader is referred to such passages as Isaiah 26:19 and Daniel 12:2-3, where the Resurrection of the dead is taught. This view was elaborated during the period between the Testaments, was held strongly by the Pharisees, and became the basis of early Christian faith, such as recorded in I Thessalonians 4:14, Acts 24:15, John 5:29. We do not argue here for the literal accuracy of these convictions but rather cite them as religious utterances of Hebrew belief.

Second, involved with this view of history is the Hebraic interpretation of human nature, which we also have discussed, especially in Chapter V. This again contrasts with the Greek picture of an eternal soul imprisoned in a body. Rather, as we have seen, for the Hebrew, man is a total personality responding in acceptance or rejection of God's demand upon him. At death, man's personal existence comes to a halt. "His body returns to the dust and his 'shade'—a vague double of his former self—goes down to Sheol, the land of darkness and death. Consistent with this view of human nature, if a man is to have a future *life* there must be a new miracle, a *re*-creation. God must raise up the body from death, reanimate it with his life-giving Spirit, and restore man to the God-relationship which is the source of his life." [4]

This Hebraic view of history and man, with its frank and forthright belief in the resurrection of the dead, does not imply escape from history into some realm of eternity, as with the Greek view. Thus the Resurrection is to take place at the end of history when faithful individuals will be raised up to become members of the messianic community. It is in this context, then, that the Resurrection of Jesus became meaningful for the early Christians. For them the crucifixion-Resurrection was a sign that God's triumph was already on its way as the culmination of all of God's dramatic acts throughout Israel's past. This was the "New Exodus," more

[4] *Ibid.*, pp. 212-213.

significant even than the old; for now God had brought about deliverance from sin and death. However difficult this perspective is for modern-minded men and women to grasp, this is the enduring theme of biblical religion: God active in human history to bring about reconciliation between man and Himself. It was with difficulty that succeeding generations maintained this view in the face of Greek thought. Some Christians called Gnostics argued that soul was separate from body; that Jesus Christ was only an appearance from an eternal realm; that he only *seemed* to suffer, die, and arise from the grave. Other Christians saw that this Gnostic perspective meant death to Christianity as a historical religion. They believed, as the very essence of Christianity, that God did disclose Himself in events of history and climactically through a real birth, an actual suffering, death, and Resurrection of Jesus Christ.

In summation of this historical perspective, Professor Anderson states a viewpoint and raises some searching questions:

The Resurrection, then, is the dominant category of a religion which rests upon a conviction intolerable to Greek thought: God's action, his coming into history, his self-revelation in historical events. The question as to what happened on Easter morning lies out on the fringe. We are dealing here with an issue of historical interpretation which cannot be put aside easily. Is history what the men of the Bible declared it to be: a meeting place between God and man? Is the Crucifixion-Resurrection, as Christians claim, the historical event in which men encounter the Lord of history and witness his triumph? On this issue Christianity cannot surrender without ceasing to be Christian. As Paul reminded Christians at the Greek city of Corinth, "If Christ be not risen, then is our preaching vain, and your faith is vain" (I Corinthians 15:14). Surely it is no exaggeration to say that if Christianity were severed from its rootage in the soil of the resurrection faith, it would soon lose its vitality and wither away.[5]

SCRIPTURAL ACCOUNTS OF THE RESURRECTION

As to the scriptural records of the Resurrection, we must face two preliminary issues frankly and squarely. The first is that the

[5] *Ibid.*, p. 216.

New Testament simply does not present a clear and consistent account of what actually occurred at the Resurrection. In this connection, we must review briefly the story as recorded in the Gospels, the affirmation of Paul, and the message of the apostles as uttered during the oral period. It will be noted here that we begin with later testimony and then with earlier utterances. As we do so, a second issue confronts us as to the kind of historical evidence we may expect to find concerning the Resurrection. As is the case with all recorded history, these events are not immune from the close scrutiny of historical investigation. But again, at the risk of unnecessary repetition, we state that all history is interpreted history and behind interpretation lie the background of presupposition and convictions of faith. As with all the recorded events of the Scriptures, especially those of the miracles, so now the Resurrection must be interpreted by presuppositions shared by those who were committed to Christ as the disclosure of God in their midst. This is to derive the principles for weighing evidence from the Scriptures themselves and not from some other standpoint, especially one which pretends to be "objective," taken without any presuppositions whatever.[6]

Mark's Gospel (16:1-8) describes how on the first Easter morning the women ran from the empty tomb in terror and bewilderment over the words of "a young man" robed in white: "Do not be amazed; you seek Jesus of Nazareth, who was crucified. He has risen . . . he is going before you into Galilee; there you will see him, as he told you."[7] The original ending of Mark has probably been lost and the passage (16:9-20) contained in our familiar Bibles added by early editors. Therefore, in its earliest known form, Mark's Gospel did not include the appearance of the resurrected Christ but ended, "for they were afraid" (16:8).

In the Gospel of Matthew the author starts from the Marcan narrative, "he is going before you into Galilee." He then tells how,

---

[6] See *ibid.*, p. 217, and Ramsey, *op. cit.*, pp. 56-58.
[7] Mark 16:6-8, Revised Standard Version.

in the midst of earthquake when the angel rolled away the stone, Jesus' appearance to the fleeing women was like lightning (28:2-10). This Gospel also records an appearance to the eleven disciples on a mountain in Galilee, where he charged them to go into all the world and promised his continuing presence. In Matthew there is no mention of appearances in Jerusalem itself except for the occasion on which Jesus appeared at the tomb (28:9-10).

As for Luke's Gospel, this writer relates the story of the empty tomb and how the women brought the news to the astonished eleven. He records appearances to the two disciples on the road to Emmaus and at eventide in the breaking of bread, as well as to Peter and to the eleven and others in Jerusalem. In Luke there are no recorded appearances in Galilee.

The final Gospel, that according to John, tells how Mary Magdalene discovered the empty tomb, and how Peter and the beloved disciple ran to the tomb to confirm her report. This Gospel writer harmonizes the Mark-Matthew tradition of Galilee appearances with the tradition of Jerusalem appearances recorded by Luke. Thus he pictures Jesus as appearing mainly in Jerusalem and then, in an epilogue, to the disciples by the shore of the lake in Galilee.

Taken simply as they read in the Gospels, these accounts are vivid and lifelike. But although these stories have an authentic ring, we cannot bring all the details into a consistent, harmonious narrative. Each writer takes the basic tradition of the empty tomb and Jesus' appearances to his disciples, and builds on certain details of his own. But this lack of consistency is precisely what we should expect; for if every detail fitted in with some artificially blocked-out plan, we should be more suspicious of the main tradition. These are the utterances of men writing under deep conviction in the attempt to tell their contemporaries the significance of the victorious Christ.

The earliest documentary account of the Resurrection is that written by Paul in I Corinthians 15 about the year A.D. 55. There Paul speaks of a "tradition" of the Church which dates back to the first decade after the Crucifixion and is hence the expression of early Christians:

> For I delivered to you as of first importance what I also received, that Christ died for our sins in accordance with the scriptures, that he was buried, that he was raised on the third day according to the scriptures, and that he appeared to Cephas, then to the twelve. Then he appeared to more than five hundred brethren at one time, most of whom are still alive, though some have fallen asleep. Then he appeared to James, then to all the apostles. Last of all, as to one untimely born, he appeared also to me.[8]

The very wording of this statement by Paul, particularly the repeated "that," indicates that it is an oft-quoted formula perhaps taught traditionally to all new converts. But the final clause is Paul's own personal witness and is not a part of the formula. Here he seems to be saying that his own vision of the Risen Lord was of exactly the same kind as that of the early apostles. Moreover, Paul's argument throughout the rest of this chapter is that the resurrected body of the Christian is of a different order, "a spiritual body," for "flesh and blood cannot inherit the kingdom of God." Christ's Resurrection was evidently not just a material event. Rather, the physical body which was buried in the grave was somehow transformed into a spiritual body, new, glorified, and ready for the conditions of a different order of life. In this new form Jesus revealed himself to the early followers. It is held by many scholars that as the story of the Resurrection was handed on within the Christian community, it came gradually to place greater emphasis on the detailed physical aspects of the Resurrection event.

As for the period of the early oral transmission of the Gospel, the main stress was placed on Jesus' appearances to the disciples themselves, that is, to the closest circle of those who had followed him throughout his earthly ministry. Here scholars point out that the apostolic sermons as recorded in Acts make no mention of the women at the empty tomb. In fact, their own conviction is based

[8] I Corinthians 15:3-8, R.S.V.

not upon any discovery of an empty tomb but rather upon their own personal experience of "seeing" the risen Christ. (See Acts 3:15, 10:40, 13:30-31.)

The foregoing is the briefest account of the biblical evidence upon which Christian belief in the Resurrection is based. It is easy to debate literal details and become dogmatic on one side or the other. One tradition stresses Christ's first appearance to Peter, most likely in Galilee, and another insists on the primacy of the women's testimony at the tomb in Jerusalem. Some scholars think that the first of these is the oldest tradition and that the stress on the empty tomb is secondary, although Ramsey, whom we have cited, argues that the empty tomb is an integral part of the earliest testimony, to be taken together with the affirmation that Jesus appeared to the disciples.

Beneath all these varieties of interpretation lies the solid core of belief that Christ had conquered death. For bold courage had overcome cringing fear and the community was now established on a new level of creativity. They had *experienced* the victorious, risen Christ. Without this event, the Christian Church never would have come into being. Also the very existence of the New Testament itself depends upon the Resurrection experience. For if Jesus had ended his life as an executed revolutionary, there is little likelihood that the scriptural record would have been made. The New Testament itself is the living expression of conviction that Christ was the Risen Lord in their midst. Then too there is the very existence of the Lord's Day. It seems probable that no Christian reared in the Jewish tradition would have changed the sacred day from the Sabbath (Saturday) to the first day of the week (Sunday) except for the extraordinary reason that on this day Jesus Christ was first seen risen from the dead. In short, if this phase of the total divine-human event known as the Resurrection had not occurred, the company of his followers never would have become the Christian Church with its Scriptures and special day of observance. John Knox speaks of "the resurrection as a fact, not as a belief." Then he adds: "The resurrection is a part of the concrete empirical meaning of Jesus, not the result of mere reflection upon that meaning. Beliefs were based upon the resurrection; it was not itself a belief. It was something given. It was a reality grasped in faith. It was the reality of all the concrete meaning of the man Christ Jesus recognized as present in the community after, and despite, his death." [9]

This real event in the experience of the Christian community was the bearer of a central meaning on which all the records of the New Testament agree: God had acted in their midst to redeem and save his people from sin and death. In this connection Bernhard W. Anderson states:

The sifting of the historical evidence does not necessarily lead us any closer to the meaning or the truth of the Resurrection. Even though we could demonstrate scientifically that the tomb was empty on Easter morning, we would not arrive at the biblical meaning of the miracle. The skeptic, admitting that some freakish event may have occurred two thousand years ago, would say in good collegiate style: "So what?" Conversely, even though the gospel evidence concerning the empty tomb falls like a house of cards when examined critically, the reality of Christ's resurrection would not be affected in the slightest. In the final analysis, the truth of the Resurrection lies not in the field of factual inquiry, but in the field of historical interpretation. Was Jesus truly God's Messiah? Did he manifest God's sovereignty over history? Was he the one who actualized God's power and grace? These questions are answerable not by examination of the evidence, but by a faith which either affirms or denies. The Christian interpretation of history, like any view of history, rests finally upon decision.[10]

THE DOCTRINE OF JUSTIFICATION BY FAITH

What are the implications of the Resurrection for that doctrine called "justification by faith," which is central to the thought of Paul and of the Protestant Reformation? It may seem strange to

[9] John Knox, *Christ the Lord*, Chicago, Willett, Clark & Company, 1945, p. 60.
[10] Anderson, *op. cit.*, pp. 223-224.

THIS BOOK IS SENT TO YOU

WITH THE COMPLIMENTS OF

Alan N. Stone

AND HARPER & BROTHERS

WHEN YOU HAVE HAD AN

OPPORTUNITY TO EXAMINE IT

WE SHALL BE PLEASED TO

HAVE ANY COMMENTS YOU

MAY CARE TO MAKE

THE ORIGINAL ESTABLISHMENT IN CLIFF STREET,
(FROM AN OLD PRINT)

HARPER & BROTHERS

College Department

49 East 33d Street • New York 16, N. Y.

some that we do not move immediately from discussion of the Resurrection into consideration of the doctrine of Eternal Life or the Life Everlasting. This latter discussion we shall reserve for the final chapter as a topic for independent treatment. The reason for this is twofold: first, belief in Eternal Life, important as it is for Christian conviction, comes as a consequence of much else besides that the Christian holds as faith; and second, as we have indicated, the early Christians did not regard the Resurrection directly or primarily as evidence for an afterlife and certainly not for immortality in the Creek sense of separation of soul from body. For them, the Resurrection is a sign of God's victorious act in conquering sin or separation from God.

Man, in rebellion against the God in whose image he is created, really destroys his own life. For if man, according to the Christian faith, is destined to fulfill his very being in dependence upon his Creator, then deliberate separation from God is death brought about by himself and upon himself. However this separation may be brought about, sin is closely connected with death. "The sting of death is sin," said Paul (I Corinthians 15:56); or again, "the wages of sin is death" (Romans 6:35). Many a man or woman may "look alive" or "feel alive," this view is saying, but may actually be estranged from God and from his or her own self in a kind of "living death." Then when the reality of physical death approaches, as it must soon or late to everyone, the ultimate futility of such an existence apart from God is disclosed in all its grimness and emptiness. But in the biblical tradition, over against this kind of "death" stands "life" as fulfillment of human selfhood. For the earliest Christians, it was this new life in relation to the divine which the Resurrection of Christ made possible. In this climactic event God had even now won the victory over "the law of sin and death" (Romans 8:2). God and man were reconciled. The gift of life was theirs. They had but to reach out and grasp it. This is the "power of the Resurrection."

For the Christian, the grasping of such power over sin and

"living death" is the strategic point in his religious affirmation and commitment. It is a matter not of theory but of practice. Paul worked it out from the depths of his own personal experience and gave expression to his convictions in his Letter to the Galatians and also in his Letter to the Romans. How can a man or woman find oneness with God and a right relation with his fellow men? What is the source of peace and freedom within one's own inward life? How can one move beyond endless self-justification into justification in the sight of God?

Let an illustration serve as point of departure for answers to these questions. An altogether human incident occurred one day, involving teen-agers, children, a dogfight, a dead mouse, guilt, self-justification, rebellion, and the bid for freedom that is within us all. A huge dog rushed suddenly out of the house and shouting young people pounded down the front steps after the dog. Yelps and snarls of a dogfight echoed along the street. After panicked struggles to separate the beasts, there was peace once more—until the human beings involved began the process of analysis and self-justification. Sitting on the porch steps, one girl exclaimed: "It was my fault. I let the dog out. But I didn't know the basement door was open." And so the discussion continued on and on, as it has a way of doing among both young and old, until, all-unannounced in the midst of self-justification, the teen-ager saw a chance to ease her own discomfiture. "Peggy!" she shouted. "Don't you dare leave that dead mouse there on the lawn!" For, following her own devices, little Peggy was having her own kind of fun, until the voice of authority, touched with self-justification, spoke. "Get a shovel out of the house and take that thing away!" Peggy obeyed. But as she disappeared around the corner of the house, she was heard to mutter: "Don't give me any of your corny lectures."

This incident illustrates impulses in every man or woman. None of us likes to be told what to do, either by insistent pressures of tradition or by external compulsions. We all claim that we do not belong to anybody. What is good is within our own grasp. We want to be free.

But the insistent question arises sooner or later: *Are* we free? Are we ever free from ourselves? Can we really manage this world of human relationships? Can anyone manage himself? Dare he try to manage other people? Students often become involved in discussion of the role of campus regulations in the holding of standards and moral practices. Shall it be by insistence on more specific rules of conduct with penalties definitely graded to fit the seriousness of each offense? Or, as against this living by pre-scribed patterns, would it be better to let each individual act on the basis of inner decision and insight? As someone comments: "One makes for respectability that is dead; the other makes for originality that is very much alive."

This is the kind of situation that Paul faced as he wrote to mem-bers of the Christian community in Galatia and again in his Letter to the Romans. Paul, like Jesus before him, struggled with the problem of dead respectability that passed for religion. How can the Christian attain acceptance in the sight of God and with him-self? According to their tradition, the Jewish teachers of Paul's day believed that within each man two forces contended with each other: a "good impulse" and an "evil impulse." These two were in such equal balance, so they claimed, that through serious study of the demands of the Jewish Law and much sincere effort a man *could* be righteous. Paul, himself a former rabbi, did not have this experience; for out of intense moral struggle, he wrote: "I do not understand my own actions. . . . For I do not do the good I want, but the evil I do not want is what I do. Now if I do what I do not want, it is no longer I that do it, but sin which dwells within me. . . . Wretched man that I am! Who will deliver me from this body of death?" [11]

Paul was resolved that Christians should move beyond mere

[11] Romans 7:15-24, R.S.V.

223

conformance to the commandments of God, as contained in the old
Law, into a new freedom. But the Law, as the expression of God's
will for man, reminds him of the meaning of sin and how difficult
it is to achieve righteousness under one's own unaided power.
How, then, is he to come into right relations with God? To use
his word, how is a man *justified* in the sight of God? His answer
is contained in the exclamation: "For the law of the Spirit of life
in Christ Jesus has set me free from the law of sin and death." [12]
Or again, in his Letter to the Galatians, Paul writes: ". . . a man
is not justified by works of the law but through faith in Jesus
Christ." [13]

Justification by faith seems like a strange doctrine to our modern
minds. The term *justification* is borrowed from the context of the
law court. To be justified means to be known as guilty and yet
to be treated as innocent or as righteous. In our world of business,
politics, and courts of law this sounds like an absurd idea. If a
man is guilty, we would say, then he is guilty. How can he then
be treated as innocent?

But this perspective is not so foreign to ordinary human experience as it sounds. Within the context of family life, for instance,
a son may misuse opportunities given him and yet be received
into a new relationship by his father as if nothing had happened
to break their mutual trust. We say the boy is justified. He is known
to be guilty. Perhaps he carries about with him the very physical
marks of his guilt branded into his face and character. But, though
he is known to be guilty, in the ideal family he is treated as if
he were innocent.

By analogy with family life, men and women come into right
relationship with God, Paul holds, not simply by the things they
do, but by what they freely affirm. They are justified before God
by their willing acceptance of what God in his love for mankind
has already done and is doing through the life, death, and Resur-

[12] Romans 8:2, R.S.V.
[13] Galatians 2:16, R.S.V.

rection of Jesus Christ. *Justification comes not by works but by God's loving grace through faith.*

But what happens to law? We might expect Paul to throw established law over altogether and claim that all folk need is inner decision and insight. This might suit the modern temper, which says: Be free. You need no law of any sort any longer!

Dr. George Buttrick tells an incident from his own experience. The Buttricks had a small son whose tonsils were to be removed.

The bribe offered him for taking the anaesthetic bravely was two goldfish swimming in a glass bowl. The small boy was duly brave, and the goldfish were duly given. "What shall we call them?" we asked. "Tonsils and Adenoids," came the reply. So Tonsils and Adenoids they were baptized, they swimming meanwhile in their waters of baptism. Came a day when Tonsils died (or was it Adenoids?), and we were dispatched forthwith to purchase a successor. The successor was carried home in a tiny carton; and we, ruminating on life in general and on the inhabitant of that carton in particular, spoke to ourselves as follows: "This goldfish would be justified in joining the revolt of modern youth. He is not meant to swim in a carton; he is made to swim in a sunflecked pool. But supposing he were in such a pool and there rebelled—supposing he said, 'This pool has stone edges and I am against stone edges'—and supposing he jumped clear of the pool onto the path—and supposing he squirmed on the path and told everybody what a good time he was having now and was free and in a vaster world—would he be free? No, he would be dead." [14]

Man is free, we say. But freedom has its price. To be free means to be bound. To be free is not to escape all law. It is to move from one orbit of law to another. Everything has a law: automobiles, airplanes, organisms, human beings, peoples, nations. You are free to jump from yonder tower. But you are not free from the consequences. If you are gifted in music, you are free to soar to heights of creative imagination. But you are not free from the octave of notes which rules music. You are free to live your life in indifferent

[14] George Buttrick, *Jesus Came Preaching*, New York, Charles Scribner's Sons, 1931, pp. 68-69.

unconcern for the welfare of others. But you are not free to escape the moral consequences of self-seeking in a world where men outstretch the limits of coöperation only at their peril. You are never free from law. You are free *in* law. This is the Christian perspective as expressed by Paul and many another closer to our own day within the Protestant tradition. For Paul wrote in his Letter to the Galatians: "For you were called to freedom, brethren; only do not use your freedom as an opportunity for the flesh but through love be servants of one another. For the whole law is fulfilled in one word, 'You shall love your neighbor as yourself.' . . . Look to yourselves, lest you too be tempted. Bear one another's burdens, and so fulfill the law of Christ." [15]

It is the Christian conviction that this is the *vocation* to which men and women are called: to be free from blind tradition for its own sake, from dead respectability, from oneself, from constant attempts at self-justification. For there is a persuasive power from beyond men themselves. It is a love which broods over men, disturbing, wooing them into a new kind of freedom. Yet in the face of that, folk still keep muttering to themselves and to their neighbors: "I did it because. . . . I did not do it because. . . . I am this way because." It is the genius of Christianity, so it claims, to cut clear through this monotonous process of self-justification. People are already justified in the sight of God, accepted as they are for what they are, and therefore no longer belong simply to themselves. This is to be free from "sin and death."

In the Christian view of human freedom, we do not need to posture or win favor with each other, on the campus, in our homes, work, or friendships. We do not stand or fall by the many things we do or do not do. There are important concerns of personal and social life, of course. They have to do with common decency, respect, service, justice, equity, peace. But they are not the road to freedom; they are the issues of freedom. In the face of this chal-

[15] Galatians 5:13-14, 6:1b-2, R.S.V.

lenge, we do not need to justify ourselves to ourselves, to our neighbors, or to God. Paul especially is saying that God's love in Christ takes all this need out of us. God stands ready, in the Christian affirmation, to make men free like this, free from within in decision and insight, so that they may be enabled to go out into the wider world and help make that free from tyranny, oppression, suffering, and want. But God begins with the men themselves— not with wings built onto the house, but with foundations. Policies, activities, and programs, in this view, are necessary expressions of Christian concern, as are agencies and institutions for the common welfare. But God makes a start not with these but with men's honest acceptance of the power and love of God as disclosed in the person and work of Jesus Christ.

These are the practical bearings of the Resurrection as God's continuing action within human history and experience to redeem men from sin and death. Fulfillment and freedom come as men and women are justified before God and by his loving concern through their willing acceptance and commitment in faith to a new way of life. "Carry each other's burdens," says Paul, "and so fulfill the law of Christ." But does this take place for each individual in solitude? It is once again the Christian conviction that it does not. For, throughout our entire discussion, we have spoken of the Christian community as an integral part of the total event through which God acts. This is the social context within which Christian faith comes alive. To this question of the nature and function of the Church within history we now turn our attention.

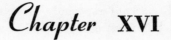

Chapter XVI

The Church as Community

George Hedley tells this story:

From China came a young graduate student who had grown up in a Methodist mission and had been trained in Methodist schools. Some weeks after his arrival, a Methodist professor in the University looked him up. "Are you happy in your classes?" "Yes, thank you." "Are you comfortable in your quarters?" "Yes, thank you very much." And so on, until, "Have you found a Church to attend?" "Oh yes, thank you; I go to the First Church." "Oh, of course: at 6th and Q Streets." "No: at 9th and Y." "Oh, the First *Christian* Church!" "But certainly, the Christian Church: I am a Christian."

The Methodist missionaries who brought up that boy did well to impress on him that he was a Christian more than he was a Methodist. And the boy did naturally enough in asking, on his first Sunday in a new land, for directions to "a Christian Church." But neither the missionaries nor he had thought of "Christian" as a term of denominational separation.[1]

Members of leading churches within many different denominations sometimes speak of "the *First* Church." They do not always specify. It might be any one of a number of different churches: First Christian, First Methodist, First Baptist, First Congregational, First Presbyterian, etc. The assumption is evidently made on the

---

[1] George Hedley, *The Christian Heritage in America*, New York, The Macmillan Company, 1947. Used by permission.

part of some Christians that theirs is the *first* church. This sounds to many nonchurch members as if they were saying, "Ours is the *only* Christian Church." Whether intended or not, such assumptions as these have become to many men and women outside the church a most serious obstacle to entrance into the Christian fellowship. In fact, to these folk, their friends who are members of churches seem possessed of the most appalling lack of humility.

Yet, on the other hand, there does exist throughout the several churches a growing band of members who are trying in every possible way to reach hands across divisive barriers of denominationalism, creed, and ritual to embrace a common fellowship. They believe that it is possible to be loyal to one's own particular church without renouncing larger loyalty to the Universal Church. They seek to do this without contempt or indifference toward those who differ from themselves in particular doctrines or practices. Even within denominational groups there are many shades of judgment about essential articles of belief and fortunately a growing freedom of discussion and more accommodating hospitality among those who differ. For the things in which they agree are becoming more important than the things in which they disagree. The battle for this kind of mutual understanding is far from won, but at least there are many who are honestly and sincerely creating the conditions under which men may differ but do so in respect and creative good will.

Among students, and men and women in other walks of life as well, it is fairly easy to evoke heated discussion on the question: What is wrong with the churches? Such objections as these may be listed (the reader may have his own list): obscure language, strange ritualistic forms and practices, overorganization, insistence on conventional taboos, hypocrisy of behavior among church members in which it seems difficult to distinguish business and social practices of Christians from those of non-Christians.

Such criticisms as these have led many Americans to say that it is possible to be religious without benefit of any church. These men and women claim to believe in God, yet they believe that participation in the worship and work of the church is unnecessary. Obviously, some are sincere about it while others have adopted this view as a cloak to cover up their own unconcern or indifference. Yet many of those who are honest in their convictions at this point believe that we can find a disembodied religion that will heal individuals and cleanse society without the encumbrances of church organization. More specifically, in terms of biblical faith, we are led to ask: Is it possible to be Christian outside the fellowship of the Church?

With these preliminary issues before us, we propose in this chapter to discuss (1) the nature of the Church as integral to Christian faith and life, and (2) specific functions of the Church expressed through the many particular churches. In the following chapter, "Ecumenical Christianity," we shall discuss the origins of diverse denominations, obstacles to realization of the ecumenical goal, and positive steps now in progress toward completer understanding and coöperation among the churches.

THE NATURE OF THE CHURCH

As we move into consideration of the nature of the Church, we need to admit honestly that there are men, women, and young people who live decent lives without benefit of the Church. Many are loyal in intent and purpose to Christian principles of justice, concern, and love for their fellow men. Christianity is personal and intensely individual. Religion, as Alfred North Whitehead put it, is what a man does with his own solitariness. Each person's convictions are his own. "In the end," someone has said, "the individual must walk by his own insight." We hold these days the conviction that we cannot afford to retreat to stubborn dogmatism, accepting views simply because they belong to age-old tradition. If we have any convictions at all, many of us say, they will not be borrowed from anybody else. This, then, is an important conviction: Religion, especially Christianity, is always *inescapably personal.*

The Church as Community

But this insight about it does not stand alone among basic Christian beliefs. There are those who would remind us of the other side of this personal emphasis, a truth we sometimes forget. It is this: there is no area of human existence, no matter how personal, that is wholly private. It is said that in the high Swiss Alps, climbers inching along the lofty passes dare not speak above a whisper; for a noise even as loud as a whisper reverberating along canyon walls may start an avalanche of snow crashing down the mountainside. Human relationships are even more sensitive than that. Nothing in the universe is utterly isolated, this point of view is saying, but each thing, event, or person finds its true being in relationship to other things. "The disease of the world," said Jan Smuts, "is fragmentation; the cure of the world is holism . . . ours is a whole-making universe. We are all interrelated." "The disease of the world is brokenness; the cure of the world is unity," writes Paul Tillich. E. Stanley Jones says: "It is time that the Church and Christians cease being part of the disease and become a part of the cure." To men and women attempting to find their own religion in solitariness John Baillie replies: "I cannot be a Christian all by myself. I cannot retire into my own shell or into my own corner and live the Christian life there. A single individual cannot be a Christian in his singleness." Whatever faith we take for our own, therefore, it is always attained most fully in fellowship with others.

Brought down to cases, this is the basic reason for the fellowship which is the Christian Church as it surges down through the ages. Recovering the perspective expressed throughout these chapters, we recall that the most basic of all Christian beliefs is that God has acted and is acting in and through events in history. He discloses His nature through that divine-human event which includes in his wholeness the life, teaching, death, and Resurrection of Jesus, the Christ. But it also includes his continuing presence as the very spark that brought about the creation of the Christian community. The very good news of the Gospel itself is mediated to the generations through this fellowship of faith. The New Testament is the product of this community as the record of God's self-disclosure and the response of men and women in commitment to the Father of the Lord Jesus Christ. The Christian Church was something distinctively new and yet it was continuous with the Jewish community out of which it grew and within which Jesus Christ made his appearance among men. In fact, this new fellowship is inseparable from the Christ who was remembered, interpreted, and held in reverence as the dynamic center of its very life. John Knox reminds us that "the new community is an essential aspect of the meaning of Christ." He adds: "The Church came into existence, not *after* the event, but *along with* the event, and is really inseparable from it at every stage, just as the event is inseparable from the Church. In every reference we have made to the elements comprising the historical event through which the revelation occurred, the creation of the community has been included. The Church is thus not so much the consequence of the event as its culmination." [2]

The coming of Jesus Christ, as we also have stated in previous chapters, meant the founding of a New Covenant between God and men onto the dynamic tradition of the Old Covenant, and the Church became the God's people who had entered into this new relationship. Through this community of the New Covenant, they believed that God who had acted in days past now continued to work and act through the continuing power in their midst of Christ, their crucified and risen Lord.

In the words of Daniel Jenkins:

It is important to remember that the group of disciples whom Jesus gathered around Him during His earthly ministry were not yet properly constituted as the Church. They became that only after His death, resurrection and ascension, when the spirit descended upon them. These mighty events constituted the Church of the New Testament, just as the Exodus and the Law and the tabernacling presence in the Ark con-

[2] John Knox, *On the Meaning of Christ*, New York, Charles Scribner's Sons, 1947, p. 97.

The Church as Community

stituted the community of Israel in the Old. It was only when He who was the true Israel had bridged the gulf between God and mankind, had demonstrated the victorious power of God over sin, and had borne our mortal natures back to the Father's presence with Him, covered with His righteousness, that the work was complete which inaugurated the new community of God's people and released His Spirit to dwell in their midst.[3]

Out of this historical perspective thus emerges a functional definition of the Church as a community which lives even today; for the event is still occurring and members of the Church are integral parts of it. *The Church is the community of people who have entered into a New Covenant relation with the Father of Jesus Christ.* The Church exists to fulfill God's purpose in the world. At the same time it stands in prophetic judgment over against the world and against itself in criticism for injustice, disharmony, separation, arrogance, inhumanity, unbrotherliness, hatred. The Church is a society within a society. Sometimes it is true to its own essential purpose and at other times it is false—in substitution of outward form, bigotry, narrowness, dogmatism for a living relationship with God.

The figure of speech which Herbert H. Farmer suggests concerning the Church is simple but effective. He asks whether you have ever gone into one of these fun houses at the amusement park and found yourself in front of the distorting mirrors. There is one that makes you look like a clothes prop and another that makes you look like a barrel. You vaguely recognize yourself in both mirrors; for it is your coat, your hat, your face. But the exaggeration causes you to smile or wince, depending on your mood. At any rate, it is a relief to turn again to the plain mirror, where despite all the imperfections you have learned to put up with all your life, at least it is *you* as a somewhat normal human being. You wish it might be better, but you are glad it is no worse.

[3] Daniel Jenkins, *The Strangeness of the Church*, New York, Doubleday & Company, 1955, p. 43.

It is something like this when we look at the Church as it actually is and then turn to an undistorted vision of the Church as it ought to be, indeed, as it is essentially in fulfillment of God's purpose in the world. The many particular denominational churches which we know on this corner and that are like the queer caricatures of the distorting mirrors. Now there is this element exaggerated and now that. In most cases the elements are all there in varying form, but all essential: the Bible read and interpreted, a duly ordained ministry, local congregations, orders of worship, observance of the sacraments, ecclesiastical government, doctrinal tradition, works of service and charity, and continuing fellowship with Christ as its dynamic center. Every existing church possesses these elements in greater or lesser degree, for these are the functional marks of a church. But, like the images in the queer mirrors, these elements become distorted. Some have one form of government and some another. Some have one way of worshiping or ordaining ministers or observing the sacraments or stating their doctrinal traditions. Others may have entirely different patterns and forms.

To many a bewildered modern-minded person this variety of beliefs and practices seems most discouraging. Some simply give up all effort to understand. Others become carping and critical. Even once-active church members who may have undergone some unfortunate personal experience in human relations now have become bitter and cynical. The Church is divided, they begin to say. The Church is behind the times and blind and deaf to human need across the world. The Church is full of hypocrites who rarely do the things they profess. So run some of the critical comments about the churches.

What shall those who stand inside the Christian community reply? That word *inside* is the key to the situation in which the member of the Church stands. It is essential here to remember our discussion in Chapters VIII and IX. There is a profound difference between "history as lived" and "history as seen," between

234

participant and observer. The Christian community is even now a historical reality continuous with the long centuries of significant events through which God has acted. As throughout past years, men and women today may respond in faith. But there can be no faith of this sort for the coldly objective observer looking in from the outside. For to respond to God's self-disclosure through events in history means to participate in those self-same events, to become personally involved in them in a fresh and decisive way. Thus the way of response to God is the way, not of detachment, but of involvement in a long chain of events. This is one's *Heilsgeschichte* or *redemptive history* which illuminates all the partial histories of his many immediate concerns and interests. These latter define only fragments of man's being: family, allegiances, associations. But through man's redemptive history his life is released from triviality and meaninglessness.[4] This is the history within which faith as response to God becomes alive and dynamic. To be a member of the Christian community in ours or any age is to be possessed of this kind of committed faith toward God who acts and demands responsible decision. Conversely, to have this kind of faith is to be a member of the Christian community.

Belief in the Church as the Christian community is of the same sort as belief in God, Jesus Christ, the Bible, or the Resurrection. Standing aside in the attempt objectively to weigh evidence for or against is futile. In this case also, faith is prior to reason. Faith in the Church means participation and personal concern within a community where even now God speaks and acts, and men may hear and respond. But this confidence in *the Church* does not mean that participants need be blind to the imperfections of the actual churches. There is a difference between the many churches and *the Church*. The Church is an order of reality far beyond the imperfect thing humans make of it. The Church is something more than the sum total of existing churches. The figure of the mirrors

[4] See Chap. VIII, note 3.

suggested above breaks down because the Church is more than an image. It is a reality that keeps coming alive in every age when dynamic encounter takes place between God and men. These men who sincerely love the Church thus would make this kind of answer to nonparticipating critics: We are not members of the historic fellowship of Christians because we think we have arrived, but precisely because we know we have not. God knows that those who profess His Name fail. They twist and distort his commission in their hypocrisy, faithlessness, and even by the intense "busyness" of church organization and activity. But, beyond its weaknesses, worldliness, indifference, and hypocrisy, is *the Church* as it ought to be and as it is essentially. It is called the Church Triumphant, the Church Invisible, the Body of Christ, the Universal Brotherhood, the One, Holy, Catholic (universal), and Apostolic Church.

This, despite what is wrong with existing churches on this corner or that, is the Church of Christian faith. It is a historic fellowship, a world community, a company of seekers. There is the Church as *ecclesia*—that which is called out—summoned to take up specific business and to fulfill a particular public purpose. But also the Church is the *koinonia* or fellowship. H. Paul Douglass makes the point in this connection that the Church as *ecclesia* existing today means the visible institution or organizational life of the churches. As these are many and various, this institutional phase of the Church is characterized by disunity. Yet, beneath all this disunity, a unity already exists. It is the *koinonia,* possessing a unity that is "truly objective, definable, not merely indefinite and subjective nor 'a mere ideal and disembodied ghost,' to use Professor George Thomas' phrase." [5] This *koinonia* even now is in existence. It is that real community to which Christians of many different institutional churches believe themselves to belong. But such unity as this does not destroy individual freedom or differences of religious

[5] H. Paul Douglass, "Eumenicity in America," in *Toward World-Wide Christianity* (The Interseminary Series, ed. O. Frederick Nolde, Vol. IV), New York, Harper & Brothers, 1946, Chap. 5, p. 170.

expression. Men and women today desperately seek to "belong," and yet no totalitarian regime or organization that swallows up individuals can satisfy this need; for persons need their freedom as well as the security of membership within a larger fellowship.

In this connection, Daniel Day Williams writes:

> The Christian Church in essence is the one universal community which answers to the deepest need of men. It is not a substitute for family, nation, trade union or club. But it differs from all of these because it relates men to eternal destiny and holds up the one loyalty to God above all other loyalties. The community of the Church unites personal freedom and a shared life in one social organism. It offers the kind of human relationships which are appropriate to sinners who are reconciled to one another through God's grace. It is just this community of reconciliation and eternal life which no secular order by itself can bestow. The profound tension between individualism and collectivism is met within the Church, and finds the foundation for its solution there. If in faith we hold this to be true, then the Church as the "new people among the people" can bear in its own life a practical witness to hope for a new, decent and peaceful order for the peoples of the world. In spite of manifest failures, the churches show signs of a renewal from within to achieve a more adequate demonstration of this possibility.[6]

SPECIFIC FUNCTIONS OF THE CHURCH

But how does the Church, through the many particular churches, set about to bring men, women, and young people into a living fellowship with the Father of the Lord Jesus Christ? What are the specific functions of the Church? This involves what theologians call "church order." Church order is more basic than "church polity," or institutional organization. Rather, church order is the shape or form through which the Church seeks to carry out Christ's purpose in the world. For Christians, as members of the fellowship of which Christ is the Head, believe they have a responsibility for the fulfillment of his mission among men and nations. In order to ensure this, they must provide for the carrying out of certain

[6] Daniel Day Williams, *What Present-Day Theologians Are Thinking,* New York, Harper & Brothers, 1952, pp. 126-127.

specific functions. We shall list briefly these essential phases of church order.

1. The people who belong to the Christian community must provide for the winsome and thorough preaching of the living Word of God by an adequately trained ministry. The *Word,* in terms of our discussion on revelation, means God's disclosure of Himself to men in such a way as to call forth response in faith. God's Word is God's speech to men, not in words merely, but through events. Jesus Christ is "the Word made flesh," and hence the central revelatory event. Deeds and words, speech and acts, are inseparable in the Hebraic-Christian tradition. The Scriptures are thus the record in words of God's self-disclosure. To become really sensitive of insight into the living Word of God contained in the Scriptures requires training. This is a task for the minister in his interpretation of God's Word and its application to the needs of the contemporary world. But the individual believer also must read and interpret for himself. For the danger is, especially in the Protestant churches, that a brilliant sermon delivered from the pulpit by a chosen professional will be considered the whole fulfillment of Christian response and life. The Word of God is channeled *through* the preaching into the hearts and minds of the Church's members and must find its way out into commitment and action in the world of everyday affairs. Thus preaching is not a "show" and a congregation is not an "audience." Rather, preaching is a corporate act in which all share as together members of the worshiping community wait expectantly for God's living Word in their midst until they make response in faith. When this happens, the Church as community comes into being in fresh and exciting ways for each succeeding generation.

2. The next phase of church order is that of the administration of the sacraments, especially the Lord's supper, Communion, Eucharist, or Mass as it is called in different traditions. Christians of Catholic persuasion will say that this ought to have been placed first, before the preaching of the Word. Protestants understand the

function of preaching well enough, but find stress on the sacraments a strange business. Sometimes Protestants regard the sacraments of baptism and the Lord's Supper as beautiful ceremonies with aesthetic appeal and at others as simply a memorial of past events or inspiration to dedicated service. Are the sacraments more significant than this? Are they necessary to the fostering of dynamic faith and action? Beneath all the differing interpretations of the sacraments, the consensus of Christian conviction is that Jesus Christ is present in the midst of the living community during the observance of these rites. This is a *real* presence. The Catholic view of transubstantiation is that the substance of bread and wine in the Mass is changed into the body and blood of Christ; certain Protestants believe that the Lord's Supper is simply a rite of remembrance. Unfortunately, the various churches are more seriously divided over the sacraments than over any other issue. Yet, however it may be conceived, the sacramental act stands at the very center of the Church's life. As one classic statement affirms, a sacrament is "an outward and visible sign of an inward and spiritual grace given unto us; ordained by Christ himself, as a means whereby we receive the same, and a pledge to assure us thereof." [7] Through ordinary physical things, that is, God gives Himself to men and is known by them until the whole corporate and individual life of the community becomes infused with His Spirit.

3. The Church, as expression of its order, also manifests its life in certain specific functions. The Church organizes itself into structures of government with appointed offices among both the clergy and laity. Again, wide variation of form and authority is to be observed. Provision must be made for the education, ordination, and installation of ministers. Christian education of children, youth, and adults must be undertaken, with adequate curricular materials and trained teachers. The work of missions both at home and abroad is also a major enterprise of the various churches, as well

[7] *The Book of Common Prayer . . . According to the Use of the Protestant Episcopal Church in the United States of America*, p. 581.

as responsibility in the field of higher education. The churches' concern and responsibility for social education and action are important as expressions of devotion to love and justice, as well as care for the sick, the distrait, the needy, the dying, and those enduring a living death of degradation, despair, and separation from God. In all these ways and many more, the people who are called of God believe they have grave responsibility to create the means through which God's gracious gift of love may be made known among men.

Chapter **XVII**

Ecumenical Christianity

We have spoken of the movement among the many churches toward greater realization of the world-wide or ecumenical fellowship. It is important to note that it is a *movement* to which we refer and not a completed fact. The goal of this movement, as one writer states it, is "church unity within a world context." Or again, "The ecumenical movement is a movement towards Christian solidarity in life and work throughout the inhabited globe." The proper usage of this word in our century dates from the Oxford Conference on Church, Community and State which gathered Christians (with the exception of Roman Catholics) from all across the earth in 1937. The ecumenical movement may be discerned, at city, county, state, and national levels, wherever men and women reach across denominational barriers toward better understanding. There have been a series of conferences throughout our century at every level, culminating in the formation of the World Council of Churches in Amsterdam in 1948 and meeting again at Evanston in 1954. To this latter gathering came some 1300 official participants, of whom 500 were voting delegates and another 500 were accredited visitors. These persons represented 54 countries and 179 distinct churches and denominations. The theme of this Second Assembly was "Christ—the Hope of the World." The exciting drama of preparation for and actual conduct of the Evanston 1954 gathering cannot possibly be reproduced in a volume of this scope. The literature on this meeting, as culmination of the ecumenical movement in our century, is readily accessible.[1]

To aid our understanding of the ecumenical movement in our own century, we need in this chapter to grasp (1) something of the sweep of history as we trace the origins of the diverse denominations in America. (2) We shall discuss some of the main obstacles to realization of the ecumenical goal. (3) We shall consider positive steps now in progress toward completer understanding and coöperation as the several churches stand face to face, but, more important, as all alike confront a world of bewildering confusion and challenge.

ORIGINS OF DENOMINATIONS

What is the origin of all these diverse denominations? Why did they divide in the first place? In the United States there are some 254 different Protestant and Orthodox church bodies and these represent about 59 percent of all church membership throughout the country. But of these 254 denominations, by far the larger number are splinter groups and contain a very small proportion of the country's total membership. There are only about 80 denominational bodies with over 50,000 members each, and these 80 bodies report over 98 percent of the total Protestant membership. But about 30 of these churches group themselves into the main denominational "families" which make up the central movement of

[1] Among the books suggested in the Appendix, the reader will find helpful the volume prepared in anticipation of the Assembly, published by Harper & Brothers, entitled *The Christian Hope and the Task of the Church*. Also noteworthy are James Hastings Nichols, *Evanston, An Interpretation;* James W. Kennedy, *Evanston Scrapbook;* Cecil Northcott, *Evanston World Assembly;* issues of the *Christian Century*, August–September, 1954; in addition to slides and documentary films which are available. Also the official report of the Second Assembly, entitled *Evanston Report*, edited by W. A. Visser t'Hooft and published in 1955 by Harper & Brothers. Publication lists are available from the World Council of Churches office.

Protestantism in the United States: Baptist, Methodist, Lutheran, Presbyterian, Reformed, Episcopal, Disciples of Christ, and Congregational-Christian. And these are all different from the Roman Catholic and Orthodox bodies, which date back to the beginnings of Christian history.[2]

In tracing the main reasons for these differences, it is essential to remember that churches always grow and take on specific form within the larger social environment in which they do their work. The Church, as "a society within society," is thus in dynamic interaction with culture. Throughout the centuries organized religion performs two distinct but closely related functions. One is its *conservative* function and the other is its *prophetic* function. Reaching back into Hebrew history, we see an Amos in the eighth century B.C. come striding from the country into the city only to find that the religious order and the political order were indistinguishable. Men, and even priests, had lost sight of the demands of the covenant relation for purity of worship and deep concern for justice among their fellow men. In the name of covenant religion, Amos became the critic of a religion that consisted in little more than giving its sanction to unjust social and economic practices. It is important for organized religion to conserve in a constructive way the best values and practices of a given cultural order. But the danger is always myopic contentment with things as they are that can lead only to stubborn attempt to keep things as they are at all costs, no matter if religion itself is used to sanctify injustice. Then it is that a prophet of God like an Amos must bring to bear the other function of religion, that of protest against a complacency that fondly imagines it is already fulfilling the demands of covenant religion. This dynamic process of conservation interacting with prophetic protest repeats itself over and over again throughout the course of history. Thus within the Church itself, living in vital

[2] See *Year Book of American Churches,* Benson Y. Landis (ed.), published each year by the Office of Publications and Distribution, National Council of the Churches of Christ in the U.S.A.

responsiveness to a changing cultural environment, there rise up from time to time individuals and groups sensitive under God to the need of reform. Such persons are confronted with two choices: either to stay within the existing order in church and society to seek new levels of spiritual life and morality or, on the other hand, to move outside the established community to begin again the construction of new forms of belief and practice. No matter which of these options is chosen, the peril is that of human pride which says: "My way is the right way and my way is God's way." But this pattern of involvement and protest, within the Church and between the Church and society, helps us understand the root causes of what we call *sectarianism* through the ages.

The earliest Christian community played its role as a society within the larger society of the Roman Empire and was at first a people apart. Then in the fourth century the empire officially became "Christian." Thus through the intervening period, until the Reformation of the sixteenth century, the very force of integration for European society as a whole was that of Christianity. The Church and empire were two organs of the same society. The Reformation movement loosened the forces of freedom and protest, and what John Baillie calls "compulsory Christianity" was supplanted by an "open Christian civilization." For long centuries, that is, whole communities were baptized into Christianity under compulsion of their leaders. But later the relation of the Christian movement to civilization included larger degrees of free choice.

Always within this movement there arose groups which objected to the Church's compromises and accommodations to the secular order and thus insisted on stricter discipline. Here in a sense emerged a new "faithful remnant" as protests against the Established Church became stronger: Waldensians, Lollards, Hussites, and then followers of Zwingli, Luther, and Calvin. Thus the latter of these comprise what are sometimes called Right Wing Protestants, for they did not separate themselves from society in their sweeping condemnation of the Roman Church. Then followed others, called Left Wing in their extreme sectarianism, who thought that the earlier reformers had left their work half-done, for example, the Anabaptists, or "rebaptizers," with their stricter standard of church membership. These Left Wing Protestants, finding society corrupt, withdrew into exclusive communities where they believed they could live out the austere and literal demands of the Gospel ethic.

But underlying these differences lay broad areas of agreement among the various branches of the Protestant movement as men made their bid for the worship and service of God in what they believed to be an authentic way. Detailed understanding of the principal insights and contributions of Reformation Christianity is a study in itself, and the reader is referred to the Appendix for a suggested list of books in this field. Here, however, we would say that the Reformation is a many-sided movement. It is a revolution within other revolutions of the modern world, such as the geographical, cultural, political, and economic, through which new perspectives and ways of doing things opened up to imaginative men. The Reformation is complicated and morally ambiguous. But it is primarily a radical reorientation of religious faith. It is dynamic, fresh, and creative and yet a vital rediscovery of aspects of the Christian message that had been smothered for centuries. Protestantism did not begin suddenly, even though its most dramatic expressions seem to have burst upon the world within a comparatively short period. Traces of this emphasis may be found in Augustine, Francis of Assisi, Duns Scotus, the Dominicans, Tauler. Through the years, lay movements sprang up, such as the "Brethren of the Common Life," seeking to lead dedicated Christian lives independent of ecclesiastical authority.[3]

Key impulses of Reformation Christianity include the repudiation of monasticism and special priestly orders and the access of

[3] See George F. Thomas (ed.), *The Vitality of the Christian Tradition,* New York, Harper & Brothers, 1945, Chap. 5; and James Hastings Nichols, *Primer for Protestants,* New York, Association Press, 1947.

every man through faith that is a free and willing acceptance of God's gracious love for mankind. After the first dynamic contributions of men such as Luther and Calvin in the sixteenth century, there came the task of expressing in systematized doctrine and dogma the significance of new insights. Thus there developed a Protestant Scholasticism which tended to regard faith as *assent* to certain theological propositions and was often even farther removed from original sources of Christian experience than pre-Reformation religion. This occurred in the late sixteenth and early seventeenth centuries and developed into the fundamentalism of a day nearer our own. It is essential, therefore, to distinguish classical Protestantism from these other trends.

Among the main tenets of classical Protestantism, as expressed by Luther and Calvin, the following may be listed briefly.

1. *Justification by faith,* which we discussed in a preceding chapter, finds its source in the insights of Paul and Augustine. Man is justified by faith alone and not by the works which he performs. For faith is an inner experience of willing acceptance of God's own gift of Himself through Jesus Christ.

2. *The Sovereignty of God* is the emphasis especially of John Calvin. A sovereign, majestic God gives power, meaning, and being to the whole universe. For He is all-powerful will and ultimate source of all events in nature and human history. Men rebel against God's will, but can be saved from themselves and their pride only by God's own grace as loving forgiveness. As God is the One who originates and controls life, it is not through mere acts of penance and men's good works that things are accomplished in history, but by the majesty and power of God. This is a doctrine of assurance, but it does not rob men of moral responsibility. Men need not fear parliaments and kings, for God alone possesses ultimate authority over human life and destiny. No matter how humble or insignificant a person may be, if he reaches out and accepts Christ, God assures him that his life ultimately will not be lost.

3. As to the *role of Jesus Christ and the Scriptures,* Christ is

the self-disclosure of God; for through him, God's grace is made available to men. This is the unique, indispensable, self-authenticating focus of God's Word. The Bible thus, as words, is the record of God's self-disclosure to man. It does not possess, for these reformers, literal authenticity, as if the book itself were an "infallible and untouchable record." Rather, it becomes again, as it has been said, "a prompter's script for the dialogue of man and God."

4. The *Reformation conception of the Church* asserts that Jesus Christ himself is Head of the Church, as men of faith exercising their right and responsibility of private judgment recognize him as Lord, as "the Word made flesh." Central to this view is "the priesthood of all believers," which means basically that every man is "priest" to his fellow believers within the Christian community. Here involved is the conception of the Church as "the community of the forgiven and the forgiving," within which there is mutuality of concern rather than submission to externally imposed authority. It follows that the clergy are technically not priests, but that, so far as fundamental matters are concerned, the minister is only another "believer" seeking out God's Will for our human situation. The sacraments also stress fellowship, within which God moves with His power and mercy. And, as for church government, it is the Protestant view that all believers have the privilege and responsibility of decision concerning matters that come before church bodies.

Although these basic convictions are characteristic of the broad movement of classical Protestantism, there are also differences between its various branches. Five great church traditions developed on European soil. The first was the Lutheran, founded in Germany and reaching out into Scandinavia and among minorities in Poland and in central Europe. The second church tradition, the Reformed, began under Zwingli and John Calvin and was influential in Switzerland, Holland, central Europe, Germany, France, and, as Presbyterianism, in Scotland, England, and the United States.

The third branch was the Anglican, first started in England under political necessity during the reign of Henry VIII and developed through the influences which came from continental Protestantism. Strong Roman Catholic sentiment remained in England and hence a middle road between Catholic and Protestant views was followed. Although the Thirty-nine Articles set forth the theological position of Anglicanism, the Prayer Book is the principal guide of devotion and Christian life for the Church and its members. Roman Catholic monasteries were confiscated in England and priests were permitted to marry. However, the office of the bishopric was maintained under conviction that none of the reforms had actually broken the line of succession carried down through the centuries by the laying on of hands from bishop to bishop. The Protestant Episcopal Church is the branch of the Anglican tradition found in the United States.

The fourth group of churches which came to birth during the Reformation are the "free churches," which above we have called churches of the Left Wing. Some of these tended toward a strictly literal interpretation of the Bible as the sole authority. Some rejected infant baptism and insisted on baptism for those who in adult years have arrived at their own decision to accept Christ. The Lord's Supper became a service of remembrance of Jesus Christ. Within this broad movement of the free churches are the Mennonites, the Baptists of Holland and England, and the Separatists of England. These latter represent strong influence from Calvinism but also the "free church" conception of the authority of the single congregation, hence the name Congregationalists. In some senses the Quakers or Friends as well as Methodists belong in this free-church movement. Although these were very different in origin and eventual outcome, they both stressed inner experience of the Christ with his power to transform the life of the individual. But characteristic of all these churches was their insistence on the separation of church and state. It is to this free-church attitude that the American conviction on this issue owes its origin, even among contemporary adherents of "classical" Protestantism.

Ecumenical Christianity

The fifth great tradition is that of Eastern Orthodoxy, or, more accurately, the Orthodox Church of the East, which dates back to the separation of Eastern churches from the West, beginning as early as the fourth century and brought to completion in the thirteenth. Adherents of this movement are found in Russia, Greece, the Balkan countries, the Middle East, and, through immigration, in smaller numbers in western Europe and the United States. The theology, liturgy, and history of Eastern Orthodoxy are studies in themselves, and those students especially interested are advised to seek reading suggestions and to visit actual services for appreciation of its rich heritage of worship.

OBSTACLES TO THE ECUMENICAL GOAL

The movement of Protestant Christianity came to America from these sources: Lutheran, Reformed, Anglican, "free church," and Orthodox. It is essential to remember now that many of the divisions among the various denominations on the American scene are due more to national and cultural differences than to those involving doctrine and practice. Successive waves of immigration from European countries caused schisms to appear even in churches of the same general ecclesiastical tradition. These folk would come here at different times. As later arrivals reached America, they found their fellow believers who had come earlier already changed in language, customs, and practices. They thus set up new churches to express this sense of separation. In turn, the more progressive elements moved on toward the West and became assimilated more rapidly to American ways. Often they even separated from the original denomination. Thus, on the American scene, these non-theological factors have played a decisive role in shaping the varieties of church life on this continent. In more recent years, cultural equalization and secular assimilation are gradually overcoming these barriers to closer understanding among the various churches.

But there remain in our day deep cleavages between churches

of varying traditions that have to do with the very nature of the Church itself. We advanced the idea in the previous chapter, and as the basis of the ecumenical goal in this chapter, that the Church is a universal *koinonia* or fellowship already in existence. Yet the Church as community contains within its own life serious obstacles to community. These difficulties are many and various, and involve such issues as the nature of the sacraments, infant versus adult baptism, the practice of open or closed communion, the source of qualification for ministers, apostolic succession, the necessity of bishops, whether or not there is any salvation outside the Church, forms of church government. These issues seem confusing to those who stand on the sidelines. Yet men have taken such controversies very seriously and have been led by their convictions to break off fellowship with other churches because of disagreement over such problems. But, as Walter Marshall Horton points out, "the meaning of each such conflict remains obscure until it is related to a larger issue of which it is only a local manifestation." [4]

Three main disagreements, according to Horton and also to Craig, stand in the way of closer unity: (1) If there is one church, what are its limits? (2) Is there a form which the Church everywhere must follow? (3) How can continuity be maintained within the one church? "Detailed disagreements," says Horton, "are simply nondiscussable until these larger issues are confronted."

As to the first principal issue, according to these authors, there are three main positions. The first is, "We are the Church," as asserted by the Roman Catholic Church and the Eastern Orthodox Church. For, beyond the limits of the *one* true Church, there can be no real church. This same basic point of view is sometimes adopted by Southern Baptists, Missouri Synod Lutherans, and some

---

[4] Walter Marshall Horton, *Christian Theology, An Ecumenical Approach*, New York, Harper & Brothers, 1955, p. 219. Horton in turn expresses indebtedness to C. T. Craig, *The One Church*, New York, Abingdon Cokesbury Press, 1951. We follow here their analysis of the central issues involved.

Anglicans who say that the one true Church exists in several "branches," Anglican, Orthodox, perhaps Roman, and Swedish Lutheran. A second perspective on this issue is a reaction against the first and asserts that the Church "does not exist" at all. The reason for this assertion is that "unity is an essential mark of the Church," and such unity transcends the multiplicity of existing churches. The ecumenical movement does not agree at all with this second view because it does claim to find an actual unity in the midst of all the divisions that separate the churches. Thus the churches that take part in the ecumenical movement, according to Horton, adopt a third view, that "the one church is found wherever God's saving grace is operative." The implication to be drawn is that the true Church is "by schisms rent asunder, by heresies perplexed," and yet it does not cease to exist.[5]

The second main issue has to do with the *form* of the Church. Some churches are convinced that there is only one form of church order that is grounded in New Testament Christianity, and that therefore there can be no other, be it Episcopal, Presbyterian, or Congregational. Other churches hold that the form of church orders is the result of historical conditions, and that therefore these may undergo change from time to time. Horton points out that it is these latter churches which are willing to unite with other churches, even though they operate under different forms of order. Those of the first type, on principle, cannot unite with others. It is to be noted that the First World Conference on Faith and Order (Lausanne, 1927) stated that "the episcopate, the council of presbyters, and the congregation of the faithful" are all authentic elements in the early Church and therefore "have an appropriate place in the order of life of a reunited church." [6] This combination of elements has actually been adopted into the polity of the Church of South India, which is an outstanding example of diversity in unity in the contemporary world.

[5] Horton, *op. cit.*, p. 220.
[6] *Ibid.*, pp. 220-221; see note 20.

Essentials in Christian Faith

The third serious issue is that of *continuity* in the Church. Those churches which take the most clearly definitive stand at this point are the Catholics, the Orthodox, and the Anglicans, who insist on the apostolic succession. Their conviction is that the authority of the ministry rests upon the succession of bishops from the time of the Apostles down to the present. This recognizable succession, they believe, not only authorizes that ministers and priests may be ordained by the laying on of hands but also that bishops, by virtue of their office, in continuous succession are actually guardians of the faith. If this continuity in the line of succession were to be broken at any point, they hold, this would destroy the very validity of ministerial ordination. Such a breach would also destroy the validity of the sacraments administered under an unauthorized ministry. Thus the whole "Catholic" conception of the Church, its authority, its ministry, and the sacraments as means of grace, depends upon this unbroken line of apostolic succession.

By contrast to the "Catholic" view of the visible continuity of the Church, the "Protestant" perspective stresses, not the historic episcopate, but God's immediate self-disclosure through His Word and the response of the faithful throughout each of the succeeding ages. This is a "vertical" relationship with the living Lord rather than a "horizontal" line of unbroken continuity. Protestants thus are less concerned with visible structure and claim rather that the Church is to be found "where the Word of God is rightly preached and the sacraments are rightly administered." The most extreme form of this conception of the Church is that held by the "free" churches. Here the Church is characterized as the "gathered community" in which the faithfulness of the witnessing congregation is the dynamic center of Christ's Spirit. In the middle, between the extremes of the "Catholic" and "Congregational" conceptions, lies that of "classical" Protestantism, Lutheran and Calvinistic (Reformed and Presbyterian). This latter view, for example, holds in high regard both the authority of the ministry and of church order. Robert S. Bilheimer writes of the Presbyterian position:

Ecumenical Christianity

The grounds for this position are chiefly two: scriptural and theological. The scriptural ground points to the dominant role of the Apostles in the life of the New Testament churches. The Presbyterian Church believes in an apostolic ministry, but does not regard the manner of succession as definitive. The marks of the apostolate are derived from the commission of Jesus to preach and to teach, and from faithfulness to the "Word of God" revealed in the Bible. The theological ground for the Presbyterian view of the ministry is derived from John Calvin's insistence upon the fact that God works instrumentally and from the importance which Calvin attached to the "right" preaching of the Word and the administration of the sacraments in the Church.[7]

POSITIVE STEPS TOWARD UNDERSTANDING

What positive steps are now in progress toward completer understanding and coöperation among the several churches and in view of their basic differences? The representatives of the churches which met in 1948 in Amsterdam for the first assembly of the World Council of Churches stated their resolve "to stay together" and never again to drop back into easy acceptance of their divisions. Thus were brought to consummation, in this resolve, long years of conversation between adherents of different traditions.

There are several misconceptions of the goals of the ecumenical movement in general and of the World Council of Churches in particular. Ecumenical unity does not mean the achievement of a world community; for that is a secular goal and a matter for governments. Nor does it mean a mere prudential reunion of unreconciled churches, as if unity were to be gained by mechanical shifting of organizational apparatus. Ecumenical unity does not mean *uniformity* of order throughout the whole Church in a fixed hierarchy of authoritarian rule. In like manner the World Council of Churches "is not and must never become a Super-Church," for "each Church retains the constitutional right to ratify or to reject utterances or actions of the Council." Again, the purpose of this

[7] Robert S. Bilheimer, *The Quest for Christian Unity*, New York, Association Press, pp. 166-167.

body "is not to negotiate unions between Churches, which can only be done by the churches themselves acting on their own initiative, but to bring the churches into living contact with each other. . . . The World Council cannot and should not be based on any one particular conception of the Church," nor "the acceptance of a specific doctrine concerning the nature of church unity." [8]

In positive terms, what is the goal of the ecumenical movement? It is that of unity in faith, life, and work conceived in terms of concrete corporate allegiance to Jesus Christ. For, fundamentally, Christians are not devoted to a program but to the *Person*. The Church is essentially a fellowship, the *koinonia*, infused with the Spirit of Christ. This is, of course, the way it started as an organism and not a mere society. It is "the Body of Christ." He is the Head and those who belong to Him are members. Thus the Church in this sense is already in existence as an instrument to be used more and more effectively by God to bring the power of reconciliation among men and nations. If this is the case, then the several churches are the particular expressions of this larger ministry, each contributing in its own way and according to its special gifts to this ecumenical goal.

In this same spirit, the member churches of the World Council hold among its basic assumptions "that conversation, cooperation and common witness of the churches must be based on the common recognition that Christ is the Divine Head of the Body." Again, they "believe on the basis of the New Testament that the Church of Christ is one." Also the "member churches recognize that the membership of the Church of Christ is more inclusive than the membership of their own church body. They seek, therefore, to enter into living contact with those outside their own ranks who

[8] *The Christian Hope and the Task of the Church,* New York, Harper & Brothers, 1954, pp. 10-11. These quotations and those which immediately follow are from a statement discussed in 1950 by the Central Committee at Toronto, and thus called the "Toronto Statement." This is not the final word, but part of the continuing discussion through which greater understanding may come.

254

confess the Lordship of Christ." The Toronto Statement concludes: "None of these positive assumptions, implied in the existence of the World Council, is in conflict with the teachings of the member churches. We believe therefore that no church need fear that by entering into the World Council it is in danger of denying its heritage." [9]

James Hastings Nichols cites a comment made at a meeting of the British Council of Churches by Archbishop Fisher of Canterbury. To someone who stated that a certain church "would not feel at home in the World Council," he replied, "There is no member church of the Council which feels at home there." Nichols adds:

A genuinely ecumenical enterprise is precisely one where no one feels at home, where all are challenged, threatened, embarrassed, and yet remain in conversation. An ecumenical gathering is one where our associates are not just those with whom we agree or with whom we feel at home. For most American supporters of the World Council good test questions might be, "Do you really accept the responsibility of relating yourself positively to Roman Catholics and to fundamentalists, as part of the task of manifesting the oneness of the Church?" Merely regional or confessional conferences are places where people feel "at home," because the invitations have been sent out on some criterion of those whom we like, rather than of those whom Christ has called. An ecumenical movement concerns the *whole* Church of Christ and its total task. Nothing less than this universal Christian perspective is properly ecumenical.[10]

Yet it must be added that it is not only division within the Church which ecumenical Christianity proposes to face in all honesty and understanding. For outside the Church, as well, new and challenging problems confront the Christian community on a world-wide scale. The Church has always been faced with new situations. Thus, through the years, one section of the ecumenical movement has been concerned with the relation of the Christian Gospel to the social, political, economic, and international problems

[9] *Ibid.*, pp. 12-15.
[10] James Hastings Nichols, *Evanston, An Interpretation*, New York, Harper & Brothers, 1954, pp. 97-98.

which confront peoples and nations everywhere. "Doctrine divides, service unites," was the slogan. If we cannot agree on doctrinal matters, advocates of this view argued, we can at least agree upon common plans of action in the social order. Time and experience have shown, however, that this is one way but *only* one way toward the ecumenical goal. Study of the proposed theme of the Evanston Assembly brought the issue to a head: "Christ—the Hope of the World." But what kind of hope? many asked. Is this hope oriented toward specific historical goals or is it a hope that can be consummated only at the end of history? American practical concerns for this world seemed seriously at variance with European preoccupation with an ultimate goal when God would bring this order to completion in final judgment. Those charged with working out the theme of the Evanston Assembly sought to strike a balance between these extremes. They stated: "The new hope is still hope in God, the maker and ruler of all things, but it is hope at once fulfilled and expectant. . . . Christ is not only our righteousness and our peace; He is also present in us as the hope of glory." [11]

As the world Church faces the task of developing specific answers to specific problems, the wide diversities of perspective will doubtless create tension; for these are some of the issues proposed for consideration: the role of the state in economic life, and its limits; the role of organized labor in modern society; the place of the businessman in modern society; the problems of underdeveloped countries; the economic responsibilities of the West; the responsibility of the member churches in relation to the challenge of Communism.

"The Responsible Society in a World Perspective" was the theme to be undertaken by the third section at Evanston. The Amsterdam Assembly posited this as the goal toward which the churches should work and defined it as a society "where freedom is the freedom of

[11] *Report of the Advisory Commission on the Main Theme of the Second Assembly, The Christian Hope and the Task of the Church*, New York, Harper & Brothers, 1954, p. 5.

men who acknowledge responsibility to justice and public order and where those who hold political authority or economic power are responsible for its exercise to God and to the people whose welfare is affected by it." Beyond this general statement the Church now proposes to venture in faith and competence into fields of specific tasks. Amid all the complexities of our world situation, ecumenical Christianity affirms: "We are one in Christ. We are divided in our Churches. But we are witnesses to the fact that God has led us to move together in our disunity toward the Lord who has given us our Oneness and who will glorify Himself in His Church." Again, "Because our hope is in Christ, we are saved from frustration where our efforts to influence public opinion or social action are seemingly in vain, and we are saved from despair when all human hopes collapse." And James Hastings Nichols comments, "In its ecumenical character, moreover, the people of God must seek to become the kind of community which God wishes the world to become. Christians of nations in tension must visit one another and in their fellowship nurture the possibility of reconciliation of all races, nationalities and classes in love of Christ." [12]

[12] Nichols, *op. cit.*, p.143.

Chapter XVIII

And the Life Everlasting

LIFE EVERLASTING AMONG BASIC CHRISTIAN BELIEFS

When thoughtful students are offered an option among several different topics on religion, almost invariably they choose to discuss the Life Everlasting. It is the age-old question which Job asked out of the midst of his physical pain and spiritual agonizing: "If a man die, shall he live again?" Apparently, therefore, many today are interested in the question. But do the same number believe in the Life Everlasting with utter commitment of faith? Sometimes concern about this issue may be stimulated in college class or church discussion group, and thus many folk do have opportunity to talk about these matters in objective fashion. But we wonder about the large groups of people outside the range of special opportunity of classroom or church discussion for whom these questions are pushed aside by the varied demands of the world of practical affairs. One has the impression that many men and women who call themselves "modern" (because they know something of the terminology of the sciences and have attained a certain degree of success in this world) have little interest in the life to come.

It is said that in the Middle Ages they devised a refined form of torture more dreaded than any other. The man to be punished was not killed or his flesh burned with hot irons. He was just put in a prison cell where he could never quite stand straight. Above him was a tiny window with light streaming through, but he could not quite stretch to it. He might sit, or he might lie down, but he could never stand erect or see the sky.

Symbolically this is something like the oppressive feeling that came upon mankind with the modern era. The human race rebelled against the authoritative tyrannies of church and state and grew restive within the confining limitations of ignorance and superstition. Thus modern men wanted to stretch, to stand upright, to think for themselves, to investigate, to learn, to achieve creativity in arts and literature, moral independence, and political freedom. Men and women of our twentieth century are heirs of this kind of hope; for we have come to believe in the power to order our own lives, to think our own thoughts, to build a society that embodies our dreams.

Clearly the gains of this self-reliant outlook on life are not to be underrated, for it has helped give us the civilization and culture of the modern West. But we begin to wonder in the midst of self-congratulation whether or not we are justified in thinking of the world "as man's own show." For some among us, disillusionment begins to set in as we see horizons closing in. There are limits within which human beings must live; and the final limit—the "iron ring around existence"—beyond which we cannot pass, is *death*.

In the words of the Epistle to the Hebrews: "Here we have no continuing city." Central to Christian conviction, suggests John Baillie, "there lies the tragic realization (a) that all human and earthly things must come to an end, and (b) that they must come to an end *before* they are made perfect."[1] This kind of realism is essential to Christian faith. It is negative and only half the complete affirmation which the Christian would make. Yet this frank facing of the fact that this life appears to be bounded by horizons

[1] John Baillie, *Invitation to Pilgrimage*, New York, Charles Scribner's Sons, 1942, p. 96.

beyond which we humans cannot pass is an essential ingredient. On this side of the horizon there seems to be final defeat. Yet the Christian believes that on the other side lies the completion of man's highest good and fulfillment of his most perfect destiny, beyond all the bounds and possibilities of this present life.

But what of those men and women who still feel competent in this life? Will all this talk about a life to come make very much appeal? One has an idea that those who are successful in the practical world will find little appeal in the selfish advantage of securing further competence in a world to come. Yet, unfortunately, this is the burden of much that passes for Christian belief. The rewards and punishments of a future world are sometimes held out to people as to little children. "You'd better be good," they are told. "But why be good?" they ask. "Because it pays in the long run," is the apparent answer.

But genuine Christian concern and conviction are grounded more deeply than this. Basically, even the most worldly among us want a different standard applied in this area of our lives from that by which we conduct our everyday business and seek our pleasure. Most honest folk have only contempt for holding the life to come as a reward in that fashion, morality as just an extension of worldly expediency into another world, and religion as just a cheap way of keeping us good.

If this kind of appeal does not convince men and women of modern mind, then men of Christian faith must make it clear what they *do* mean when they speak of the Life Everlasting. But their frank insistence is that the main business of Christianity is not to demonstrate the reality of the future life, nor its chief motive that of securing for oneself a haven of security in another world. The chief concern of Christianity is that of bringing men and women into vital relationship of encounter and response with God through Christ, and consequent release and freedom of fellowship and service among one's fellow men—whether here or hereafter. All that we have said about this in preceding chapters comes to focus on this point, and the student of Christianity is encouraged to recall these matters in his own summation of faith.

From this background, the following observations become important:

1. The Life Everlasting does not mean simply quantitative extension of life into an indefinite future, but rather qualitative difference of life beginning in the present moment and continuing on into each succeeding moment.

"Immortality is one thing," said Joseph Fort Newton, "eternal life is another. The one may be mere duration, the other is depth, richness, radiance of life, overflowing, sparkling, free. . . . The fate of civilization rests with those who are citizens of eternity in time."

What this insight indicates is that the main task of the Christian is with *this* life. Such a view is frankly "this-worldly" in the deepest sense of that term. Only in this way can it properly be "other-worldly." That is to say the Christian holds that committed intent to live out God's purposes here and now is more truly "spiritual" than the selfish hope of reward as the only motive for being "good." For there is so much of God's justice and love that must be made actual within the sphere of human relationships.

2. It follows from these considerations that belief in the Life Everlasting does not stand by itself among Christian convictions. Just as this affirmation is not and ought not to be first in motive, it is not first in logical order of our thinking. For the Christian holds other beliefs first and this follows from them.

Among these convictions is that the world is more than a machine. It is alive with purpose, order, meaning—moving and being moved in the direction of completer truth and goodness. The universe is a person-producing universe, conserving, promoting all that is highest in value and personal life. It is a moral universe. Behind, in and through it all is the God who is creative Will to goodness actively at work in wooing the world to Himself. God discloses Himself in the events of history and in the experience of men. Even though men are created in His image, they rebel and separate themselves from God. Yet God acts to overcome this separation and thus to reconcile men to Himself. The same God who moves in history also discloses Himself in the order, beauty, and purposiveness of nature. But God reveals Himself, so the Christian affirms, as righteousness, justice, and love in and through the personality, teaching, life, death, Resurrection, and continuing presence of Jesus Christ—thus saving men for a life of fulfillment and devoted service.

If this view of the universe, God, and the significance of human life makes no sense as a meaningful world hypothesis, then there is no need even to raise the question of the Life Everlasting. But if it does make sense as a meaningful faith, then the Life Everlasting or Eternal Life, not just quantitative extension of years, but qualitative difference of intention, character, and conduct, becomes a genuine option. Such a view affirms the conviction that all the richness of personal existence and value will not ultimately be destroyed. The literal details as to precisely what a future life involves may vary, but it remains an affirmation of an essential insight about the ultimate destiny of all that is of worth in human experience, as rooted and grounded in the God of justice and love.

It is our purpose now in this chapter to discuss (1) the different ways in which the Life Everlasting is understood; (2) positive evidences which are frequently cited as ways of stating in the symbolic form of imagic language this basic affirmation of faith.

DIFFERENT UNDERSTANDINGS OF THE BELIEF

Generally under influence of the nonbiblical heritage (both Greek and Eastern), the doctrine of the Life Everlasting is interpreted as *immortality*. Four views of immortality are frequently cited. Some hold only the first; others, the first and second; others, the first, second, and third; and still others, the fourth. The fourth is the view which most distinctively belongs to the Christian perspective.

1. *Biological immortality* is a view held by naturalists and scien-

tific humanists who hold this natural order of space and time to be the whole of reality. Here the only "immortality" there is consists of the biological continuity of the human race handed down from generation to generation.

2. *Social immortality* is the view that what survives of an individual, in addition to biological factors, is the social influence of what we do, say, and achieve as these live after us through succeeding generations. George Eliot expresses this affirmation in verse:

> O may I join the choir invisible
> Of those immortal dead who live again
> In minds made better by their presence; live
> In pulses stirred to generosity,
> In deeds of daring rectitude, in scorn
> For miserable aims that end with self,
> In thoughts sublime that pierce the
>   night like stars,
> And with their mild persistence urge
>   men's search
> To vaster issues. . . .
> So to live is heaven. . . .[2]

3. *Impersonal immortality* is the view, which takes varying forms, that we as individuals or our souls are absorbed again into the universe, the realm of eternal being or the world soul, from which we originally came. That universal life moves on. As a part now of the great reality we move on also, but swallowed up—not conscious but yet merged into the world soul. This position sometimes takes the form of *pantheism,* in which the one reality, God or the universe, receives the individual person to itself as the drop of water is lost in the vast ocean. Views similar to this are also taught by Eastern religions which hold that the soul of the individual is absorbed into some huge reservoir of soul stuff within which it is but a tiny particle. In our Western tradition, this general perspective usually takes the form of Platonism. Greek thought rests on a

[2] From the poem, "O May I Join the Choir Invisible."

distinct dualism of body and soul as we described this view of human nature in Chapter V. The essential element in man is a deathless or immortal soul which belongs in its real nature to the realm of eternal forms. It is imprisoned for a time in the body, but it awaits release to realize its destiny. When Paul preached to the Athenians, philosophers holding this classical position listened to what he had to say. But what the Apostle proclaimed to them only startled and shocked them. For Paul stated that the Day of Judgment was near as the close consummation of history. The sign of this, he said, is the good news that God had raised Jesus Christ from the dead. The New Testament records the response which Paul's words elicited from them: "Now when they heard of the resurrection of the dead, some mocked; but others said, 'We will hear you again about this.'" [3] These Greeks shared Paul's confidence about a future life, but what they could not accept was Paul's confidence in the resurrection of the body and his statement that such a Resurrection had actually taken place in the case of Jesus Christ.

4. *Personal immortality* is thus even too pale a term to describe the Christian belief in the continuance of the whole person after death. The basis for such a claim as this is *faith in the character of the God who acts, comes into history, reveals himself to men and women, and conquers sin and death through the crucified and risen Christ*. Moving from this postulate—just as in the case of our discussion concerning the being of God, the divine-human character of Jesus Christ, the Resurrection—now the philosophical arguments have their place. But here also faith is prior and the so-called evidences which are adduced become symbolic or analogical statements of that prior faith and commitment.

W. Norman Pittenger writes that

. . . the *final* basis for the Christian belief in the persistence of man's personality beyond the grave is the nature of God as that has been dis-

---

[3] Acts 17:32, Revised Standard Version.

And the Life Everlasting

closed in religious experience, in history, and in meditation upon the meaning of life in the Christian fellowship. Furthermore, it is supremely founded upon the victory of Christ over death. . . .

If the eternal Reality is most adequately conceived as the heavenly Father, who created man in his image, who has given men the completed human image of himself in Christ, and who raised that human nature from death in the great events which we call Resurrection, eternal life would seem to follow as an inevitable corollary. Such a God must desire the fullest self-realization for every son of man, and clearly that is impossible in this short and problematical life.[4]

The Life Everlasting, within the Christian context of historic faith, thus means that the *unique and whole person* never dies, but lives on in fellowship with God and other persons through sharing in Christ's life and way. The resurrection of the body does not mean that human beings will have physical bodies after death exactly like those which they possess in life. Rather, this Hebraic way of stating the hope of life to come is vivid, pictorial, imagic language. It states that human persons will not be absorbed into some great reservoir of reality as in other conceptions of immortality. Humans in all their wholeness will, through an act of God, retain their uniqueness and individuality in community with Him. Paul expressed this perspective in I Corinthians 15 as he spoke of the resurrection of the dead:

But some will ask "How are the dead raised? With what kind of body do they come?" You foolish man! What you sow does not come to life unless it dies. And what you sow is not the body which is to be, but a bare kernel, perhaps of wheat or of some other grain. But God gives it a body as he has chosen, and to each kind of seed its own body. . . . So it is with the resurrection of the dead. What is sown is perishable, what is raised is imperishable. It is sown in dishonor, it is raised in glory. It is sown in weakness, it is raised in power. It is sown a physical body, it is raised a spiritual body. If there is a physical body, there is also a spiritual body.[5]

[4] W. Norman Pittenger, *The Christian Way in a Modern World,* Louisville, Cloister Press, 1944, p. 142.
[5] I Corinthians 15:35-44, R.S.V.

In this passage Paul is thus trying to avoid the view that some sort of separate "soul" or "spirit" is raised up. But rather, what is resurrected is a new and revitalized person. He knows that we are face to face with a mystery here, just as in the case of the experience of the risen Christ. It is impossible to be literal and exact; for all he can express is a conviction and a hope, based upon all that has happened of fulfillment through Jesus Christ, that the unique and total personality will live on in new fellowship with God. Says Paul: "Lo! I tell you a mystery. We shall not all sleep, but we shall all be changed . . . the dead will be raised imperishable, and we shall be changed." [6]

POSITIVE STATEMENTS IN RELIGIOUS LANGUAGE

What role do the arguments and positive evidences which are frequently cited play? The Christian clearly begins with his whole faith in God, the world, and man as illumined through commitment to Jesus Christ. As James Martineau has said: "We do not believe in Immortality because we have proved it, but we forever try to prove it because we believe in it." "Where is the proof?" still ask men and women of modern mind. The answer must be that there is no verifiable, scientific evidence for the Life Everlasting. But out of Christian faith grow hope and desire. Then the conviction emerges that hope and desire cannot be better than reality itself. The Christian then proceeds to make honest attempt at living on a new dimension of concerned and creative good will within the contagious presence of Christ's Spirit. As the whole of human existence begins to make sense in fresh and creative ways, the "proof," so the Christian believes, will come out of the depths of personal experience. With this perspective in mind, we now cite four evidences for the Life Everlasting as more specific ways of

[6] I Corinthians 15:51-52, R.S.V.

stating in symbolic form this confidence and hope which is central to Christian faith.

1. There is a line of argument which takes its clue from the evolutionary development of organic life, including that of man. It is an argument from analogy and is dangerously misleading if it is pressed too far beyond intended limits. This view is that *for every capacity and function of organic and human life, some corresponding answer in the world of reality seems to be found.*

We have thirst. In response to that need there is water. Desire for food is implanted in us. And out in the world food actually exists to satisfy the need. Every step of evolutionary development is marked by attainment of some physical or mental faculty which enables the organism to adjust to a larger environment. Every new faculty or ability is response to some actual existence in the outer world. For example, life was originally blind, then the nerves of vision developed in response to outwardly existing radiant light; result, the eye. Life was originally deaf; then in response to outwardly existing acoustic vibrations, ears developed with ability to hear.

John Haynes Holmes writes:

Every attribute we possess has been brought into being by some existing outward fact, and by that token is a living demonstration of the abiding reality of the fact. The eye proves the reality of light, the ear the reality of sound . . . the living organism is related to the universe as a coin is related to a die. The unmarked gold is placed in the stamping machine and slowly the die sinks into its texture until every mark upon the die has been transferred to the surface of the gold. The mere appearance of a line or a figure on the surface of the finished coin is all the proof that is needed of the original presence of that line or figure on the die. In the same way, the organism is placed in what we might call the stamping-machine of the universe. Slowly, through the long ages of the past, the die of outward reality has been pressed down upon the yielding texture of the organism, until every fact in the environing universe has made its indelible impression in the shape of organ, faculty, idea. And as with the coin, so with the organism, the presence of each inner attribute and power proves the actual existence in the outer world of the reality by which it has been created and to which it corresponds.[7]

In the same fashion, so this argument runs, there developed the family, social ideals, standards of right and wrong, moral and spiritual powers, as human beings made response to an ever new and larger environing universe. Then by analogy, parallel is drawn with man's belief in the Life Everlasting. Holmes adds: "The fact that man from the very earliest period of his existence has *had* the extraordinary idea of an Eternal Life . . . has never been able to get away from it . . . all this would seem to be the sure adaptation of the struggling spirit to the unseen reality of the universe." [8]

The conclusion to be drawn, according to this perspective, is that there must be some reality which corresponds to this persistent hope. But from the point of view of Christian faith, aside from its misleading interpretation of the evolutionary mechanism of heredity, this argument is valuable only if employed with extreme caution. It bears close resemblance to the arguments for the being of God, especially the ontological argument. There the very question of God's being is asked because an awareness of God has already taken place within the inner experience. With this as the basic presupposition of faith, the seeker finds kinship between his own mind and the order which pervades the universe. Also, in the case of this argument for Eternal Life now under discussion, perhaps the question and the search are more significant than any proof. For there are intimation and awareness, in which man's persistent hope is grounded, to which reality seems to make response.

Emerson in his "Essay on Immortality" tells of two men who had been engaged in earnest search for an answer to the agelong question of Eternal Life. An accident separated them for 25 years. When they met, they shook hands long and cordially, and one

[7] John Haynes Holmes, *Is Death the End?* New York, G. P. Putnam's Sons, 1915, p. 69.
[8] *Ibid.*, pp. 72-73.

friend asked, "Any light, Albert?" "None," replied Albert. "Any light, Lewis?" "None," he replied. And thus they parted, their long search still unended. But Emerson comments "that the impulse which drew those two minds to this inquiry through so many years was a better affirmative evidence for immortality than their failure to find a confirmation was a negative." [9]

In the Christian perspective, this kind of approach is but a tenuous beginning, for biblical faith is much more robust than this. But at any rate, we have here indication of the force of the very question itself concerning man's ultimate destiny, asked by countless men and women in age after age. To such a persistent impulse it seems reasonable to suppose that there is an answering reality and that man's hope and expectation are not in vain.

2. This argument is akin to the first because it also makes reference to the realm of nature, of which man is a part. This view states that *we live in a universe which conserves all its energies.* These apparently static things we see around us, chairs, tables, books, are not what they seem to be. What we call matter is made up of swirling centers of energy. Nothing stands still. Everything moves with ceaseless force. Light changes into heat; heat changes into motion; but there is no annihilation. By analogy, the question is then posed: Will a universe that so carefully guards all these physical energies then destroy man with his power to think, will, and love?

Again, what this argument is asserting is a corollary to the world view, held in faith, which affirms that man himself in his total personality is not reducible to the level of the material. Man is more than a thing. Human beings are justified in asserting the importance of their spirits. Men need not cower before the bigness of nature, for man is the only part of the universe that is aware of itself. Only human minds can order things into significance; create the beauty of a painting, poem, or symphony. Shall the

[9] Ralph Waldo Emerson, "Essay on Immortality," *The Complete Writings of Ralph Waldo Emerson,* New York, William H. Wise & Co., 1939, pp. 827-828.

269

beauty, truth, and goodness of life pass away into nothingness? The belief in Eternal Life is one way of saying that what is of worth shall endure through the continued self-conscious existence of the total personality after death. However, Christian belief in its sharper affirmation would add that this expectation is grounded in the love of God Himself in whose image man has been created and in whose everlasting fellowship fulfillment of human destiny will take place.

3. This is again a consequence of the Christian faith in God and His loving concern for each individual person. Here the hope of Life Everlasting is based on *our constant human craving for the completion of our individual lives.* Our days on earth are full of loose ends: tasks begun but not finished, dreams unrealized, powers wasted, opportunities lost beyond recall. But we do not feel this so much for ourselves as for those we have learned to love and respect. Our deepest dread is that their individuality will be lost. It is our hope that those who have gone on before us will be able somehow to keep on enriching the universe, in which we all live together, according to their special abilities.

Says blind and deaf Helen Keller: "Here and now our misfortune is irreparable. Our service to others is limited. Our thirst for larger activity is unsatisfied. The greatest workers for the race—poets, artists, men of science . . . are at times shaken with a mighty cry of the soul, a longing more fully to body forth the energy, the fire, the richness of fancy and of human impulse which overburden them. What wonder, then, that we with our more limited senses and more humble powers should with passionate desire crave wider range and scope of usefulness."

4. But there is one more word that must be stated, for it is the beginning and the end of all evidence for the Christian. *The hope of Everlasting Life is based on our experience of Christ.* The Christian faith is no refashioning of ancient philosophies or dim reflection of what wise men of all ages have said. It is fresh, new, sprung

270

And the Life Everlasting

from the soil of personal experience. It all came about because a certain man was born on earth. A few simple disciples trudged around after him, listening to his teaching and discovering new truths about life. Then suddenly He was dead, their friend gone, and for three days their grief was soul-shaking. All that they had hoped or dreamed was shattered. Then came Easter morning. Their faith was vindicated once more. "He lives," they said. "Death cannot defeat Him. He is the Son of God." Then later they added: "Because He lives, we shall live also."

There it is: a simple, world-shaking story. It is difficult to help modern men and women to interpret it, for there is so much doubt that gets in the way of faith. But if it does not mean what it says, that all that is divine within us shall live on, then the Christian Church will have to reverse two thousand years of history, find a new Gospel, rewrite the whole New Testament, and find another Saviour. Christ lives! So shall the sons of men. This is the climax of Christian affirmation.

Probably the aptest illustration out of all the modern writing on this subject comes from Professor John Baillie of Edinburgh University. He tells of visiting a friend who was soon to die. The friend told him of what he found to be helpful as he faced the end. More than anything else, he said, he had been thinking of the account he had heard long since of another man who, like himself, had come to his closing hours upon earth. That man's Christian physician told him that his days were but few. He said to his doctor: "Have you any conviction as to what lies beyond? Can you give me any idea of what awaits me in the future life?" As the doctor was fumbling, silently praying for an answer, there came a scratching at the door. The physician took the hand of his patient and said: "That's my dog. He has followed me into the house. He wants to come into this room. He doesn't know what's here. It's a mystery to him. All he knows is that I, his master, am here. And that's enough." He pointed above. "You do not know what lies beyond that door. Your Master and mine is there. He says, 'Where I am, there ye shall be also.' Is not that enough?" [10]

"If a man die shall he live again?" The Christian answer is an affirmative, and all of life is based on the conviction that the fullest life is one of fellowship with God, made accessible through Jesus Christ, a fellowship that may begin now and will persist throughout all eternity.

[10] John Baillie, *And the Life Everlasting*, New York, Charles Scribner's Sons, 1948, pp. 237-238.

Appendix

Major Ecumenical Conferences
of the Twentieth Century [1]

Conferences on World Missions

World Missionary Conference, Edinburgh, Scotland, 1910

International Missionary Meeting, Geneva, Switzerland, 1920

International Missionary Council

Constituting Meeting, Lake Mohonk, N.Y., U.S.A., 1921

Jerusalem, Palestine, 1928

Madras, India, 1938

Whitby, Ontario, Canada, 1947

Willingen, Germany, 1952

Conferences on Life and Work

Stockholm, Sweden, 1925

Oxford, England, 1937

Conferences on Faith and Order

Lausanne, Switzerland, 1927

Edinburgh, Scotland, 1937

Lund, Sweden, 1952

World Conference on Christian Youth

Amsterdam, The Netherlands, 1939

Oslo, Norway, 1947

Kotayam, Travancore, South India, 1952

World Council of Churches

Constituting Assembly, Amsterdam, The Netherlands, 1948

Second Assembly, Evanston, Illinois, U.S.A., 1954

[1] Lists of publications concerning the ecumenical movement in all its phases are available from the offices of the World Council of Churches and the National Council of Churches in the U.S.A. in New York City as well as from local city, county, and state council offices.

Suggested Reading

Students as well as general readers will think their way through their own beliefs through wide reading. Here listed are some of the books available in the various special fields of concern. Both the books of general interest and more advanced treatments include chapters on the special topics. Wise use of tables of contents will aid in finding relevant materials. Other works are listed under topical headings for more detailed reading. Corresponding chapter numbers within this volume are indicated. When this volume is used as a text, students will bring enriched background to class discussion by wide reading and the actual writing of critical reports.

WORKS OF GENERAL INTEREST ON BASIC CHRISTIAN BELIEFS

Bosley, H. A., *A Firm Faith for Today*, New York, Harper & Brothers, 1950.

Gray, Henry David, *A Theology for Christian Youth*, New York, Abingdon-Cokesbury Press, 1951.

Harkness, Georgia, *Conflicts in Religious Thought*, New York, Harper & Brothers, 1949.

Harkness, Georgia, *Foundations of Christian Knowledge*, New York, Abingdon-Cokesbury Press, 1955.

Harkness, Georgia, *Understanding the Christian Faith*, New York, Abingdon-Cokesbury Press, 1947.

Harner, Nevin, C., *I Believe*, Philadelphia, Christian Education Press, 1950.

Hedley, George, *The Symbol of the Faith, A Study of The Apostles' Creed*, New York, The Macmillan Company, 1948.

Horton, W. M., *Our Christian Faith*, Boston, Pilgrim Press, 1947.

Houf, H. T., *What Religion Is and Does*, New York, Harper & Brothers, 1945.

Suggested Reading

Lewis, C. S., *Beyond Personality*, London, G. Bles, Centenary Press, 1944.

Lewis, Clive Staples, *The Case for Christianity*, New York, The Macmillan Company, 1943.

Nichols, James Hastings, *Primer for Protestants*, New York, Association Press, 1951.

Phillips, J. B., *New Testament Christianity*, New York, The Macmillan Company, 1956.

Pike, James A., and Pittenger, W. Norman, *The Faith of the Church*, Greenwich, Conn., Seabury Press, 1951.

Rall, Harris Franklin, *The God of Our Faith*, New York, Abingdon-Cokesbury Press, 1955.

Richardson, Alan, *The Gospel and Modern Thought*, London, Oxford University Press, 1950.

Sayers, Dorothy L., *Creed or Chaos?* New York, Harcourt, Brace and Company, 1949.

Smart, James D., *What a Man Can Believe*, Philadelphia, Westminster Press, 1953.

Sockman, Ralph W., *How to Believe*, New York, Doubleday and Company, Inc., 1953.

Spurrier, William A., *Guide to the Christian Faith*, New York, Charles Scribner's Sons, 1953.

Vidler, A., *Christian Beliefs*, New York, Charles Scribner's Sons, 1950.

Among series of books in process of completion, the three following will be found readable and helpful:

Christian Faith Series, Reinhold Niebuhr, Consulting Editor, New York, Doubleday and Company, Inc.
    Cherbonnier, E. La B., *Hardness of Heart*, 1955.
    Jenkins, Daniel, *The Strangeness of the Church*, 1955.
    Miller, Alexander, *The Renewal of Man*, 1955.
    Pike, James A., *Doing the Truth*, 1956.
    (Other titles to be published.)

The Hazen Books on Religion, New York, Association Press, 1937.
    Bowie, Walter R., *The Bible*.
    Calhoun, Robert L., *What Is Man?*

Harkness, Georgia, *Religious Living.*
Horton, Walter M., *God.*
Lyman, Mary E., *Jesus.*
Stewart, George, *The Church.*

The Layman's Theological Library, Robert McAfee Brown, General Editor, Philadelphia, Westminster Press. When complete this series will include:

Brown, Robert McAfee, *The Significance of the Church.*
Coburn, John, *Prayer and Personal Religion.*
Denbeaux, J. Fred, *Understanding the Bible.*
Forman, Charles, *A Faith for the Nations.*
Hamilton, William, *The Christian Man.*
Jenkins, Daniel, *Believing in God.*
Johnson, Robert, *The Meaning of Christ.*
Kee, Howard Clark, *Making Ethical Decisions.*
Langford, Norman, *Barriers to Belief.*
Loew, Cornelius, *Modern Rivals to Christian Faith.*
Miller, William Lee, *The Protestant and Politics.*
Shinn, Roger L., *Life, Death and Destiny.*

MORE ADVANCED TREATMENTS

Aulen, G., *The Faith of the Christian Church,* Philadelphia, Muhlenberg Press, 1948.

Barth, Karl, *Credo,* New York, Charles Scribner's Sons, 1936.

Brunner, E., *Our Faith,* London, Student Christian Movement Press, 1949.

Brunner, E., *Systematic Theology,* Chicago, University of Chicago Press, 1951, Vol. I.

De Wolf, L. Harold, *A Theology of the Living Church,* New York, Harper & Brothers, 1953.

Farmer, Herbert H., *Towards Belief in God,* New York, The Macmillan Company, 1947.

Herberg, Will, *The Writings of Martin Buber,* New York, Meridian Books, 1956.

Hodgson, Leonard, *Christian Faith and Practice,* Oxford, Basil Blackwell, 1952.

Suggested Reading

Hordern, William, *A Layman's Guide to Protestant Theology*, New York, The Macmillan Company, 1955.

Horton, W. M., *Christian Theology: An Ecumenical Approach*, New York, Harper & Brothers, 1955. (See especially list of references classified as to various shades of view, pp. 275 ff.)

Quick, O. C., *Doctrines of the Creed*, 9th impression, New York, Charles Scribner's Sons, 1951.

Rall, Harris F., *Christianity: An Inquiry into Its Nature and Truth*, New York, Charles Scribner's Sons, 1940.

Reinhardt, Kurt, *The Existentialist Revolt*, Milwaukee, Bruce Publishing Co., 1952.

Richardson, Alan, *Christian Apologetics*, New York, Harper & Brothers, 1947.

Richardson, Alan, *The Gospel and Modern Thought*, London, Oxford University Press, 1950.

Temple, William, *Nature, Man and God*, New York, The Macmillan Company, 1934.

Tillich, Paul, *Biblical Religion and the Search for Ultimate Reality*, Chicago, University of Chicago Press, 1955.

Tillich, Paul, *The Protestant Era* (trans. James Luther Adams), Chicago, University of Chicago Press, 1948.

Tillich, Paul, *Systematic Theology*, Chicago, University of Chicago Press, 1951, 1957, 2 vols.

Weber, Otto, *Karl Barth's Church Dogmatics*, Philadelphia, Westminster Press, 1953.

Whale, J. S., *Christian Doctrine*, Cambridge, Cambridge University Press, 1941.

Whale, J. S., *The Protestant Tradition*, Cambridge, Cambridge University Press, 1955.

Williams, Daniel Day, *What Present-Day Theologians Are Thinking*, New York, Harper & Brothers, 1952.

WORKS ON THE PHILOSOPHY OF RELIGION

Bertocci, P., *Introduction to the Philosophy of Religion*, New York, Prentice-Hall, Inc., 1951.

Burtt, E. A., *Types of Religious Philosophy*, rev. ed., New York, Harper & Brothers, 1951.

277

Essentials in Christian Faith

Casserley, J. V. L., *The Christian in Philosophy*, New York, Charles Scribner's Sons, 1951.

Collins, James Daniel, *The Existentialists*, Chicago, Henry Regnery & Co., 1952.

Hutchison, John, *Faith, Reason and Existence*, New York, Oxford University Press, 1956.

Lyman, Eugene W., *The Meaning and Truth of Religion*, New York, Charles Scribner's Sons, 1933.

Nevins, W. N., *Religion as Experience and Truth*, Philadelphia, Westminster Press, 1941.

Pratt, J. B., *The Religious Consciousness*, New York, The Macmillan Company, 1920.

Roberts, David E., *Existentialism and Religious Belief* (ed. Roger Hazelton), New York, Oxford University Press, 1957.

Trueblood, Elton, *Philosophy of Religion*, New York, Harper & Brothers, 1957.

Wieman, H., *The Source of Human Good*, Chicago, University of Chicago Press, 1946.

Wieman, H., and Meland, Bernard E., *American Philosophies of Religion*, New York, Harper & Brothers, 1936.

THE MORAL PREDICAMENT AND VALUES

(Chapters I and II)

Bennett, J., *Christian Ethics and Social Policy*, New York, Charles Scribner's Sons, 1946.

Brightman, Edgar S., *Nature and Values*, New York, Abingdon-Cokesbury Press, 1945.

Bronstein, D. J.; Krikorian, Y. H.; and Wiener, P. P. (eds.), *Basic Problems in Philosophy*, New York, Prentice-Hall, Inc., 1947.

Brunner, H. E., *The Divine Imperative*, Philadelphia, Westminster Press, 1947.

Dewey, John, and Tufts, James H., *Ethics*, rev. ed., New York, Henry Holt & Co., 1932.

278

Suggested Reading

Herberg, W., *Judaism and Modern Man*, New York, Farrar, Straus and Young, 1952.

Hill, Thomas E., *Contemporary Ethical Theories*, New York, The Macmillan Company, 1950.

Niebuhr, Reinhold, *Christian Realism and Political Problems*, New York, Charles Scribner's Sons, 1953.

Niebuhr, Reinhold, *An Interpretation of Christian Ethics*, New York, Harper & Brothers, 1935.

Pepper, Stephen C., *"A Brief History of the General Theory of Value,"* in *A History of Philosophical Systems* (ed. Vergilius Ferm), New York, Philosophical Library, 1950.

Ramsey, P., *Basic Christian Ethics*, New York, Charles Scribner's Sons, 1950.

Stace, W. T., *Religion and the Modern Mind*, Philadelphia, J. B. Lippincott Company, 1952.

Stevenson, C., *Ethics and Language*, New Haven, Yale University Press, 1944.

Thomas, George F., *Christian Ethics and Moral Philosophy*, New York, Charles Scribner's Sons, 1955.

Tillich, Paul, *Love, Power and Justice*, New York, Oxford University Press, 1954.

Trueblood, Elton, *Alternative to Futility*, New York, Harper & Brothers, 1948.

Trueblood, Elton, *Foundations for Reconstruction*, New York, Harper & Brothers, 1946.

Trueblood, Elton, *The Predicament of Modern Man*, New York, Harper & Brothers, 1944.

Trueblood, Elton, *Signs of Hope*, New York, Harper and Brothers, 1950.

Van Dusen, H. P. (ed.), *The Christian Answer*, New York, Charles Scribner's Sons, 1945.

Wheelwright, Philip, *A Critical Introduction to Ethics*, rev., ed., New York, Odyssey Press, 1949.

Wheelwright, Philip, *The Way of Philosophy*, New York, Odyssey Press, 1954.

Essentials in Christian Faith

THE PHILOSOPHICAL PREDICAMENT

(Chapters III and IV)

Ayer, A. J., *Language, Truth and Logic*, New York, Dover Publications, Inc., 1951.

Beck, Lewis White, *Philosophic Inquiry*, New York, Prentice-Hall, Inc., 1952.

Brightman, Edgar S., *An Introduction to Philosophy*, rev. ed., New York, Henry Holt & Co., 1951.

Collingwood, R. G., *Essay on Philosophical Method*, New York, Oxford University Press, 1933.

Emmett, D., *The Nature of Metaphysical Thinking*, London, Macmillan & Company, Ltd., 1945.

Ewing, A. C., *The Fundamental Questions of Philosophy*, New York, The Macmillan Company, 1952.

Fuller, B. A. G., *History of Philosophy* (rev. Sterling M. Mac Murrin), New York, Henry Holt & Co., 1955.

Kaufmann, Walter, *Existentialism from Dostoievsky to Sartre*, New York, Meridian Books, 1957.

Mead, Hunter, *Types and Problems of Philosophy*, rev. ed., New York, Henry Holt & Co., 1953.

Pepper, Stephen C., *World Hypotheses*, Berkeley, University of California Press, 1942.

Pratt, James B., *Naturalism*, New Haven, Yale University Press, 1939.

Randall, John Herman, Jr., and Buchler, Justus, *Philosophy, An Introduction*, New York, Barnes and Noble, Inc., 1942.

Tillich, Paul, *Biblical Religion and the Search for Ultimate Reality*, Chicago, University of Chicago Press, 1955.

Titus, Harold H., *Living Issues in Philosophy*, New York, American Book Company, 1953.

Wheelwright, Philip, *The Way of Philosophy*, New York, Odyssey Press, 1954.

Suggested Reading

THE PERSONAL PREDICAMENT AND THE NATURE OF MAN

(Chapter V)

Buber, Martin, *Between Man and Man*, London, Kegan Paul, 1947.
Buber, Martin, *I and Thou*, Edinburgh, T. & T. Clark, 1937.

Cassirer, E., *An Essay on Man*, New Haven, Yale University Press, 1944.
Calhoun, R., *What Is Man?* New York, Association Press, 1939.
The Christian Understanding of Man (Oxford Conference preparatory
volume), London, Allen and Unwin, 1937.

Dewey, J. A., *A Common Faith*, New Haven, Yale University Press, 1934.

Fromm, E., *Escape from Freedom*, New York, Rinehart and Company,
1941.
Fromm, E., *Man for Himself*, New York, Rinehart and Company, 1947.

Harkness, Georgia, *The Modern Rival of Christian Faith*, New York,
Abingdon-Cokesbury Press, 1952.

Lamont, Corliss, *Humanism as a Philosophy*, New York, Philosophical
Library, 1949.

Maritain, J., *True Humanism*, London, Centenary Press, 1946.
May, R., *Man's Search for Himself*, New York, W. W. Norton and Com-
pany, 1953.
Miller, Alexander, *The Renewal of Man: A Twentieth Century Essay on
Justification by Faith*, New York, Doubleday and Company, Inc., 1955.
(See especially his note on books, pp. 181 ff.)

Newbigin, Lesslie, *Sin and Salvation*, Philadelphia, Westminster Press,
1957.
Niebuhr, Reinhold, *The Nature and Destiny of Man*, New York, Charles
Scribner's Sons, 1941-1943, Vol. I.
Niebuhr, Reinhold, *The Self and the Dramas of History*, New York,
Charles Scribner's Sons, 1955.

Reese, Curtis W., *The Meaning of Humanism*, Boston, Beacon Press,
1945.

Temple, William, *Nature, Man and God*, London, Macmillan & Company,
Ltd., 1934.

Tillich, Paul, *The Courage to Be,* New Haven, Yale University Press, 1952.

Tillich, Paul, *Systematic Theology,* Chicago, University of Chicago Press, 1951, Vol. I.

THE SCIENCES

(Chapter VI)

Burtt, E. A., *The Metaphysical Foundations of Modern Science* (Doubleday Anchor Books), New York, Doubleday and Company, Inc., 1955.

Butterfield, H., *The Origins of Modern Science,* New York, The Macmillan Company, 1951.

Conant, James B., *On Understanding Science,* New Haven, Yale University Press, 1947.

Conant, James B., *Science and Common Sense,* New Haven, Yale University Press, 1951.

Dampier, W., *A History of Science,* New York, The Macmillan Company, 1932.

Heim, Karl, *Christian Faith and Natural Science,* New York, Harper & Brothers, 1953.

Hocking, William E., *Science and the Idea of God,* Chapel Hill, University of North Carolina Press, 1944.

Jeans, Sir James H., *The Growth of Physical Science,* New York, The Macmillan Company, 1948.

Knedler, John W., Jr., *Masterworks of Science,* New York, Doubleday and Company, Inc., 1947.

Owen, D. R. G., *Scientism, Man and Religion,* Philadelphia, Westminster Press, 1952.

Richardson, Alan, *Science, History and Faith,* London, Oxford University Press, 1950.

Sullivan, J., *The Limitations of Science,* New York, New American Library, 1954.

Taylor, F. Sherwood, *A Short History of Science and Scientific Thought,* New York, W. W. Norton and Company, 1949.

Suggested Reading

THE NATURE OF RELIGION AND LANGUAGE

(Chapter VII)

Baillie, John, *Natural Science and the Spiritual Life,* London, Oxford University Press, 1951.

Bewkes, E. (ed.), *The Nature of Religious Experience,* New York, Harper & Brothers, 1937. (See especially Chap. 6, "The Truth in Myths," by Reinhold Niebuhr.)

Casserley, J. V. L., *The Christian in Philosophy,* New York, Charles Scribner's Sons, 1951.

Cassirer, E., *An Essay on Man,* New Haven, Yale University Press, 1944.

Cassirer, E., *Language and Myth,* New York, Harper & Brothers, 1946.

Hackman, George C.; Kegley, Charles W.; and Nikander, Viljo K., *Religion in Modern Life,* New York, The Macmillan Company, 1957.

Harkness, Georgia, *Religious Living,* New York, Association Press, 1940.

Hutchison, John, and Martin, J. A., *Ways of Faith,* New York, The Ronald Press Company, 1953.

James, William, *The Varieties of Religious Experience,* New York, Longmans Green & Co., 1902.

King, Winston L., *Introduction to Religion,* New York, Harper & Brothers, 1954.

Langer, Suzanne, *Philosophy in a New Key,* New York, Penguin Books, 1948.

Malinowski, B., *The Foundation of Faith and Morals,* London, Oxford University Press, 1936.

Pratt, J. B., *The Religious Consciousness,* New York, The Macmillan Company, 1920.

Stevenson, Charles L., *Ethics and Language,* New Haven, Yale University Press, 1944.

Widgery, A. C., *What Is Religion?* New York, Harper & Brothers, 1953.

Wheelwright, Philip, *The Burning Fountain,* Bloomington, Indiana University Press, 1954.

Essentials in Christian Faith

THE BIBLE AND HISTORY
(Chapter VIII)

Anderson, B. W., *Rediscovering the Bible,* New York, Association Press, 1951.

The Bible Today: Historical, Social, and Literary Aspects of the Old and New Testaments, Described by 28 British Scholars, New York, Harper & Brothers, 1956.

Blair, Edward P., *The Bible and You,* New York, Abingdon-Cokesbury Press, 1953.

Buber, Martin, *The Prophetic Faith,* New York, The Macmillan Company, 1949.

Burrows, Millar, *The Dead Sea Scrolls,* New York, Viking Press, 1955.

Burrows, Millar, *An Outline of Biblical Theology,* Philadelphia, Westminster Press, 1956.

Dodd, C. H., *The Authority of the Bible,* London; Nisbet & Co., Ltd., 1955.

Grant, Frederick C., *How to Read the Bible,* New York, Morehouse-Gorham Co., 1956.

Harkness, Georgia, *Toward Understanding the Bible,* New York, Abingdon-Cokesbury Press, 1952, 1954.

Neil, William, *The Rediscovery of the Bible,* London, Hodder and Stoughton, 1955.

Niebuhr, H. R., *The Meaning of Revelation,* New York; The Macmillan Company, 1941.

Rece, E. H., and Beardslee, William A., *Reading the Bible,* Englewood Cliffs, N. J., Prentice-Hall, Inc., 1956.

Richardson, Alan, *Preface to Bible Study,* Philadelphia, Westminster Press, 1944.

Shinn, Roger L., *Christianity and the Problem of History,* New York, Charles Scribner's Sons, 1953.

Swaim, J. Carter, *Do You Understand the Bible?* Philadelphia, Westminster Press, 1954.

Swaim, J. Carter, *Right and Wrong Ways to Use the Bible,* Philadelphia, Westminster Press, 1953.

Suggested Reading

Wright, G. Ernest, *The Biblical Doctrine of Man in Society*, London, Student Christian Movement Press, 1954.

Wright, G. Ernest, *The Old Testament Against Its Environment*, Chicago, Henry Regnery & Co., 1951.

REVELATION AND FAITH

(Chapter IX)

Baillie, John, *The Idea of Revelation in Recent Thought*, New York, Columbia University Press, 1956.

Brightman, Edgar S., *Introduction to Philosophy*, New York, Henry Holt & Co., 1925.

Brightman, Edgar S., *Religious Values*, New York, Abingdon-Cokesbury Press, 1925.

Brown, W. A., *Beliefs That Matter*, New York, Charles Scribner's Sons, 1928.

Brown, W. A., *Pathways to Certainty*, New York, Charles Scribner's Sons, 1930.

Brunner, H. E., *The Divine-Human Encounter*, Philadelphia, Westminster Press, 1943.

Fosdick, Harry Emerson, *The Meaning of Faith*, New York, Abingdon-Cokesbury Press, 1917.

Harkness, Georgia, *Foundations of Christian Knowledge*, New York, Abingdon-Cokesbury Press, 1955.

James, William, *The Will to Believe*, New York, Longmans, Green and Co., 1896.

Niebuhr, H. R., *The Meaning of Revelation*, New York, The Macmillan Company, 1941.

Otto, Rudolph, *The Idea of the Holy*, New York, Oxford University Press, 1936.

Thomas, George (ed.), *The Vitality of the Christian Tradition*, New York, Harper & Brothers, 1944.

Tillich, Paul, *Dynamics of Faith*, New York, Harper & Brothers, 1957.

Trueblood, Elton, *The Knowledge of God*, New York, Harper & Brothers, 1939.

Trueblood, Elton, *The Logic of Belief*, New York, Harper & Brothers, 1942.

Essentials in Christian Faith

GOD AND THE PROBLEM OF EVIL

(Chapters X and XI)

Anselm, *Writings* (trans. S. N. Deane), Chicago, Open Court Publishing Co., 1910.

Aquinas, *Basic Writings of Saint Thomas Aquinas* (ed. A. C. Pegis), New York, Random House, 1945.

Aquinas, *Introduction to Thomas Aquinas* (ed. A. C. Pegis), New York, Modern Library, 1948.

Augustine, *Basic Writings of Augustine* (ed. W. Oates), New York, Random House, 1948.

Baillie, John, *Our Knowledge of God*, New York, Oxford University Press, 1939.

Bertocci, Peter A., *Introduction to the Philosophy of Religion*, New York, Prentice-Hall, Inc., 1951.

Dixon, W. Macneile, *The Human Situation*, New York, Longmans, Green and Co., 1937.

Farmer, Herbert H., *God and Man*, New York, Abingdon-Cokesbury Press, 1947.

Ferré, Nels F. S., *The Christian Understanding of God*, New York, Harper & Brothers, 1951.

Ferré, Nels F. S., *Evil and the Christian Faith*, New York, Harper & Brothers, 1947.

Hazelton, R., *On Proving God*, New York, Harper & Brothers, 1952.

Hodgson, Leonard, *Doctrine of the Trinity*, New York, Charles Scribner's Sons, 1944.

Horton, Walter M., *God*, New York, Association Press, 1937.

Hutchison, John A., *Faith, Reason and Existence*, New York, Oxford University Press, 1956.

Kant, I., *Selections* (ed. T. M. Greene), New York, Charles Scribner's Sons, 1929.

Lewis, C. S., *The Problem of Pain*, New York, The Macmillan Company, 1943.

Trueblood, Elton, *The Logic of Belief*, New York, Harper & Brothers, 1942.

Suggested Reading

Whale, J. S., *The Christian Answer to the Problem of Evil*, New York, Abingdon-Cokesbury Press, 1936.

CHRIST, HIS CROSS, RESURRECTION, AND JUSTIFICATION

(Chapters XII-XV)

Anderson, B., *Rediscovering the Bible*, New York, Association Press, 1951.

Aulen, G., *Christus Victor*, New York, The Macmillan Company, 1937.

Baillie, D. M., *God Was in Christ*, New York, Charles Scribner's Sons, 1948.

Baillie, John B., *The Place of Christ in Modern Christianity*, New York, Charles Scribner's Sons, 1929.

Bowman, John W., *The Intention of Jesus*, New York, The Macmillan Company, 1943.

Brown, William A., *How to Think of Christ*, New York, Charles Scribner's Sons, 1945.

Cullmann, Oscar, *Christ and Time*, Philadelphia, Westminster Press, 1950.

Dibelius, Martin, *Jesus* (trans. Charles B. Hedrick and Frederick C. Grant), Philadelphia, Westminster Press, 1949.

Dillistone, F. W., *The Significance of the Cross*, Philadelphia, Westminster Press, 1944.

Goodspeed, Edgar J., *A Life of Jesus*, New York, Harper & Brothers, 1950.

Grant, Frederick C., *An Introduction to New Testament Thought*, New York, Abingdon-Cokesbury Press, 1950.

Hodgson, Leonard, *The Doctrine of the Atonement*, New York, Charles Scribner's Sons, 1951.

Hunter, A. M., *Introducing the New Testament*, Philadelphia, Westminster Press, 1946.

Hunter, A. M., *The Work and Words of Jesus*, Philadelphia, Westminster Press, 1950.

Knox, John, *Christ the Lord*, Chicago, Willett, Clark & Company, 1945.

Knox, John, *The Man Christ Jesus*, Chicago, Willett, Clark & Company, 1942.

Knox, John, *On the Meaning of Christ*, New York, Charles Scribner's Sons, 1947.

Lyman, Mary Ely, *Jesus*, New York, Association Press, 1937.

Manson, William, *Jesus the Messiah*, Philadelphia, Westminster Press, 1946.

Miller, Alexander, *The Renewal of Man: A Twentieth Century Essay on Justification by Faith*, New York, Doubleday and Company, Inc., 1955.

Niebuhr, Reinhold, *The Nature and Destiny of Man*, New York, Charles Scribner's Sons, 1941-1943, Vol. II.

Phillips, J. B., *Making Men Whole*, New York, The Macmillan Company, 1953.

Ramsey, A. Michael, *The Resurrection of Christ*, Philadelphia, Westminster Press, 1946.

Richardson, Alan, *The Miracle-Stories of the Gospels*, New York, Harper & Brothers, 1942.

Weatherhead, Leslie D., *Over His Own Signature*, New York, Abingdon-Cokesbury Press, 1955.

Wolf, William J., *Man's Knowledge of God*, New York, Doubleday and Company, Inc., 1955.

THE CHURCH AND ECUMENICAL CHRISTIANITY

(Chapters XVI and XVII)

Bennett, John C., *Christianity and Communism*, New York, Association Press, 1951.

Bilheimer, Robert S., *The Quest for Christian Unity*, New York, Association Press, 1952.

The Christian Hope and the Task of the Church (Evanston preparatory volume), New York, Harper & Brothers, 1954.

Dillenberger, John, and Welch, Claude, *Protestant Christianity*, New York, Charles Scribner's Sons, 1955.

Hedley, George, *The Christian Heritage in America*, New York, The Macmillan Company, 1947.

Herberg, Will, *Protestant-Catholic-Jew*, New York, Doubleday and Company, Inc., 1956.

Horton, W. M., *Toward a Reborn Church*, New York, Harper & Brothers, 1949.

Hutchison, J. (ed.), *Christian Faith and Social Action*, New York, Charles Scribner's Sons, 1953.

Suggested Reading

Jenkins, D. T., *The Strangeness of the Church,* New York, Doubleday and Company, Inc., 1955.

Kennedy, James W., *Evanston Scrapbook,* Lebanon, Pa., Sowers Printing Company, 1954. (Pamphlet giving first-hand impressions of the Second Assembly.)

Latourette, Kenneth S., *The Emergence of a World Christian Community,* New Haven, Yale University Press, 1949.

May, Henry F., *Protestant Churches and Industrial America,* New York, Harper & Brothers, 1949.

Muehl, William, *Politics for Christians,* New York, Association Press, 1956.

The Nature of the Church (Lund Conference preparatory volume), New York, Harper & Brothers, 1952.

Nichols, James Hastings, *Democracy and the Churches,* Philadelphia, Westminster Press, 1951.

Nichols, James Hastings, *Evanston, An Interpretation,* New York, Harper & Brothers, 1954.

Niebuhr, H. R., *Christ and Culture,* New York, Harper & Brothers, 1951.

Niebuhr, H. R., *The Purpose of the Church and its Ministry,* New York, Harper & Brothers, 1956.

Niebuhr, H. R., *The Social Sources of Denominationalism,* Hamden, Conn., Shoe String Press, 1929, 1954.

Northcott, Cecil, *Evanston World Assembly,* London, Lutterworth Press, 1954.

Nygren, Anders, *Christ and His Church* (trans. Alan Carlsten), Philadelphia, Westminster Press, 1956.

Nygren, Anders (ed.), *This Is the Church* (trans. Carl C. Rasmussen), Philadelphia, Muhlenberg Press, 1952.

Rouse, Ruth, and Neill, Stephen, *The History of the Ecumenical Movement, 1517-1948,* Philadelphia, Westminster Press, 1954.

Temple, William, *Christianity and Social Order,* New York, Penguin Books, 1942.

Thomas, George, *The Vitality of the Christian Tradition,* New York, Charles Scribner's Sons, 1955.

Van Dusen, Henry P., *World Christianity,* New York, Abingdon-Cokesbury Press, 1947.

Essentials in Christian Faith

Visser t'Hooft, W. A. (ed.), *Evanston Report* (Official report of the Second Assembly), New York, Harper & Brothers, 1955.

Visser t'Hooft, W. A., *The Renewal of the Church*, Philadelphia, Westminster Press, 1957.

Wedel, Theodore O., *The Coming Great Church*, New York, The Macmillan Company, 1945.

Whale, J. S., *The Protestant Tradition*, Cambridge, Cambridge University Press, 1955.

Williams, D., *God's Grace and Man's Hope*, New York, Harper & Brothers, 1949.

Williams, J. Paul, *What Americans Believe and How They Worship*, New York, Harper & Brothers, 1952.

World Council of Churches, *Ecumenical Book Shelf*. (A list of publications, available from the World Council of Churches, 156 Fifth Avenue, New York 10, N. Y.)

THE LIFE EVERLASTING

(Chapter XVIII)

Baillie, John, *And the Life Everlasting*, New York, Charles Scribner's Sons, 1948.

Brown, William A., *The Christian Hope*, New York, Charles Scribner's Sons, 1912.

Fosdick, Harry Emerson, *The Assurance of Immortality*, New York, The Macmillan Company, 1913.

Grant, F. C., *Can We Still Believe in Immortality?* Louisville, Cloister Press, 1944.

Hardman, Oscar, *Resurrection of the Body*, New York, The Macmillan Company, 1934.

Holmes, John Haynes, *Is Death the End?* New York, G. P. Putnam's Sons, 1915.

Lewis, C. S., *The Great Divorce*, New York, The Macmillan Company, 1946.

Lyman, Eugene W., *The Meaning of Selfhood and Faith in Immortality*, Cambridge, Mass., Harvard University Press, 1928.

Perry, Ralph B., *The Hope of Immortality*, New York, Vanguard Press, 1945.

Taylor, A. E., *The Christian Hope of Immortality*, New York, The Macmillan Company, 1947.

Index

Index

Burtt, E. A., 84 n.
Buttrick, Dr. George, 201, 207, 225 n.

Calvin, John, 244, 246, 247, 253
Canaan, 113
Carlyle, Thomas, 72
Casserly, J. V. Langmead, 44, 48, 98, 100, 101, 102
Chalcedon, Council of, 175
Cherbonnier, E. La B., 125
Chesterton, G. K., 31
Christ, *see* Jesus Christ
Christ the Lord, 170, 176, 220 n.
Christian Answer to the Problem of Evil, 151 n., 200 n.
Christian Apologetics, 135, 182 n.
Christian Ethics and Moral Philosophy, 67
Christian Faith and Natural Science, 45 n.
Christian Heritage in America, 228 n.
Christian Hope and the Task of the Church, 242 n., 255 n.
Christian in Philosophy, 44, 98
Christian Science, 150-151
Christian Theology, An Ecumenical Approach, 250 n.
Christian Way in a Modern World, 26, 265
Christianity, biblical, 75
  and Buddhism, 135
  commitment to, 93-95
  conception of self in, 72-73, 74
  core of, 57
  credibility of, 46
  ecumenical, 241-257 ff.
  and faith, 129-130
  as a faith-principle, 135
  as a force for integration in European society, 244
  Hebraic-Christian historical perspective in, 108-110
  Hebraic tradition in, 121
  historical tradition of, 187-188
  and moral order, 21-22
  obstacles to ecumenical, 249-253
  and philosophy, 44-48, 97-98
  and secularism, 45

three sources of Protestant, in America, 249
  view of man in, 71-75
  and Western civilization, 23
Church, "catholic" conception of, 252
  as the Christian community, 235-236
  as community, 169, 228-240 ff.
  conservative function of, 243
  continuity in, 252
  definition of, 233
  as development of Jewish community, 232
  in dynamic interaction with culture, 243
  elements of, 234
  established, protests against, 244
  as fellowship, 236-237, 254
  the "first," 228
  form of, 251
  government of, 239-240
  nature of, 230-237
  obstacles to community within, 250
  prophetic function of, 243
  Protestant, 242-243
  Protestant conception of, 252
  religion without, 229-230
  specific functions of, 237-240
  universal, 229
Church of South India, 251
Communion, 199-200, 238, 250
  See also Lord's Supper
Communism and the Church, 256
Congregational-Christian Church, 243, 248
Copernicus, 83
Corinth, 215
Corinthians, 204, 215, 217-218, 221, 265
Covenant, New, 120, 121, 169
  Old, 120
  parity and suzerainty, 117-121
Craig, C. T., 250
Cross, for man, Christ, and God, 197-203
  meaning of, 210
  and resurrection, in Hebrew tradition, 211-215
Cunningham, G. W., 160

292

Index

Index

294

Index

Index

Man—*Continued*
  personal and religious predicament
    of, 57-60
  philosophical dilemma of, 28-30
  and reason, 66-67
  rebellion against God of, 75
  in relation to universe, 27
  and self, 56-75 ff.
  self of, awareness of, 269-270
  separated from God, 73, 75
  between social and animal world,
    62-63
  as social being, 70
  and the Universe, 161
  vs. the world, 26-35 ff.
Manson, William, 182 n., 199
Mark, St., 172, 174, 204, 213, 216-217
  Gospel of, 175, 177, 185, 199
Martineau, James, 266
Mary Magdalene, 217
Mass, 238, 239
Materialism, 78
Matthew, St., 216-217
  and Atonement, 207
  Gospel of, 172
Mead, Hunter, 52
Meaning of Christ, On the, 232 n.
Meaning of Humanism, The, 70
Meaning of Revelation, 128-129, 188
Mendenhall, George E., 117
Mennonites, 248
Messiah, 119-120
*Metaphysical Foundations of Natural
  Science,* 84
Metaphysics, 34, 59
Metaphysics, as analogical art, 97
  as hypothesis, 39
  quest for, 39-44
  root-metaphor method, 41-42
  speculative, 39
  technical, 38
  verification in, 48
  and world hypothesis, 40-43, 140
Methodists, 243, 248
Micah, 114, 119
Ministers, 239
  adequate training of, 238
  authority of, 252
  Presbyterian view of, 253

Miracles, Old Testament, 181-182
Miracle Stories of the Gospels, 182 n.
Missions, 240
Missouri Synod Lutherans, 250
Modernism, 123
Montague, W. P., 47
Morals, relativity of, 9-12
Morgan, Lloyd, 62, 158
Moses, 114, 126, 127
  law of, 179
Mother of Pearl, 209 n.
Mountain Meadow, 94
Myths, Babylonian, 158
  primitive, 102-104, 125

Natural Science and the Spiritual Life,
  105 n.
Naturalism, 69, 182
  and Christianity, 75
  contemporary, 78
  and science, 79
Nature, Man and God, 134 n.
Nature and Destiny of Man, The, 65
Nature of Religious Experience, 104
Neo-Platonism, 99, 100
Newton, Isaac, 86
Newton, Joseph Fort, 261
Nichols, James Hastings, 242 n.,
  245 n., 255, 257
Niebuhr, H. Richard, 116, 128, 188
Niebuhr, Reinhold, 65, 72, 104-105,
  133
Nietzsche, 7
Northcott, Cecil, 242 n.
Northern Kingdom, 114

One Church, The, 250 n.
Ontology, 34, 59
Oxford Conference on Church, Com-
  munity and State, 241

Palestine, 113
Palmer, Albert W., 136
Pascal, Blaise, 47, 72, 133
Passion, the, 213
  in the Gospels, 212
Passover, 200
Paul, St., 23, 154, 172, 191, 204, 215,
  216-227 ff., 246, 264, 265, 266

Index

Index

Index

Date Due

Demco 293-5